Cases on Organizational Communication and Understanding Understudied Groups

Jessica A. Kahlow
University of Wisconsin, Milwaukee, USA

IGI Global
PUBLISHER of TIMELY KNOWLEDGE

A volume in the Advances in Human Resources Management and Organizational Development (AHRMOD) Book Series

Published in the United States of America by
IGI Global
Business Science Reference (an imprint of IGI Global)
701 E. Chocolate Avenue
Hershey PA, USA 17033
Tel: 717-533-8845
Fax: 717-533-8661
E-mail: cust@igi-global.com
Web site: http://www.igi-global.com

Library of Congress Cataloging-in-Publication Data

Names: Kahlow, Jessica A., DATE- editor.
Title: Cases on organizational communication and understanding understudied groups / Jessica A. Kahlow, editor.
Description: Hershey, PA : Business Science Reference, [2022] | Includes bibliographical references and index. | Summary: "This publication will help instructors by providing a set of cases to use in their classes to explain concepts pertaining to understudied groups to students so they can more easily apply them in their lives and future careers"-- Provided by publisher.
Identifiers: LCCN 2022970012 (print) | LCCN 2022970013 (ebook) | ISBN 9781668437537 (hardcover) | ISBN 9781668437544 (paperback) | ISBN 9781668437551 (ebook)
Subjects: LCSH: Communication in organizations--Case studies. | Employee motivation--Case studies.
Classification: LCC HD30.3 .C37147 2022 (print) | LCC HD30.3 (ebook) | DDC 354.75--dc23/eng/20220223
LC record available at https://lccn.loc.gov/2022970012
LC ebook record available at https://lccn.loc.gov/2022970013

This book is published in the IGI Global book series Advances in Human Resources Management and Organizational Development (AHRMOD) (ISSN: 2327-3372; eISSN: 2327-3380)

British Cataloguing in Publication Data
A Cataloguing in Publication record for this book is available from the British Library.

All work contributed to this book is new, previously-unpublished material.
The views expressed in this book are those of the authors, but not necessarily of the publisher.

For electronic access to this publication, please contact: eresources@igi-global.com.

Advances in Human Resources Management and Organizational Development (AHRMOD) Book Series

ISSN:2327-3372
EISSN:2327-3380

Editor-in-Chief: Patricia Ordóñez de Pablos, Universidad de Oviedo, Spain

MISSION

A solid foundation is essential to the development and success of any organization and can be accomplished through the effective and careful management of an organization's human capital. Research in human resources management and organizational development is necessary in providing business leaders with the tools and methodologies which will assist in the development and maintenance of their organizational structure.

The **Advances in Human Resources Management and Organizational Development (AHRMOD) Book Series** aims to publish the latest research on all aspects of human resources as well as the latest methodologies, tools, and theories regarding organizational development and sustainability. The **AHRMOD Book Series** intends to provide business professionals, managers, researchers, and students with the necessary resources to effectively develop and implement organizational strategies.

COVERAGE

- Worker Behavior and Engagement
- Employee Benefits
- Personnel Retention
- Recruitment Process
- Succession Planning
- Employee Evaluation
- Change Management
- Corporate Governance
- Upward Feedback
- Disputes Resolution

IGI Global is currently accepting manuscripts for publication within this series. To submit a proposal for a volume in this series, please contact our Acquisition Editors at Acquisitions@igi-global.com or visit: http://www.igi-global.com/publish/.

The Advances in Human Resources Management and Organizational Development (AHRMOD) Book Series (ISSN 2327-3372) is published by IGI Global, 701 E. Chocolate Avenue, Hershey, PA 17033-1240, USA, www.igi-global.com. This series is composed of titles available for purchase individually; each title is edited to be contextually exclusive from any other title within the series. For pricing and ordering information please visit http://www.igi-global.com/book-series/advances-human-resources-management-organizational/73670. Postmaster: Send all address changes to above address.

Titles in this Series

For a list of additional titles in this series, please visit:
https://www.igi-global.com/book-series/advances-human-resources-management-organizational/73670#titles

International Perspectives and Strategies for Managing an Aging Workforce
Fatma Ince (Mersin University, Turkey)
Business Science Reference • copyright 2022 • 346pp • H/C (ISBN: 9781799823957) • US $215.00 (our price)

External Events and Crises That Impact Firms and Other Entities
Heather C. Webb (Higher Colleges of Technology, Dubai, UAE) and Hussain Al Numairy (Higher Colleges of Technology, Dubai, UAE)
Business Science Reference • copyright 2022 • 303pp • H/C (ISBN: 9781799883463) • US $200.00 (our price)

Multidisciplinary Approach to Diversity and Inclusion in the COVID-19-Era Workplace
Rilla Hynes (Northwood University, USA) Carlos Tasso Aquino (Gettysburg College, Gettysburg, USA) and Josephine Hauer (University of Phoenix, USA)
Business Science Reference • copyright 2022 • 348pp • H/C (ISBN: 9781799888277) • US $215.00 (our price)

Religion and Its Impact on Organizational Behavior
Ebtihaj Al-Aali (University of Bahrain, Bahrain) Meryem Masmoudi (University of Bahrain, Bahrain) and Gardenia Jassim AlSaffar (Royal Bahrain Hospital, Bahrain)
Business Science Reference • copyright 2022 • 326pp • H/C (ISBN: 9781799893196) • US $195.00 (our price)

Navigating the New Normal of Business With Enhanced Human Resource Management Strategies
Perfecto Gatbonton Aquino Jr. (Independent Researcher, Philippines) and Revenio Cabanilla Jalagat Jr. (Al-Zahra College for Women, Oman)
Business Science Reference • copyright 2022 • 313pp • H/C (ISBN: 9781799884514) • US $195.00 (our price)

For an entire list of titles in this series, please visit:
https://www.igi-global.com/book-series/advances-human-resources-management-organizational/73670#titles

IGI Global
PUBLISHER of TIMELY KNOWLEDGE

701 East Chocolate Avenue, Hershey, PA 17033, USA
Tel: 717-533-8845 x100 • Fax: 717-533-8661
E-Mail: cust@igi-global.com • www.igi-global.com

Table of Contents

Section 2
Non-Traditional and Minority Groups

Detailed Table of Contents

Section 1
Groups With Invisible Differences

This case study serves as an impetus to begin discussion about how communication theories uniquely contribute to understanding mental health communication during transitions from organizational life as a college student to subsequent post-college workplaces. This case illustrates communication privacy management theory and the organizational socialization model by following a student, Valerie, as she enters college, works through mental health issues, and enters her job after college. Through conversations, internal dialogue, and events, the case reveals the ways that communication functions to shape Valerie's understanding of what and with whom she can share her mental health needs.

The National Institute of Mental Health has reported that approximately 51.5 million people in the U.S. experience some form of mental illness and that anxiety is one of the most prevalent mental illnesses, with 31.1% of Americans experiencing some form of anxiety disorder in their lives. In this case study, one of the most common discriminatory behaviors toward all minority groups, microaggressions, is explored through the lens of leader-member exchange theory (LMX). LMX has been the foremost leadership theory used to understand the dynamics of mental illness in the workplace and how leaders interact and motivate those with disabilities or mental illness. The authors apply LMX to help leaders better understand their role in creating a more inclusive workplace.

Mental health issues, such as depression, anxiety, and post-traumatic stress disorder, are increasing in the U.S. However, people diagnosed with mental illnesses often experience stigmatization and discrimination in their workplace. The chapter examines how people with mental illness make decisions around revealing and, importantly, concealing their mental illness in the workplace. The concepts stigma and communication privacy management theory are used to examine the challenges associated with living with mental illness in the workplace. A case study is used to illustrate these concepts and provide a pedagogical context in which the factors around concealing mental illness in the workplace are situated. Finally, an analysis of the case study is presented using the conceptual and theoretical frameworks applied in the present chapter.

In college, people who have learning differences or ADHD are provided an array of different resources (e.g., notetakers, tutoring, additional test time, counseling, etc.). People with these differences learn ways to manage them, but these strategies do not directly translate to the workplace. Resources are often not available in the workplace, leaving people with learning differences to manage on their own. The case study follows Suzie—a young professional diagnosed with ADHD at an early age—through a day in her new role as a communication coordinator. Suzie has accepted ADHD as a part of her identity, but she often questions the accuracy of her notes, has difficulty interpreting her notes, and finds it difficult to remember conversations. The case begins with Suzie in a meeting with her supervisor. After the meeting, she goes back to her desk to interpret her notes. In doing so, she attracts attention from her coworkers. The case provides opportunities to discuss concepts such as minority stress, stigma, self-disclosure, invisible disabilities, and workplace accommodations.

Preface

Since the pandemic, organizational communication has been at the forefront of our lives more so than it has ever been in the past; this is clear from the variety of self-help-like books about working from home and navigating the workplace and the plethora of articles online about how organizations can retain employees amidst the great reshuffle. People are now more aware of terms like work-life balance and what that means for them. This shift in the way people approach work profoundly impacts organizational communication, and it is redefining our workspaces. Now is a particularly fascinating time to be studying organizational communication because, as Mangia (2020) says, "the line between work and home isn't just blurred—it's been erased" (p. 1). This relates to many concepts discussed throughout this book, including work-life balance and spillover. Mangia (2020) goes on to explain how the current state of the world is not what anyone asked for, but it is what it is. However, and interestingly, the current state of the world provides a good backdrop for studying organizational communication because of how quickly things have changed and how unlikely it is that everything will completely return to how it was—for better or worse. This reconsideration of priorities has inadvertently led to what has become known as the 'great resignation' or the 'great reshuffle' as people attempt to land more fulfilling and balanced positions. To combat this 'great reshuffle,' organizations have begun prioritizing diversity, equity, and inclusion (e.g., Lawley, 2022). Given this transition to DEI efforts, there is still a lot to learn in terms of creating workplaces that are diverse, equitable, and inclusive.

Organizations' refocus on DEI efforts means that more focus will be put on people most impacted by those efforts (e.g., understudied and under-discussed groups). The phrase 'understudied groups' calls attention to understanding the array of areas that are often overlooked in research, teaching, and in practice. As such, the chapters in this book use a very broad definition of what constitutes an understudied group. In general, an understudied group can be interpreted to mean any group of people who could be considered overlooked, glossed over, or otherwise under-discussed or underrepresented in terms of research, teaching, or in practice. The chapters in this book, *Cases on Organizational Communication and Understanding Understudied*

Groups, highlight two main areas of understudied groups with distinctive challenges: 1) workers with invisible differences and 2) non-traditional and minority groups. Many of the chapters in this book call out the prevalence of these understudied groups and the challenges they face in day-to-day interactions, even though many of them remain understudied and under-discussed.

This book presents ten case studies to examine various types of understudied groups that comprise the modern workplace and several plausible issues that affect those individuals as they navigate the workplace. Each case also explores a related topic in organizational communication, including work-life spillover, communication privacy management theory, relationship quality, self-disclosure, organizational assimilation, work-life balance, cultural differences, and microaggressions. Through these case studies, students will develop a better understanding of how communication can develop, enrich, and limit individuals in understudied groups as they navigate the workplace.

In addition to being topically relevant, the cases in this book introduce several emerging theories in organizational communication as they pertain to studying stigmatized, minority, and non-traditional workers. Theories explored in these ten cases include communication privacy management, leader-member exchange, minority stress, work-family border, communication accommodation, social penetration, and resilience. Amidst the growing popularity and normalization of mental health and neurodiversity-related topics in the constantly evolving workplace, this book offers a timely set of case studies to help people navigate the modern workplace.

This book is intended for use in undergraduate courses in organizational, business, and professional communication. Each chapter includes an overview of relevant theories and concepts related to the case, the case itself, a discussion of how those concepts and theories apply to the case, engaging discussion questions, and a list of keywords and definitions.

The first part of this book focuses on understudied groups in the stigmatized groups category, which includes individuals struggling with their mental health, neurodiverse individuals, and other invisible differences. While the stigma associated with being a part of these groups has been on the decline, there remains a general lack of information as to how to best support these individuals in the workplace.

The opening chapter of this book, "'Who Can I Trust?': Mental Health Communication Privacy Management and Organizational Socialization," by Dr. Sarah Riforgiate and Alexis Madson, explores the transition from college to the workplace and how a young adult manages this transition—including the disclosure decisions regarding her mental health. The case explores the organizational assimilation process and some challenges associated with it, including finding access to mental health care during her probationary period at her new employer. In this dilemma, she must also navigate whether to disclose—and what to disclose—regarding her mental health, which is aptly used by the authors as an opportunity to highlight the value of communication privacy management theory in organizational communication contexts. This chapter is particularly useful because it sheds light on a transitional period all college students will experience with the added layer of mental health.

The following chapter, "Relationship Quality Matters: Leader-Member Exchange and Mental Health Disabilities in the Workplace," by Dr. Anne Hubbell and Dr. Greg G. Armfield, explores the importance of relational quality between leaders and individuals with disabilities or mental illness. The case follows a leader and an employee with generalized anxiety to highlight how harmful microaggressions can be, especially when the leader does not understand the employee's difference. To overcome this barrier, this case uses the leader-member exchange theory to describe how organizational leaders can create a more inclusive work environment. This case is particularly valuable as it will prepare students to step into organizations that value diversity and inclusion with ways to be more inclusive and the know-how to provide accommodations for a diverse range of employees.

The third chapter on mental health is titled "Concealing Mental Illness in the Workplace: Applying Communication Privacy Management Theory to Managing Mental Health Privacy in the Workplace" and is written by Dr. Andrea Meluch. The case highlights the value of therapy and getting help for mental health-related issues and how difficult it can be to manage when a supervisor fails to see the value of therapy. This case study also uses communication privacy management theory to understand how, when, and why an employee may disclose this information, including for reasons such as helping others get the help they need and possibly needing time away from work. The case is an important addition to this book as it considers how and when to speak up about—often invisible and unknown—mental health concerns in the workplace.

The next two chapters focus specifically on ADHD as a form of neurodiversity and its associated stigmas. The fourth chapter, "'Stop Trying So Hard!': Disclosing ADHD in the Workplace," by Dr. Jessica Kahlow, follows another recent college graduate into the workplace and highlights the challenges imposed by the workplace on individuals with ADHD. The case provides a look into the brain of someone with ADHD and how ADHD can make even simple tasks unnecessarily complicated. The case approaches the stigma surrounding ADHD using minority stress theory and encourages readers to consider how different accommodations may or may not be helpful in this situation. This chapter is important because it raises awareness of what it is like to struggle with ADHD and how people without ADHD may better accommodate and consider the needs of their coworkers.

The final chapter in this group, "Seeing (Speaking) Through Her Eyes (Brain): Louisa's Journey," by Courtney D. Fallon, provides another take on the challenges associated with navigating ADHD disclosures, seeking accommodations in the workplace, and how—if implemented—those accommodations impact other working relationships. This case takes a structuration approach to understand how organizational culture can inhibit neurodiverse perspectives and indirectly promote ableism in the workplace. This case is an important one for understanding how to best accommodate ADHD and other invisible disabilities in the workplace.

The second half of this book examines minority and non-traditional workers as understudied—and under-discussed—groups. While the first section of this book focused on often invisible differences, the second half focuses on understudied groups who often have distinct trait-based or role-based differences and their positionality within their respective workplaces.

This section leads off with a chapter on adventure workers (or 'gig' workers). "Avoiding 'Beige Cubicle Hell': Emotion and Work-Life Spillover Among Adventure Workers," by Kari J. Pink and Emily A. Godager, artfully depicts some of the challenges related to emotions and spillover that non-traditional workers encounter. Their case follows the exciting ups and downs in the lives of ski resort workers and compares this lifestyle to that of a traditional office worker. As more and more people opt out of traditional jobs and become part of the gig economy, it is important to understand their choices and the unique challenges they face. With so many employees considering leaving their current traditional roles in light of the great resignation, gig workers are here to stay and need to be better understood.

The next chapter, "Convergence and Divergence at Work: Cross-Cultural Interactions With a Difficult Coworker," by Seulgi Park and Dr. Patricia Gettings, explores the experience of an immigrant nurse working in the United States. Their case follows a nurse and explores the different pressures and challenges she faces while working alongside people from differing backgrounds and how these cultural differences lead to communication-related challenges and decrease overall job satisfaction. The case also explores the factors one considers when deciding whether to leave an organization, which is also valuable in the era of the great resignation. This case is important because immigrants experience a whole host of unique workplace challenges, and these have only been compounded in the nursing industry since the onset of the pandemic.

"'You're Very Smart for a Black Woman': A Case of Microaggressive Communication," by Dr. Electra Gilchrist-Petty, follows an academic to a conference, where her presentation is deemed excellent, but not without its associated microaggressions. The case highlights the all too common struggles that women—and particularly women of color—face in the world of academia. The case is important because it shows how it really is not all that difficult to simply treat people like people, regardless of who they are, what they look like, or where they came from—everyone is capable of having excellent ideas. As the case points out, people are often unaware of how their words are microaggressions, and this chapter provides one case to open people's eyes so they can be more aware of the impact of their words.

Another understudied minority group impacted by stigma includes the LGBTQ+ community. The chapter "I Am Me: Transgender Communication in the Workplace" by Victoria Bray follows an individual who is transgender and their experiences in the workplace. Among other challenges related to finding one's place in the organization, this case also explores self-presentation and how transgender individuals often feel the need to present themselves in a certain way in the workplace. The case highlights generational differences in the workplace and how older coworkers may not have the same inclusive mindset as younger ones, and the challenges resulting from this. This case is important because it is the only one in this book that focuses primarily on workplace-related issues that the LGBTQ+ community faces.

The remaining two chapters in this book examine resilience. "Workplace Resilience During Cancer Treatment: An Exploration of Workplace Communication Processes That Lead to Resilience for Female Employees" by Dr. Donna M. Elkins follows an individual navigating the workplace through a cancer diagnosis. The case uses the communication theory of resilience to understand the diagnosee's perspective on navigating work post-diagnosis. This case is particularly important because while we hope that nothing bad ever happens to our coworkers, it can be difficult to know what to do or how to react in these situations. The case is helpful because it talks about this difficult topic that everyone will likely eventually encounter, and it will hopefully provide a way to help navigate that difficult time.

The final case study in this book is titled "It's Just a Part of Life" by Dr. Patrice M. Buzzanell and Dr. Suzy D'Enbeau. It cleverly and insightfully unpacks the messiness of everyday life and the weight of feeling the need to excel professionally and personally. The authors thoughtfully incorporate how the couples use various communication concepts to articulate how they can be used to make the best out of an overwhelming situation. This case takes a more family-oriented approach to resilience by following two couples through job changes and infertility to construct resilience and balance. The case draws attention to childlessness and infertility as under-discussed groups as well as to challenges with parenting while also trying to excel professionally. The case is important because it applies communication concepts to everyday life.

It is my hope that by using these cases in your classes that students will become more open-minded and aware of the specific issues that certain groups face while engaging with related concepts in communication. In thinking more broadly about the groups studied within the chapters of this book, it becomes apparent that understanding the unique positions of others is important for workplace communication. As these chapters so clearly highlight, the workplace is not always black and white; boundaries are not always clear, and situations with individuals with differences—invisible or otherwise—need to be heard, valued, and prioritized.

The chapters in this book also highlight how assumptions are made about people in the workplace and how even incorrect assumptions or stigmas can be hurtful to the employee. It is clear that more work needs to be done to help individuals with any kind of difference navigate their experiences in the workplace. This book provides a first step in doing this in the field of communication by identifying understudied groups and the unique challenges and pressures they face in the workplace.

Jessica A. Kahlow
University of Wisconsin, Milwaukee, USA

REFERENCES

Lawley, H. (2022). Focusing on diversity, equity and inclusion as individual concepts is key to curbing the great resignation. *BenefitsPRO*.

Mangia, K. (2020). Entering the shift. In *Working from home: Making the new normal work for you* (pp. 1–8). Wiley.

Acknowledgment

I have always believed that sometimes you need to carve your own path, and this book project is the perfect example of that. Understudied groups are understudied, and therefore, it can be challenging to find the perfect fit for manuscripts dealing with these topics. I am delighted to have been able to provide this outlet for that reason, and I am so thankful to have had the opportunity to work with such amazing authors (many of whom would make surprisingly compelling novelists), teachers, and researchers in communication to make it possible.

That said, I have to thank Dr. Sarah Riforgiate for helping me see the value of case studies, for all of her helpful feedback in the case study that inspired this book, and for instilling the "anything is possible" mindset in me during my graduate studies.

Again, thank you to each of the authors in this book for their hard work and time in putting their chapters together. I was truly so excited to read each of these chapters, and I can only hope that future readers are half as excited about these as I am. Each case is so insightful and raises awareness by discussing specific issues that people will likely encounter in their working lives.

Also, thank you to everyone who contributed a review for this book; your insights truly made each chapter even stronger. Finally, I am also thankful to everyone I worked with at IGI Global, who saw the value of this book and helped make it possible.

Section 1
Groups With Invisible Differences

Chapter 1
"Who Can I Trust?": Mental Health Communication, Privacy Management, and Organizational Socialization

Sarah E. Riforgiate
https://orcid.org/0000-0002-5933-4369
University of Wisconsin, Milwaukee, USA

Alexis Madson
University of Wisconsin, Milwaukee, USA

EXECUTIVE SUMMARY

This case study serves as an impetus to begin discussion about how communication theories uniquely contribute to understanding mental health communication during transitions from organizational life as a college student to subsequent post-college workplaces. This case illustrates communication privacy management theory and the organizational socialization model by following a student, Valerie, as she enters college, works through mental health issues, and enters her job after college. Through conversations, internal dialogue, and events, the case reveals the ways that communication functions to shape Valerie's understanding of what and with whom she can share her mental health needs.

INTRODUCTION

College is an important organization that shapes work communication expectations for many (Kramer & Dailey, 2019). College is designed to help students enhance their knowledge base, develop skills, and prepare for future careers through coursework

DOI: 10.4018/978-1-6684-3753-7.ch001

(Ruder & Riforgiate, 2019) and internships (Woo et al., 2017). Additionally, college is often the first occasion when individuals live independently, necessitating the development of life-related skills for self-care. These numerous experiences inform future work communication expectations, including what emotions and information are appropriate to communicate and how to seek necessary assistance.

Importantly, college students require active, healthy minds to learn what is needed while balancing the demands of coursework, paid work, and other adult responsibilities (John Hopkins University, 2021). However, college students also experience considerable stress that manifests from many sources including academic demands (Alsulami et al., 2018) and financial strains (Student Loan Hero, 2021), among others. COVID-19 compounded mental health concerns as many students faced increased challenges related to food insecurity, unstable housing situations, and reduced technology access (Lederer et al., 2020). In 2020, 71% of students reported feeling greater anxiety over concerns about the health of loved ones, decreased ability to complete coursework, difficulties getting adequate sleep, and feelings of isolation from social distancing restrictions (Son et al., 2020). These demands contributed to mental health declines, and college student mental health issues are on the rise (Lipson et al., 2019). The 2020 Healthy Minds Study found that 39% of college students reported having either moderate or major depression. Further, Chen and colleagues (2019) shared that 87.3% of students indicated that at some point they "felt overwhelmed by all [they] had to do" and that almost 10% of students seriously considered suicide (p. 445).

Taking these statistics to heart, colleges continue to develop resources to assist students with mental health concerns (Carrasco, 2021). Unfortunately, numerous barriers prevent students from seeking help and using resources including a lack of perceived support, concern about stigmas (e.g., shame, guilt, regret, embarrassment, etc.) (Vidourek, et al., 2014), and fear of technology privacy violations (Joyce & Weibelzahl, 2011). Experiences before and during college influence help seeking behavior related to mental health concerns (Meluch & Starcher, 2020). Learning what and to whom to disclose is an essential step in locating and using resources, and these communication behaviors have implications in future organizational contexts.

This case study is designed to generate discussion about how students and new employees make communication decisions when disclosing mental health concerns using two theoretical lenses: *communication privacy management theory* (Petronio, 2010, 2013; Smith & Brunner, 2017), and *organizational socialization* (Jablin, 2001; Kramer & Dailey, 2019; Riforgiate & Kramer, 2021). The case follows Valerie as she enters college, addresses mental health concerns during college, and subsequently enters a professional organization as an employee. Through conversations, internal dialogue and events, the case reveals the ways communication shapes Valerie's understanding of what, how, and with whom she shares her mental health needs.

The next section describes mental health and mental illness. Then, communication privacy management theory and organizational socialization are detailed as frameworks for understanding communication patterns. Subsequently, the case study is provided, followed by a section synthesizing Valerie's communication and the theories. Finally, discussion questions are included to facilitate conversations about communication, disclosure, and mental health.

Mental Health and Mental Illness

Mental health issues and mental illness are increasing in the U.S. and worldwide (Chaib & Brunier, 2017), therefore it is important to understand these terms and the scope of the concerns. According to the U.S. Center for Disease Control (2021), "mental health includes our emotional, psychological, and social well-being. … It also helps determine how we handle stress, relate to others, and make healthy choices." Whereas mental illness "refers collectively to all diagnosable mental disorders – health conditions involving significant changes in thinking, emotion, and/or behaviors [and] distress and/or problems functioning in social, work or family activities" (American Psychiatric Association, 2021). Mental health concerns and illness manifest from internal and external triggers and include conditions such as situational anxiety, depression, and obsessive-compulsive disorder (OCD). Early signs of diminished mental health include loss of interest or pleasure, weight gain/loss, sleep problems, low energy, feeling lost and alone, and mood swings among others (Mentalhealth.gov, 2020).

According to the American Psychiatric Association (2021), mental illness is common, affecting approximately one in five individuals. Further, diagnosed mental illness has increased among college students over a ten-year span from 2007 to 2017, rising from 19% to 34% (Lipson et al., 2019). Although mental illness is common, diagnosable, and treatable, many do not seek help (Chaib & Brunier, 2017). Even in high-income countries such as the U.S., "nearly 50% of people with depression do not get treatment" (Chaib & Brunier, 2017). Further, individuals between the ages of 16-24 years old are the least likely to contact a physician for mental illness assistance (Bebbington et al., 2003). These statistics highlight the importance of increasing awareness and developing communication patterns to help young adults navigate mental health challenges in organizations.

Communicating mental health concerns is vital for gaining access to resources and support. Unfortunately, individuals do not ask for mental health assistance for a variety of reasons, including concerns about stigmatization (Meluch & Starcher, 2020; Wilson et al., 2021). Mental illness stigma often occurs when individuals believe they are weaker, or are perceived as such by others, and can manifest when a person is negatively self-conscious after seeking mental health assistance (Lazard et al., 2016).

Additionally, organizational communication norms of "professionalism" create barriers for expressing negative emotions (Riforgiate & Sepúlveda, 2021), which often accompany requests for mental health assistance. Kramer and Hess (2002) found that employees identified rules for both positive and negative emotional expression; however, employees broadly expected co-workers to mask negative emotional communication. Further, organizational hiring processes preference individuals who display expected emotions and communication expectations are reinforced through organizational socialization processes (Kramer & Hess, 2002). Organizational emotional norms can cause individuals to mask or downplay felt emotions that are perceived as inappropriate, which can discourage help seeking behavior.

Specific to college, instructors also influence norms about appropriate emotional expression and mental health disclosure. White and Labelle (2019) found that some instructors were open to assisting students with mental health, acting "as an *empathic listener*," serving "as a *referral source*," or functioning as "a *first responder*," while other instructors saw themselves as a "*bystander*" because they were uncomfortable and lacked training to appropriately assist students (italics in original, p. 140). Instructor discomfort with mental health disclosures influenced how resources were provided (e.g., via a generic syllabus paragraph versus initiating personal conversations or check-ins) (White & Labelle, 2019). From the student perspective, students who disclosed mental health concerns to instructors in the past perceived greater risks for future disclosures compared to non-disclosing students (Meluch & Starcher, 2020). Additionally, Vidourek et al. (2014) surveyed 682 students about reporting mental health issues and found the three most frequent concerns were "embarrassment, denial, and not wanting to be labeled crazy" (p. 1014). Unfortunately, mental health concerns are often hidden or masked due to negative experiences and perceptions of organizational norms.

Mental illness is often considered an individual private issue, yet it has broad organizational implications. Colleges have been increasing spending and providing a variety of mental health resources to meet growing student needs for assistance (Carrasco, 2021). Additionally, when individuals with mental illness are not supported, organizations experience increased medical premiums, worker absenteeism, productivity loss (Goetzel et al., 2003), and employee turnover (Anderson et al., 2011). Organizations can enhance employee well-being and reduce mental illness issues by "modifying workloads, providing cognitive behavioral therapy, relaxion and meditation training, time management training, exercise programs, journaling, biofeedback and goal setting" (Anderson et al., 2011, p. i7). Therefore, it is necessary to understand communication patterns to communication patterns to address mental health concerns.

Communication Privacy Management Theory

When individuals make decisions to share private information about themselves and others, they consider how much, when, and with whom to disclose (Petronio, 2010; 2013). Mental health concerns are often considered private, and individuals weigh risks and benefits when making disclosure decisions (Smith & Bruner, 2017). Petronio (2010) proposed communication privacy management (CPM) theory to explain disclosure decisions; CPM "predicts that dialectical tensions are at the core of managing private information" as individuals want to protect privacy while concurrently desire to be open (p. 176).

CPM focuses on three components to manage this privacy/openness tension: 1) *privacy ownership* (to whom the information belongs), 2) *privacy control* (who has the right to contain or disclose the information), and 3) *privacy turbulence* (instances when privacy boundaries are ruptured because of perception differences of ownership and control) (Meluch & Starcher, 2020). According to CPM, individuals feel they are the sole owner of personal information, thus they have the right to conceal information and decide whom to trust with the information (Petronio, 2013). When owners share personal information with others, others become "'authorized co-owners' and are perceived by the 'original owner' to have fiduciary responsibilities for the information" (Petronio, 2013, p. 9). Thus, individuals create *privacy boundaries* around information they feel is personal and create sharing *rules* for themselves and others (Wilson et al., 2021).

For example, Brett may not disclose his mental health concerns with others because he feels they are personal (*privacy ownership*) and he wants to manage his own information (*privacy control*). However, Brett may feel it is necessary share information with his roommate to gain social support or with his teacher or employer to obtain accommodations. Once information is shared, his roommate, teacher, and/or employer co-own the information with him. Brett might assume that *privacy rules* protect his private health information with his teacher or employer, seeing the rules as implicitly communicated based on professional norms. However, he might explicitly communicate *privacy rules* to his roommate with statements such as, "Please don't tell anyone." to create *privacy boundaries*. If his roommate asks a mutual friend about Brett and discloses co-owned information, this disclosure could violate *privacy rules*, create *privacy turbulence,* and initiate rule renegotiation.

According to CPM, *contextual criteria* and *risk/benefit assessments* are important in determining when, what, and to whom to disclose (Wilson et al., 2020). *Contextual criteria* are the circumstances that influence disclosure decisions such as "life experiences (e.g., traumatic life events) or other contextual circumstances (e.g., the appropriateness of a topic being discussed at work)" (Meluch & Starcher, 2020,

p. 770). For example, if Brett is struggling with his workload because of mental health concerns, missed deadlines may create a context that necessitates disclosure to his supervisor.

Additionally, *risk/benefit assessments* occur when individuals anticipate potential negative consequences compared to positive outcomes of disclosure (Wilson et al., 2020). For example, Brett would weigh disclosure risks (e.g., fear of his supervisor viewing him as weak, concern his supervisor would see him as inappropriate or unprofessional), with the benefits (e.g., potential to gain assistance, additional work time). Past disclosure experiences shape individuals' willingness to disclose in future situations (Meluch & Starcher, 2020). If Brett's past disclosure experiences were poor, he would view disclosure as riskier.

Relationship types also have a bearing on risk/benefit assessments. Kennedy-Lightsey and colleagues (2012) found that people disclose information to a third-party, such as a friend, before a more "high stakes" person like a family member. Further, Wilson et al. (2020) explained that concerns about burdening family with mental health issues reduced disclosures to family members. Taken as a whole, CPM provides a framework to understand communication patterns about mental health concerns and help individuals productively disclose information.

Organizational Socialization

Managing and disclosing private information often occurs in organizational contexts, including colleges or workplaces, creating an intersection between CPM and the organizational socialization model. When joining an organization, "learning the ropes" occurs as new members consider existing experiences and gain new experiences (Kramer & Dailey, 2019, p. 96). This learning also involves deciding what, when, and to whom it is appropriate to disclose in the organization.

Jablin (2001) proposed the organizational socialization model, arguing that assimilation occurs in four parts: *anticipatory socialization*, *encounter*, *metamorphosis*, and *organizational exit*. *Anticipatory socialization* includes communication encounters prior to entering the organization that shape expectations about organizational member behaviors (Ruder & Riforgiate, 2019). Talking with and/or observing family members, educational experiences, and media depictions are common anticipatory socialization sources (Kramer & Dailey, 2016). Anticipatory socialization is comprised of two sub-categories: *vocational anticipatory socialization* and *organizational anticipatory socialization* (Kramer, 2010). *Vocational anticipatory socialization* involves communication related to how individuals learn what it means to be in a particular field, industry, or type of position (Kramer, 2010). For example, before entering college, individuals may hear about family members' college experiences, learn about college from guidance counselors or recruiters, talk with friends attending college, and see college students portrayed through media. While accuracy of this information varies, communication experiences work together to create expectations for what it means to be a "college student" and what behaviors are appropriate.

Organizational anticipatory socialization involves refining general expectations by obtaining information specific to an organization (Kramer, 2010). For example, before attending college, individuals may tour the college, read the website, and talk to current students. Similarly, before a job interview individuals may research the organization and then ask questions during the interview. Importantly, individuals consider vocational and organizational anticipatory socialization information when making decisions to attend college, determine their major, pursue work, and select which organizations to join (Riforgiate & Ruder, 2019). Anticipatory socialization also informs expectations about how to behave, including what information and emotions are appropriate to disclose.

Individuals enter the *encounter phase* when they begin in a new organization (Jablin, 2001). During the encounter phase, new members use direct and indirect communication strategies to learn what it means to be an organizational member and what behavior is appropriate (Heiss & Carmack, 2011). Direct communication strategies include asking questions such as "Can I have additional time on this project?" and "Where do I sent this report?" Additionally, individuals learn organizational processes and norms indirectly through observation such as arriving early and waiting in the parking lot until a co-worker enters the building to know how early is "on time." Similarly, new members observe others' reactions to communication involving positive, neutral, and negative emotions to learn expectations about regulating and communicating emotions (Riforgiate & Sepúlveda, 2021). Ultimately, new members who use proactive direct and indirect communication strategies adapt more quickly compared to those who passively learn expectations through mechanisms like unsolicited advice (Kramer & Dailey, 2016). In addition to assimilating to existing organizational norms, new members may also communicate in ways that question, test, or challenge norms (Kramer, 2010).

New members experience *metamorphosis* when they become full-fledged organizational members (Jablin, 2001). The exact time required for metamorphosis varies, ranging between approximately six to 12 months (Kramer, 2010). Even if one experiences metamorphosis, organizational changes such as employee turnover, leadership succession, changing units, or new work procedures can cause members to return to earlier socialization stages (Kramer & Dailey, 2016).

Finally, *organizational exit* occurs when individuals leave an organization for a variety of reasons (Godager et al., 2021). Organizational exit often restarts the organizational socialization process as individuals subsequently become new organizational members elsewhere, taking past experiences and applying them to future contexts. Graduating college students experience exiting from college in a series of stages where they focus on the past, focus on the future, then focus on the past and the future to prepare themselves for the next phase in their lives (Davis & Myers, 2012). This case study illustrates movement through organizational socialization when entering college and the cycle begins again upon graduation and starting a new position. Throughout the case, CPM rules and decisions are shaped by organizational socialization experiences that prompt or suppress disclosure.

CASE STUDY: "WHO CAN I TRUST?"

Stifling air pressed around Valerie's body as a drop of sweat made a winding path down her forehead and the side of her face. Valerie loaded her bedding, plastic drawers, and belongings into a large brown cardboard box on wheels and gave the box a big shove up the access ramp. All the resident hall advisers were smiling cheerfully and offering to help on dorm "move in" day. Valerie faked a smile to blend in. Her August afternoon time slot seemed like a challenge to mark the start of her college career. She had already jumped through the hoops of applying, registering for classes, and finding a roommate online, but going to college didn't seem real until she glanced at the mounds of clothing, bags of school supplies and snacks, and basket of toiletries in her "spacious" 13' by 15' dorm room. *If only the heat was my only concern*, she thought.

As Valerie and her mom walked down to the car, Valerie said, "I can take this last load up Mom." She tried to sound optimistic and confident to calm her mom and blend with the outpouring of positivity that everyone in the dorm displayed. "I can sort my stuff. I know you have a five-hour drive back."

"Oh honey, I can come back up to help you make your bed and get set up." Her mom offered.

"No, it's all right Mom. My roommate should be here soon, and I shouldn't get too settled before meeting her and deciding how to move the furniture."

Tears welled in her mom's eyes. "Are you sure you have everything? I don't mind running to the store with you before I leave with the car."

"Mom, really, I am fine. I love you. I will be all right." Valerie said as bravely as possible, then thought to herself, *how in the world am I going to pull this off?*

They hugged before her mom climbed into the car. Valerie turned quickly as her mom drove off and climbed the stairs with the last of her stuff. She felt off-balance but forced a smile as she passed others on the stairway. *Is it the heat, the physical exhaustion, or am I just nervous?*

With her hand on the doorknob and balancing a box, several bags, and clothing hanging over her arms from her last carload, Valerie took a deep breath in and held it counting to five. Exhaling, she pushed the wooden dorm room door open and stumbled over her piles of stuff, just managing to catch herself before falling face first into a desk. She was surprised by how small and stuffy the room felt.

Thank goodness the room has a window, she thought. But the walls still felt like they were closing in. She dropped her stuff quickly and sat on a pile of clothing at the edge of a bed, trying to take deep, intentional breaths. She felt like she was stepping off a spinning carnival ride and was off balance. "Breathe," she told herself aloud, counting to five again as she inhaled deeply. "Breathe," she repeated, slowly exhaling. After several minutes sitting as still as possible and focusing on her breath, she took a sip of water from the water bottle that her mother forced on her. *Thanks Mom*, she thought. They had argued if she did or didn't need a water bottle, but she was glad her mom won that battle.

Valerie sat for another five minutes and decided she should organize a bit to make room for her roommate who would undoubtably pack more stuff into the crammed space. *This is not quite how I imagined college from my campus visit and all the brochures with happy and excited students. I only feel intense anxiety and panic.*

Her roommate was a sophomore and Valerie knew little about her. Unpacking kept Valerie's mind focused on something constructive rather than all the "what ifs" she could come up with staring at the sterile beige-ish dorm room walls. The new coat of paint was thickly layered over years of wear and stories of students before her. She wondered how many students had been seeking a fresh start with a clean slate before her.

Valerie knelt on the floor, slowly emptying one shopping bag at a time. Sorting through clothing was no big deal but removing photos and the teddy bear from when she was a baby struck a chord. Valerie's eyes brimmed with tears. She blinked several times so her mascara wouldn't run. *Get it together*, she told herself. *No-one around you seems to be sad.* Despite only being gone for a few hours, she was already homesick. The longest she had been away from home was a couple of weeks at summer camp – which were a disaster. *How am I going to make it a whole semester?* Valerie worried as a tear escaped her constant blinking and rolled down her cheek easily along with the dripping sweat.

Under her breath Valerie encouraged herself, *Be strong. The last thing I want to do is ask for help or worry mom and dad. I don't even know how to begin to get help now that I am on campus. I can do this on my own.*

Startled by the door handle shaking, Valerie turned her back to the door and used a nearby sweater sleeve to dab her eyes. Smiling as broadly as possible with a bit of a squint to hide the tears and redness in her eyes, she turned to meet the gaze of a tall, slender young woman.

"Hi!" The girl said. "I'm Alicia."

"Hey Alicia." Valerie gave a shy wave and noticed that in trying to appear cheerful her voice was an octave higher and squeaky. "Nice to meet you."

Valerie unintentionally stared. Alicia's long straight brown hair rested easily on her shoulders. Her bright green eyes sparkled, and her rosy cheeks managed to show through her bronzed tan skin. Alicia stood effortlessly while conveying confidence, reminding Valerie of the "popular kids" from high school who looked away when she walked by. However, Alicia didn't look away. She seemed kind and curious about Valerie.

"Is this my side?" Alicia asked, making Valerie realize she had been staring at Alicia for a while without saying anything.

"Yeah, that's yours," Valerie pointed to the other bed. "I mean unless you want this one. I just figured it would be best to stack my stuff mostly on one side. Well, at least that was how the piles started." *Why can't I interact with people? I sound like an idiot.* Valerie criticized herself.

"I'm sorry, I didn't catch your name," Alicia commented. "Uhm, my name is Valerie, but you can call me Val."

"Nice to meet you, Val! What pronouns do you use?" Alicia flashed a welcoming smile and she seemed unbelievably confident and graceful.

"Oh, uhm, she/her/hers. Thanks for asking! And how about you?"

"She/her," Alicia smiled again allowing Valerie to notice her straight white teeth.

Valerie couldn't help but like Alicia. Alicia had a comfortable, positive presence, just like the resident hall advisers and campus tour guides. Valerie wanted a roommate she could trust and feel comfortable confiding in. Opening up to people too quickly in the past had burned Valerie in high school though. While Valerie wanted Alicia to know and understand her, she held back. *I can't share too much. This is a fresh start from high school. No-one needs to know my struggle with anxiety, think I am weak, or talk about me behind my back. This year is going to be different.*

Unpacking, Valerie and Alicia made small talk and realized they had a lot in common. They both loved reading, wanted to travel more, hated cauliflower, and were only children. In fact, they were even in the same section of ECON 101, which gave Valerie someone to sit with. *This is going to be all right.* Valerie assured herself.

A month into classes, they had an easy routine and things were going well. Living, eating, and taking a class together created lots of opportunities to develop their friendship.

"Did you see Ethan in ECON today?" Alicia asked. "He keeps looking across the room at you and smiling."

"Oh my gosh! No, he is smiling at *you*. I love the twinkle in his eyes. He is so cute and a genius."

"Val, he is not looking at me. It is all you! You should ask him to help you with your homework." Alicia encouraged with a wink. "Besides, I have my eye on Allan," she laughed.

Val giggled, then remembered her homework and sighed deeply, "Yeah, I could really use help with my papers. I can't believe I have four papers due in the next three weeks. There is no way I am going to be able to pull this off!"

"Sure you can Val. You are smart and work hard. Just sit down and get started," Alicia advised.

"Yeah, I will get going on them Saturday," Valerie agreed.

Secretly, thus far Valerie had no problem with her homework. She didn't mind the essays and she stayed on top of her assignments. Compared to high school, she couldn't believe how well she was able to keep up. She usually finished all her studying for the next day well before dinner. The only reason she complained was because it seemed like everyone lamented homework and she desperately wanted to fit in.

Two more weeks came and went, and Valerie's upcoming midterms hit her hard. She had been doing so well up to that point but overwhelm crept in and Valerie felt the pressure. She had been talking to herself a lot lately. *One thing at a time. Just take one thing at a time.* This mantra had helped before, but suddenly there was twice the amount of work with higher stakes. Valerie's heart frequently raced and she found herself short of breath, dizzy at times, and having trouble sleeping. Sometimes she couldn't sleep at all and other times she felt like all she could do was sleep. Valerie was no stranger to these symptoms, but they had never been so extreme before.

The week of midterms, right before heading to class, Valerie said under her breath more urgently, *Plan ahead. Take one thing at a time. Breathe.* She kept writing down assignments and crossing tasks off in her planner. Glancing at her planner again, she realized she missed several discussion board assignments. Her face flushed and her heart pounded. A tingling sensation moved across her body and her chest tightened. As her breath quickened to abrupt, jagged intakes, she tried to hold back the eminent sobbing, but her body acted as a separate entity from her mind. She couldn't stop.

Tears streamed down her flushed cheeks. She was grateful Alicia had already left for class as she stifled the noise from her deep sobs and running nose. Alicia was always on top of things – just like all the other students. Alicia would not understand. Her teacher would not understand.

Thoughts flooded her mind, flowing faster than her tears. *Why can't I keep up? How could I miss these assignments? Why wasn't I better organized? I am going to fail. Everyone else is keeping up. No one else seems stressed. I am going to get kicked out of college. I knew what I needed to do and simply didn't do it. And now look - the work keeps piling up more and more because I didn't do it. I didn't keep careful enough track. I know better. There is no way out. I can't make this right.* Valerie's negative self-talk was new, and she didn't know how to confront it. She felt completely alone. In high school she would have talked with the guidance counselor, but in college she had no idea who could help her or even where to start looking.

The missing discussion board posts seemed like an all or nothing proposition. *My teacher must think I am a slacker and that I don't care. I am so embarrassed.*

Valerie skipped class and buried herself under her blankets. When Alicia returned at lunchtime, Valerie pretended she was sleeping and skipped lunch. Once Alicia had returned to class, Valerie pulled out her laptop. There was a message from Professor Edwards.

"Hi Valerie - I missed you at the midterm today and noticed you haven't turned in some discussion board posts. It can be hard to acclimate during your first semester. Please let me know what I can do to help get you back on track."

Oh my gosh! Oh my gosh! Oh my gosh! The midterm was TODAY? Valerie panicked. *I want to contact Professor Edwards to tell him the stress I've been under lately, and at the very least apologize. Maybe he would still let me take the midterm. I don't want him to think I don't care, or even worse that I'm not capable or weak.*

Valerie quickly typed, "Dear Dr. Edwards – I am so sorry I missed the midterm. My alarm didn't wake me up. Is there any way I can come in now and take it during your office hours?"

Valerie read Dr. Edwards' email and her own response several times. *Should I tell him how much I am struggling? Would it help for him to know I have anxiety? Should I tell him I messed up which day was the midterm? Other students aren't struggling or asking for exceptions.* Blaming it on her alarm clock seemed like a stretch, but then she didn't have to get into her mental health history. He didn't need to know that anyway. *Plus,* Valerie reasoned, *I've dealt with stuff like this before on my own. No one needs to know about my anxiety. Telling my teachers didn't help in high school. I don't want Dr. Edwards or Alicia to think of me differently and I certainly don't want to worry my parents.*

Thankfully, Dr. Edwards responded right away and let her make up the test. He didn't question why she had missed the test and Valerie didn't volunteer any other reasons. Valerie was determined to step up her study routine and keep better track of assignments. *I can fix this,* Valerie resolved. *I will practically live in the library so I will not be tempted to crawl into bed and hide. If I am at the library, I won't need to talk with Alicia or other people about how anxious I feel.* Valerie completely shifted her study and part-time work schedule. For a few weeks it seemed to be working.

Alicia bumped into Valerie in the library after working on a group project. "Hey, Val! I haven't seen you in a while. You'd think we didn't live together! How are things going?"

Valerie looked up from her textbook. "Yeah. uhm, Sorry. I've been at the library studying late most nights. When I get home, you're already asleep."

"That's okay," Alicia took a seat across from Valerie and continued, "but you have to come up for air every once in a while. Take a break from studying. Classes aren't the end-all be-all."

"Yes, they are!" Valerie shouted, not realizing how many heads turned as she raised her voice. "How can you not care about studying? Don't you want good grades?"

Alicia leaned forward and spoke softly to calm Valerie down, "Of course, I care. I just don't want to lose my life over a couple of tests."

Valerie fumed, tightening her jaw as she responded, "Just leave me alone. I need to study," returning to look at her book to avoid eye contact. *Studying and grades are important! My parents and teachers have said so for years. I have to maintain my GPA; that is what the Dean and my advisor said during orientation. What is Alicia thinking!??!*

Alicia was stunned. Trying to sound positive she said, "Alright, but I'm here if you need me."

Valerie didn't look up as Alicia walked away. Alicia had been happy to see Valerie and left confused at the way the conversation unfolded. The next day, Alicia pushed through the crowd of students leaving her Classical Literature class.

"Emily, wait!" Alicia shouted over student side conversations.

When Alicia caught up to Emily she said, "Hey, I need to talk to you about something."

"What's up? Is everything all right?"

Alicia lowered her voice, "I'm not sure. I'm worried about Val. Have you talked with her recently?" Emily was a mutual friend from an ECON group project.

"No. Why? What's wrong?" Emily looked more concerned.

Alicia confided, "Val seems really stressed out, way beyond the normal midterm stress. I asked her to take a break yesterday and she snapped at me to leave her alone. She looks exhausted and has been studying nonstop. I don't know what to do. It's been like I am living alone in the dorm room. I am worried something is seriously wrong."

"Yikes. Well, maybe you can try talking to her again, but be more direct and ask if she is doing okay. Val hasn't said anything to me, but I haven't seen her either," Emily offered.

"Yeah. I can try that," Alicia replied hesitantly.

When Alicia returned to the dorm room, she found Valerie huddled at her desk piled with open books illuminated by a single desk lamp in the dark room.

Alicia quietly hung up her coat and gently asked, "Hey Val, can you pause to talk for a second?"

Valerie didn't look up, letting out an irritated sigh, "I guess."

"Val, I'm worried about you. You've been studying nonstop, and it's wearing you down."

Valerie blurted out defensively, "If this is about yesterday, then I'm sorry. I was stressed and..."

Alicia jumped in, "No Val, it's not about yesterday. I'm your friend and I care about you. I just want to make sure you're taking care of yourself. I talked to Emily and she agreed that I should check on you."

Rather than accepting the concern in Alicia's voice, Val focused on how she was a topic of discussion. "Wait... you talked to Emily... about me? Why would you do that?" Val tried to hold back her anger.

"I was worried about you, Val. So, I asked her for advice." Alicia said with concern.

"I would appreciate it if you wouldn't talk to other people about me." Val responded in a flat matter-of-fact tone. "I'm fine." *Val thought, the last thing I want is for all my friends to gossip about me that I have problem. That would be like high school all over again.* Val told herself, *don't cry. She will think you are weak and incapable.*

"Val..." Alicia noticed the pain in Valerie's face and stopped. "I know you'll tell me when you're ready. Just know I'm here for you."

Alicia quietly grabbed her keys to head to dinner when she noticed Valerie was fighting back tears. Alicia paused, sat on her bed and looked at Valerie with such kindness. Valerie took a deep breath and surprised herself, sharing,

"Alicia! I am... not okay, but I don't want everyone to know."

"Do you want to talk about it?" Alicia offered.

"No, but I should. Promise not to tell anyone else?"

Alicia looked Valerie in the eyes and nodded. "Promise."

Valerie took another deep breath,

"I am completely overwhelmed by school, wanting to get good grades, balancing work, and needing money. I've gotten into a pattern of studying, working, and not taking care of myself." Tears rolled down Valerie's cheeks as the words tumbled from her mouth, "I feel like with college there are a lot responsibilities ... and then you see how much money you owe. I feel like I can never escape the stress and anxiety. I thought I could work my way out of it, but I seem to be making things worse. I had issues with anxiety in high school, but I thought I had them under control. I don't want people to look at me funny or think that I am incapable, so I have been trying to cope the best that I can. Everyone here has their act together – including you. I see students answering in class, relaxing in the union, and they always know the answers and are happy. Sure, students complain about homework, but they joke about it – it isn't like they are struggling. I am at a breaking point all the time. I can't tell my family because they will worry. I don't want to give up, but I don't know how to move forward."

"I completely understand." Alicia comforted as she handed Valerie a Kleenex. "When I moved to campus last year. I also struggled with managing everything. It's already scary when you know what you're doing, but when you don't, you feel like someone's going to come knocking on your door and be like where's the money? I was terrified and felt really alone."

Valerie paused to process, "Alicia, I am sorry that happened to you. That must have been awful."

Alicia continued, "It was. I had major social anxiety too. Being a daughter of immigrants… It's just, you always see bad things happening to people around you, like deportation, and you always see what problems people have going on, but you never have a solution because you are one of those people. That's why I'm studying Political Science, to understand the system better and how it affects people like me."

Valerie felt humbled by Alicia's story. "How did you cope with your anxiety?"

Alicia sighed, "Well, I ignored it for a long time in high school because I didn't have a primary doctor or insurance and you need a doctor to give you a referral. I knew I couldn't pay for the doctor's visits. But when I started college, I heard about free counseling at the health center during Orientation. When things got bad, I went to the health center website and made an appointment. I saw a therapist who was a grad student there for a while, but then they connected me with other resources in the area and now I see a therapist outside of school."

"I didn't even know there were therapists on campus. No-one talks about it." Valerie paused, "Weren't you nervous to run into someone you knew at the health center?"

"A little bit, especially because of the social anxiety. But I saw someone I knew when I went for the appointment and it brought me a lot of comfort. It was nice knowing someone was going through similar things. I was also just happy that they were taking charge of their mental health. It made me more inspired to work on myself."

"Yeah, I could see that. Thank you for sharing with me and letting me know about the health center." Valerie let out a sigh. For the first time in a while, she felt like she could breathe.

Alicia gave her a big hug. "I am here for you Val. You are not alone."

Several weeks later, Valerie was waking back from class, lost in her own thoughts. *I made it through midterms. I should be relieved. Why am I still so anxious? Should I go to therapy? I'm not sure I'm comfortable talking to a stranger about my mental health. I would never have guessed that Alicia struggled with social anxiety. It is nice to know I am not alone, but I wish I had an adult I trusted to talk with. I don't want to worry my parents. They might make me move back home. But I feel so jittery all the time and my chest hurts from the stress. Maybe I should call home.*

Valerie grabbed her cellphone out of her back pocket, sat on a nearby bench, and looked around. No-one was nearby. She took a deep breath and scrolled through some family photos. *I should call. My parents love me and will know what I should do.* Her finger hovered over the button a while before clicking on her mom's number. The phone rang a couple of times while Valerie held her breath.

"Hi Val." her mom answered cheerfully.

"Hi Mom, uhm, can I talk to you about something?" Valerie asked.

"Sure, sweety, what's up?" Her mom replied in a loving tone.

It wasn't so hard to talk with her mom after all. Valerie shared her fears and asked for advice about going to the health center. Her mom wasn't angry and didn't demand she come home. In fact, her mom encouraged her to go to the health center and even looked up the phone number. With a phone number in hand, Valerie felt in control for the first time since starting college. "Thank you for always loving and supporting me mom, I will call now." Valerie promised.

Valerie finished her first semester, first year, and three more years of college by taking one week at a time with the help of her therapist and support of her family. Seeing people in the health center and talking with the therapist about how normal her feelings were helped her realize that it is all right to ask for help. Not everyone on campus was as happy as they appeared. The important thing was to take care of herself.

While her anxiety didn't go away and there were some rough patches, Valerie found ways to care of herself and be successful. *One more week and I will have my degree,* she thought as she walked to the library to study for finals.

Valerie was surprised to bump into Alicia in the library. "Hey, Val! How's it going?"

"I am doing well, considering I am studying for finals and looking for a job." Valerie shared. "It is great to see you. I hadn't heard from you at all last year. I figured you graduated. What are you doing back on campus?" Valerie asked.

"Sorry to be out of touch. I took last year off school to be with my family. It was best for them and for my mental health." Alicia confided.

"I totally understand." Valerie said. "It is so important to take care of yourself. Actually, I've wanted to thank you for looking out for me my freshman year. I didn't tell you at the time, but after we talked around midterms that fall, I started seeing a therapist consistently. I don't think I would have had the confidence to do that without the conversation with you. I wasn't ready to talk about it at the time. You made all the difference for me Alicia. Thank you." Valerie looked Alicia in the eyes and smiled.

"I'm so happy to hear that! How is the job search going?" Alicia asked.

"I am stressed but managing." Valerie replied. "I sent my resumé to a few places, but I haven't heard anything. I am getting nervous."

"I am in the same boat." Alicia shared. "What are you nervous about?"

"I am nervous that I will mess up at the interview, that I won't be able to find a job, or worse yet I will find one and they will fire me! It is hard to be super positive on applications and in interviews when you don't feel positive."

"You don't have an interview yet and you're already nervous about losing your job? I hope you can work through that anxiety. Relax, focus on graduating and getting through your interview when you get one!" Alicia encouraged.

"I will."

"Just take a deep breath. You have this!" Alicia said as she flashed the same bright, toothy smile she did freshman year.

"I will do my best!" Valerie replied, but thought to herself, *Yeah, like I can ever really calm down. This is something I just have to live with. At least I have some better coping strategies to make things easier now compared to when I started college.*

Alicia was right. Valerie got an interview and then a job about a month after graduation. Things were looking up. Valerie dressed up in her best "business casual" outfit and showed up early for her first day of work.

Her boss, Lauren, greeted her in the lobby and walked her to her new desk.

"So, Valerie, we're excited to have you on the team. As a new employee, you are on probation for 90 days, but after those three months, your full benefits kick in – health, dental, and two weeks paid vacation."

"Great! I understand." Valerie replied and did her best to smile sincerely. *Everyone in the office looks so positive and confident. I am so nervous! Please don't mess up. Did she say I don't have any health insurance for three months? How am I going to cover my doctor's appointments? It will be all right. I will figure something out.*

"Here is your desk. Molly will be training you, but if you need anything from me, my office is just around the corner. Feel free to stop by." Lauren offered with a confident smile.

"Thank you." Valerie replied.

"Nice to meet you, Valerie, is it? My name is Molly, and you will be hanging out with me for a week."

"Nice to meet you, Molly. You can call me Val if you'd like."

"How are you feeling? A bit nervous?" Molly asked, sensing Valerie's hesitation.

"Well, you know, first day. If I am honest, I'm a little nervous I might make a mistake." Valerie shared as she thought. *It's nice talking to someone closer to my age and Molly seems cool.*

"Well, don't worry about mistakes before you've even begun." Molly said in a reassuring tone. "We all need learn how to do the work at some point. I made plenty of mistakes and I am still here. I will help you."

Valerie breathed a small sigh of relief. *Note to self, mistakes are normal here. I can learn this job.*

The first day, and even the first couple of weeks were fine as Molly helped Valerie learn the job. But then Valerie began struggling with additional deadlines that piled up with each new responsibility and an important new project. *I have so much to do and no time. I thought this was going to be different from college and my anxiety was under control. I will never get all this work done. Everyone else is keeping up during work hours. I don't want them to think I can't do this job!* Valerie worked late into the evenings and the project deadline arrived quickly. *Oh my gosh, I'm going to be fired before my 90-day probation is up. I can't finish on time.*

The day of the project deadline, Molly approached Valerie's desk, "Hi Val. Show me what you have."

"I'm sorry, Molly. I didn't finish. I'm so so so sorry." Valerie said as tears welled in her eyes.

"Val, it is totally okay. Hey, don't be upset. I gave you a tough project. I figured you would need more time. That is no problem. All you need to do in the future is let me know. Open communication helps us stay on the same page." Molly explained, "The company truly values each employee and wants everyone to enjoy working here. You just need to figure out your limitations and time management. That takes time. This isn't college anymore - we move deadlines around. Don't be so hard on yourself."

Valerie hadn't realized until that moment that she had been hard on herself. *I have been so nervous about messing up that I made myself miss the deadline and hurt my mental health. I don't know that I can share my mental health concerns at work, but this is something I am going to need to live with. I need to keep working on my anxiety if I want to make it through this job and life.*

CASE STUDY ANALYSIS AND DISCUSSION

Communication Privacy Management (CPM) Theory

CPM and organizational socialization communication patterns are evident throughout this case study, providing an opportunity to analyze how disclosures are shaped by privacy and organizational norms. Considering CPM theory, Valerie saw her mental health and anxiety concerns as personal information belonging to her, demonstrating *privacy ownership*. Privacy ownership is further evident in Valerie's management of the information, exercising *privacy control*. Her internal dialogue, *"No one needs to know about my anxiety."* is an example of her intentional choice not to disclose and to remain in control of the information. Further, Valerie decided to attribute missing her exam to an issue with her alarm clock rather than her anxiety, allowing her to remain in control of the information.

Privacy turbulence occurred when Valerie learned that Alicia spoke to Emily about Valerie's stress and behaviors. Alicia violated *privacy boundaries* because Valerie felt that her stress was private even though it was externally observable. Valerie's angry response of, "Wait... You talked to Emily about it? Why would you do that?" communicated that Valerie perceived the violation. This *privacy turbulence* caused Valerie to explicitly renegotiate her *privacy boundaries* instructing, "I would appreciate it you wouldn't talk to other people about me." Further, the *privacy turbulence* prompted Valerie to verbally confirm *privacy rules* prior to disclosing more information when she asked, "Promise not to tell anyone?" and waited for Alicia's response of, "Promise." When Valerie disclosed that she was struggling and Alicia shared her own struggles, the roommates initiated *co-ownership* of each other's private information.

This case also demonstrates mental health disclosures based on *contextual criteria* and *risk/benefit assessments* when Valerie decided to not disclose her anxiety to her professor. Valerie acknowledged *contextual criteria* based on her assumptions of normal college student behaviors (e.g., *"Everyone else is keeping up. No one else seems stressed."*). Valerie engaged in *risk/benefit assessment* when she weighed the risks of disclosing (e.g., *"I don't want him to think... that I'm not capable or weak."*) with the uncertainty that disclosing would create any benefit (e.g., *"Telling my teachers didn't seem to help in high school."*) and decided not to disclose. Valerie's decision parallels Meluch and Starcher's (2020) finding that college students who revealed mental health issues in the past to instructors were more hesitant to reveal information in the future. However, it is also possible that if Valerie had disclosed, her professor may have been able to help connect her with campus resources (White & Labelle, 2019). Additionally, Valerie did not share her anxiety when entering her new job; this decision considered *contextual criteria* related to professionalism (Kramer & Hess, 2002) and *risk/benefit assessments* related to her 90-day probationary period and new working relationships.

Contextual criteria were also important in Valerie's decision to disclose to Alicia and her mother. Valerie's anxiety constituted a *contextual criteria* that was detrimental enough for Valerie to recognize she needed help. Valerie communicated this, telling Alicia "I am... not okay, but I don't want everyone to know." and that she did not want to talk about it "but I should." In this case, Valerie perceived the need to obtain help (benefit) as greater than the perceived risk. Valerie disclosed to Alicia first, which is in line with Kennedy-Lightsey and colleagues' (2012) finding that individuals see less risk in disclosing to friends compared to family members. Valerie was hesitant to disclose to her parents because she perceived the risk of burdening them (e.g., *"I certainly don't want to worry my parents."*) and feared that they would make her return home. Valerie's disclosure behavior mirrors Wilson et al.'s (2020) finding that individuals withheld mental health concern disclosures to avoid burdening family members.

Organizational Socialization

The four phases of *organizational socialization* – anticipatory socialization, encounter, metamorphosis, and exit – relate to CPM in terms of the organizational norms that shape disclosures. College and workplaces are organizational contexts where previous communication experiences shape expectations (Woo et al., 2017). For example, *anticipatory socialization* was evident when Valerie drew on information prior to attending college, thinking, *"This is not quite how I imagined college from my campus visit and all the brochures with happy and excited students."* Upon starting college and her new job, Valerie also drew on her prior experiences as *anticipatory socialization* information to make disclosure decisions (e.g., *"Telling my teachers didn't seem to help in high school."*). Negative past communication experiences shaped what Valerie viewed as appropriate communication in college and subsequently her job.

Valerie experienced the *encounter phase*, upon entering college and her job. In college, Valerie observed others' communication behaviors to understand what emotions were appropriate to communicate (e.g., "I see students answering in class, relaxing in the union, and they always know the answers and are happy. Sure, students complain about homework, but they joke about it – it isn't like they are struggling."). These observations led Valerie to perceive that it was not appropriate to disclose negative emotions or mental health struggles. At work, Valerie observed Molly's competence as she trained Valerie in her new position, also setting expectations for communication and expected behavior. Valerie also passively received advice and information in college when Alicia disclosed her own social anxiety, as well as at work when Lauren shared job benefit information and Molly indicated that deadlines were flexible with open communication. In each example, Valerie learned information that helped her understand organizational communication norms.

The *metamorphosis phase* of becoming an organizational member was most evident when Valerie neared graduation and recognized she would succeed, thinking *"One more week and I will have my degree."* Valerie's comments near graduation also illustrate communication patterns common for *organizational exit* (Davis & Myers, 2012) as Valerie looked back to thank Alicia for her support and looked forward to finding work after graduation. As Valerie began her new job, the organizational socialization cycle began again. Throughout this case, Valerie demonstrated CPM and organizational socialization phases, including how communication patterns shape what, when, and to whom to disclose private information.

DISCUSSION QUESTIONS

1. How does Valerie make communication decisions to manage privacy boundaries while assimilating into school and subsequently work? What are organizational factors that influence these decisions?
2. While Valerie sees her mental health and anxiety as private, how do her communication patterns make this information public in unexpected ways?

3. When Valerie confided in Alicia about her mental health, what were the benefits and risks of this decision? How did Valerie communicate in ways to minimize the risks
4. Considering organizational socialization phases, which phase seems most important to learning communication norms about CPM and why?
5. How are vocational and role anticipatory socialization both beneficial and problematic for mental health disclosures as individuals enter and metamorphosize into organizations?

REFERENCES

Alsulami, S., Omar, Z. A., Binnwejim, M. S., Alhamdan, F., Aldrees, A., Al-bawardi, A., Alsohim, M., & Alhabeeb, M. (2018). Perception of academic stress among health science preparatory program students in two Saudi universities. *Advances in Medical Education and Practice*, *9*, 159–164. doi:10.2147/AMEP.S143151 PMID:29559816

American Psychiatric Association. (2021). *Patients & Families*. https://www.psychiatry.org/patients-families/what-is-mental-illness

Anderson, P., Jané-llopis, E., & Hosman, C. (2011). Reducing the silent burden of impaired mental health. *Health Promotion International*, *26*(1, suppl 1), i4–i9. doi:10.1093/heapro/dar051 PMID:22079936

Bebbington, P. E., Meltzer, H., Brugha, T. S., Farrell, M., Jenkins, R., Ceresa, C., & Lewis, G. (2000). Unequal access and unmet need: Neurotic disorders and the use of primary care services. *Psychological Medicine*, *30*(6), 1359–1367. doi:10.1017/S0033291799002950 PMID:11097076

Carrasco, M. (2021, September 20). *Colleges seek virtual mental health services*. Inside Higher Ed. https://www.insidehighered.com/news/2021/09/20/colleges-expand-mental-health-services-students

Chaib, F., & Brunier, A. (2017). *"Depression: Lets' talk" says WHO, as depression tops list of causes or ill health*. World Health Organization. https://www.who.int/news/item/30-03-2017--depression-let-s-talk-says-who-as-depression-tops-list-of-causes-of-ill-health

Chen, J. A., Stevens, C., Wong, S. H., & Liu, C. H. (2019). Psychiatric symptoms and diagnoses among U.S. college students: A comparison by race and ethnicity. *Psychiatric Services (Washington, D.C.)*, *70*(6), 442–449. doi:10.1176/appi.ps.201800388 PMID:30914001

Davis, C. W., & Myers, K. K. (2012). Communication and member disengagement in planned organizational exit. *Western Journal of Communication*, *76*(2), 194–216. doi:10.1080/10570314.2011.651250

Godager, E. A., Coker, M. C., Davis, B. L., & Pink, K. J. (2021). Making sense of leaders' exits: Extending exit socialization research through sensemaking. *Communication Studies*. Advance online publication. doi:10.1080/10510974.2021.2011354

Goetzel, R. Z., Hawkins, K., Ozminkowski, R. J., & Wang, S. (2003). The health and productivity cost burden of the "top 10" physical and mental health conditions affecting six large U.S. employers in 1999. *Journal of Occupational and Environmental Medicine*, *45*(1), 5–14. doi:10.1097/00043764-200301000-00007 PMID:12553174

Heiss, S. N., & Carmack, H. J. (2011). Knock, knock; Who's there?: Making sense of organizational entrance through humor. *Management Communication Quarterly*, *26*(1), 106–132. doi:10.1177/0893318911414914

Jablin, F. M. (2001). Organizational entry, assimilation and disengagement/exit. In F. M. Jablin & L. L. Putnam (Eds.), *The new handbook of organizational communication: Advances in theory, research and methods* (pp. 732–818). Sage. doi:10.4135/9781412986243.n19

John Hopkins University. (2021, August 16). *School-life balance*. https://jhsap.org/self_help_resources/school-life_balance/

Joyce, D., & Weibelzahl, S. (2011). Student counseling services: Using text messaging to lower barriers to help seeking. *Innovations in Education and Teaching International*, *48*(3), 287–299. doi:10.1080/14703297.2011.593705

Kennedy-Lightsey, C. D., Martin, M. M., Thompson, M., Himes, K. L., & Clingerman, B. Z. (2012). Communication privacy management theory: Exploring coordination and ownership between friends. *Communication Quarterly*, *60*(5), 665–680. doi:10.1080/01463373.2012.725004

Kramer, M. W. (2010). *Organizational socialization: Joining and leaving organizations*. Polity.

Kramer, M. W., & Dailey, S. L. (2019). Socialization and organizational culture. In J. McDonald & R. Mitra (Eds.), *Movements in organizational communication research: Current issues and future directions* (pp. 96–115). Routledge. doi:10.4324/9780203730089-6

Kramer, M. W., & Hess, J. A. (2002). Communication rules for the display of emotions in organizational settings. *Management Communication Quarterly*, *16*(1), 66–80. doi:10.1177/0893318902161003

Lazard, A. J., Bamgbade, B. A., Sontag, J. M., & Brown, C. (2016). Using visual metaphors in health messages: A strategy to increase effectiveness for mental illness communication. *Journal of Health Communication*, *21*(12), 1260–1268. doi:10.1080/10810730.2016.1245374 PMID:27869576

Lederer, A. M., Hoban, M. T., Lipson, S. K., Zhou, S., & Eisenberg, D. (2020). More than inconvenienced: The unique needs of U.S. college students during the pandemic. *Health Education & Behavior*, *48*(1), 14–19. doi:10.1177/1090198120969372 PMID:33131325

Lipson, S. K., Lattie, E. G., & Eisenberg, D. (2019). Increased rates of mental health service utilization by U.S. College Students: 10-year population level trends (2007-2017). *Psychiatric Services (Washington, D.C.)*, *70*(1), 60–63. doi:10.1176/appi.ps.201800332 PMID:30394183

Meluch, A. L., & Starcher, S. C. (2020). College student concealment and disclosure of mental health issues in the classroom: Students' perceptions of risk and use of contextual criteria. *Communication Studies*, *71*(5), 769–782. doi:10.1080/10510974.2020.1771392

Mentalhealth.gov. (2020, May 28). *What is Mental Health?* https://www.mentalhealth.gov/basics/what-is-mental-health

Petronio, S. (2010). Communication privacy management theory: What do we know about family privacy regulation? *Journal of Family Theory & Review*, *2*(3), 175–196. doi:10.1111/j.1756-2589.2010.00052.x

Petronio, S. (2013). Brief status report on communication privacy management theory. *Journal of Family Communication*, *13*(1), 6–14. doi:10.1080/15267431.2013.743426

Riforgiate, S. E., & Kramer, M. W. (2021). The nonprofit assimilation process and work-life balance. *Sustainability*, *13*(11), 5993. doi:10.3390u13115993

Riforgiate, S. E., & Sepúlveda, S. (2021). Managing and being managed by emotions. In F. Cooren & P. Stücheli-Herlach (Eds.), *Handbook of management communication* (pp. 511–528). De Gruyter Mouton., doi:10.1515/9781501508059-028

Ruder, E. M., & Riforgiate, S. E. (2019). Organizational socialization of millennial nonprofit workers. In M. Z. Ashlock & A. Atay (Eds.), *Examining Millennials reshaping organizational cultures* (pp. 33–50).

Smith, S. A., & Brunner, S. R. (2017). To reveal or conceal: Using communication privacy management to understand disclosures in the workplace. *Management Communication Quarterly*, *31*(3), 429–446. doi:10.1177/0893318917692896

Son, C., Hegde, S., Eng, B., Smith, A., Wang, X., & Sasangohar, F. (2020). Effects of COVID-19 on college students' mental health in the United States: Interview survey study. *Journal of Medical Internet Research*, *22*(9), e21279. doi:10.2196/21279 PMID:32805704

Student Loan Hero. (2021, January 27). *A look at the shocking student loan debt statistics for 2021*. https://studentloanhero.com/student-loan-debt-statistics/

U.S. Center for Disease Control. (2021). *Mental Health*. https://www.cdc.gov/mentalhealth/learn/

Vidourek, R. A., King, K. A., Nabors, L. A., & Merianos, A. L. (2014). Students' benefits and barriers to mental health help-seeking. *Health Psychology and Behavioral Medicine*, *2*(1), 1009–1022. doi:10.1080/21642850.2014.963586 PMID:25750831

White, A., & LaBelle, S. (2019). A qualitative investigation of instructors' perceived communicative roles in students' mental health management. *Communication Education*, *68*(2), 133–155. doi:10.1080/03634523.2019.1571620

Wilson, S. R., Hintz, E. A., MacDermid Wadsworth, S. M., Topp, D. B., Southwell, K. H., & Spoont, M. (2021). Female U.S. military veterans' (non)disclosure of mental health issues with family and friends: Privacy rules and boundary management. *Health Communication*, *36*(4), 412–423. doi:10.1080/10410236.2019.1693128 PMID:31752542

Woo, D., Putnam, L. L., & Riforgiate, S. E. (2017). Identity work and tensions in organizational internships: A comparative analysis. *Western Journal of Communication*, *81*(5), 560–581. doi:10.1080/10570314.2017.1312510

KEY TERMS AND DEFINITIONS

Anticipatory Socialization: The first stage of the organizational socialization process that involves communication encounters prior to entering an organization and how those exchanges shape expectations of organizational member behaviors (Ruder & Riforgiate, 2019).

Communication Privacy Management (CPM) Theory: This theory explains that individuals experience a dialectical tension between keeping information confidential and being open to predict communication disclosure decisions. Factors such as privacy ownership and privacy control predict if individuals will experience privacy turbulence when dealing with personal information (Petronio, 2010).

Contextual Criteria: The circumstances that influence disclosure decisions such as "life experiences (e.g., traumatic life events) or other contextual circumstances (e.g., the appropriateness of a topic being discussed at work)" (Meluch & Starcher, 2020, p. 770).

Encounter Stage: The third stage of the organizational socialization process that occurs when individuals become new members of an organization and use direct and indirect communication strategies to learn what it means to be an organizational member and what behavior is appropriate (Heiss & Carmack, 2011).

Metamorphosis Stage: The third stage in the organizational socialization process when an individual feels like a full-fledged organizational member (Jablin, 2001).

Organizational Anticipatory Socialization: This occurs during the first stage of the organizational socialization process in the anticipatory socialization stage and involves refining general expectations by obtaining information specific to a particular organization (Kramer, 2010).

Organizational Exit: The fourth and final stage of the organizational socialization process when an individual leaves an organization for a variety of reasons (Godager et al., 2021).

Organizational Socialization: This four-stage model explains how individuals learn about, enter, become members, and leave organizations, including specific communication behaviors that are prevalent during each of the stages (Jablin, 2001).

Privacy Boundaries: Barriers created through communication rules that delineate what personal information belongs to individuals and others and how that information is allowed to be shared (Wilson et al., 2021).

Privacy Control: When an individual has the right to contain or disclose personal information (Meluch & Starcher, 2020).

Privacy Ownership: When an individual believes that information belongs to themself or specified others (Meluch & Starcher, 2020).

Privacy Turbulence: When boundaries around personal information are ruptured because individuals have different understandings of information ownership and control (Meluch & Starcher, 2020).

Risk/Benefit Assessments: Individuals anticipate potential negative consequences and positive outcomes to determine if they will share private information (Wilson et al., 2020).

Vocational Organizational Anticipatory Socialization: This represents part of the first stage of the organizational socialization process in the anticipatory socialization stage and involves communication related to how individuals learn what it means to be a member in a particular field, industry, or type of position (Kramer, 2010).

Chapter 2
Relationship Quality Matters:
LMX and Mental Health in the Workplace

Anne Hubbell
New Mexico State University, USA

Greg G. Armfield
New Mexico State University, USA

EXECUTIVE SUMMARY

The National Institute of Mental Health has reported that approximately 51.5 million people in the U.S. experience some form of mental illness and that anxiety is one of the most prevalent mental illnesses, with 31.1% of Americans experiencing some form of anxiety disorder in their lives. In this case study, one of the most common discriminatory behaviors toward all minority groups, microaggressions, is explored through the lens of leader-member exchange theory (LMX). LMX has been the foremost leadership theory used to understand the dynamics of mental illness in the workplace and how leaders interact and motivate those with disabilities or mental illness. The authors apply LMX to help leaders better understand their role in creating a more inclusive workplace.

INTRODUCTION

In this case study, one of the most common discriminatory behaviors toward all minority groups, microaggressions, is explored through the lens of leader–member exchange theory (LMX). LMX has been the foremost leadership theory used to understand the dynamics of mental illness in the workplace and how leaders interact with and motivate those with disabilities or mental illness. We apply LMX here to help

DOI: 10.4018/978-1-6684-3753-7.ch002

leaders better understand their role in creating a more inclusive workplace. Through the communication between a leader (Chris) and an organizational subordinate (Jo), who is experiencing Generalized Anxiety Disorder (GAD, see Casarella, 2021), the importance of the communication and how insidious and damaging microaggressions can be will be illustrated. The goal of case is to encourage discussion on improving communication between leaders and members, particularly with individuals struggling with mental health disabilities.

MENTAL HEALTH IN THE WORKPLACE

Approximately 51.5 million people in the U.S. experience some form of mental illness (National Institute for Mental Health [NIMH], 2021). Anxiety is one of the most prevalent mental illnesses, with 31.1% of Americans experiencing some form of anxiety disorder in their lives (NIMH, 2021). According to the National Institute of Mental Health, in the years 2001–2003, 19.1% of adults in the U.S. experienced a form of anxiety disorder, with the reporting being higher among women (23.4%) than men (14.3%) (NIMH, 2021). Individuals with anxiety disorders often go undiagnosed and untreated. Approximately only 37% of those with an anxiety disorder are treated (ACCESS Community Health Network, 2021). Even without treatment, those with anxiety disorders may still function well in the workplace except during those times when they are experiencing severe, or debilitating, symptoms.

A mental illness diagnosis, like a generalized anxiety disorder, changes how a person moves through the world (Rose & Thornicroft, 2011). It is usual for individuals to, at times, feel worried or concerned about something in their lives. However, according to the DSM-IV and DSM-5 (Diagnostic and Statistical Manual of Mental Disorders, volumes 4 and 5), an anxiety disorder is when an individual is experiencing extreme and overwhelming feelings of worry and anxiety over time, with impacts on sleep, muscle tension, concentration, fatigue, or restlessness (Substance and Mental Health Services Administration, 2016). Anxiety disorders include generalized anxiety disorder, panic disorder, social anxiety disorder, specific phobias, agoraphobia, separation anxiety, selective mutism (i.e., children who will not speak in public), and medication-induced anxiety disorder (Anxiety disorders, 2020).

In this case study, we will focus primarily on mental illness in the workplace and how such individuals experience ableism, or the belief that there is a perfect version of what a human should be, one who is "able." *Ableism* has been defined as

a network of beliefs, processes, and practices that produces a particular kind of self and body (the corporeal standard) that is projected as the perfect, species-typical and therefore essential and fully human. Disability then is cast as a diminished state of being human. (Campbell, 2001, p. 44)

To apply this to the workplace, disabled individuals are often perceived as unable or potentially less valuable or employable in organizations (Jammaers et al., 2016). Further, those with mental illness are treated less positively than those with physical or visible disabilities (Unger, 2002). Those with invisible disabilities, such as an anxiety disorder, must manage the potential need to disclose their disability with the stigma of how they will be treated once they have disclosed having a mental illness (Elraz, 2018). When an individual discloses a mental illness, or any form of invisible disability, they often have to prove they have a disability and mental illness. Also, as mental illness is a stigmatized disability, that proof is often more likely to be challenged or dismissed. If an individual chooses to disclose the need for support because of a mental illness, they may be exposing themselves to potential judgment based on stigma (Joachim & Acorn, 2000). They may make themselves susceptible to a range of negative outcomes such as devalued social identities, prejudice, stereotyping, discrimination, and neglect (Crocker, et al., 1998; Dahnke, 1982; Miller & Kaiser, 2001). Further, when an individual does share an invisible disability, such as a mental illness, they often are treated differently and often endure microaggressions. These become even more sensitive to an individual once they have revealed a hidden or invisible disability. In this case study a manager (Chris) finds out that their subordinate (Jo) has GAD. Once Jo discloses their mental illness, they feel more vulnerable to potential attack such that statements Chris makes where they may intend to be supportive, become microaggressions that greatly undermine the relationship between Jo and Chris.

A leader's relationship with their subordinates is central to an individual's ability to communicate a potential disability and work through any potential impairments or needed accommodations. Pairing mental illness in the workplace with LMX (leader-member exchange theory which focuses on the quality of communication between leaders and members) and microaggressions, can help start the conversation and move toward better organizational training. It can also help students think about how they would work through respecting and supporting someone with a mental illness.

MICROAGGRESSIONS

Microaggressions emerge from implicit biases, which come from stereotypical and simplistic views of individuals in marginalized groups. As described by the National Education Association's Center for Social Justice,

Implicit bias is a mental process that stimulates negative attitudes about people who are not members of one's own "in group." Implicit racial bias leads to discrimination against people who are not members of one's own racial group. Implicit bias operates in what researchers call our "implicit mind," the part of the brain that we commonly call the "subconscious" or the "unconscious." This means that implicit bias can operate in an individual's mind without a conscious awareness of this process. (Center for Social Justice, 2021, para 2).

Microaggressions are considered "micro" because they are small slights. They are considered "everyday verbal, non-verbal, and environmental slights, snubs, or insults, whether intentional or unintentional, that communicate hostile, derogatory, or negative messages to target persons solely on their marginalized group membership" (Sue, 2010, p. 3). Research on individuals with mental illness experience social rejection because of their illness (Gonzales et al., 2015b) with 48% of individuals in one study reporting negative social interactions because of their mental illness, including being treated as if there was something wrong with them (Yanos, et al., 2001). These slights are often from those closest to the individual (Lundberg, et al., 2009). As individuals spend most of their time at work, often developing close friendships with people with whom they work, microaggressions can have a profound impact on the experience of a person with a disability or a member of any other marginalized group (Luc, n.d.).

The study of microaggressions, although a relatively new area of research in the social sciences, has generated thousands of studies (Olkin et al., 2019). Marginalized populations have been the focus of these studies, although persons with disabilities have been represented in only a few of them (Olkin et al., 2019). Microaggressions apply to persons with disabilities and those with mental health and other invisible disabilities as they experience them the same as any other marginalized group and often those with disabilities fall into more than one marginalized group. For example, women with mental health diagnoses are experiencing two stereotyped identities. This can become even more complicated when experiencing additional microaggressions (for a more thorough review, see Olkin et al., 2019). Women may experience microaggressions as women, as a person with a disability, and an invisible disability. This experience of microaggressions increases exponentially for women of color. Basford et al. (2014) found that when women and men reviewed a hypothetical situation in which microaggressions on disabilities were subtle and obvious, women perceived more discrimination in the situation than men. This effect was strongest when looking at the perception of subtle discrimination, as women perceived significantly more of this than did the men in the study.

Gonzales and colleagues (2015a; 2015b) researched the microaggressions experienced by individuals with mental illness and found three categories of microaggression behaviors toward individuals with mental illness. The three categories include: Assumption of Inferiority, Patronization, and Fear of Mental Illness. Assumptions of inferiority are statements which contain the implication that an individual is incompetent, they do not have individual agency (cannot function like other people), and/or have lower intelligence (Gonzales, et al., 2015b); Olkin et al., 2019). A microaggression of this type could be when a manager tells a subordinate that they do not have to complete a project they are working on. When a manager states that an individual does not have to complete a job, the individual may perceive this as a microaggression of inferiority; sensing that the manager is communicating a belief that the person with a mental illness is incapable of completing the project. It is important to note that statements may or may not be intended to be aggressive but it is the context and lived experience of an individual which can lead to the perception that they have received a microaggression. This does not mean that the victim should be blamed. Instead, the microaggression comes from an implicit bias, potentially even overt discrimination, and not having knowledge that a microaggression can be harmful does not excuse the behavior.

Patronization is another type of microaggression experienced by individuals with mental illness diagnoses (Gonzales, et al., 2015a). Such a microaggression includes condescending or potentially insincere supportive statements (Gonzales, et al., 2015b). For example, a manager may tell a subordinate that they did a good job in such a way that it sounds like maybe that is not exactly what the manager believes and that the manager is just trying to be "nice." Another example may be when a manager tells a subordinate that they will be "fine" even when the subordinate is communicating great stress and/or is struggling. Also, if a manager says something like, "Oh, I understand how you feel, I have felt like that sometimes" while not acknowledging that a little anxiety is normal but excessive, continued anxiety, may be indicative of GAD. Such a statement is dismissive of the lived experience of an individual with a mental illness, particularly if they communicate to their manager that they are struggling because of their mental illness.

The third category of microaggressions includes statements of Fear of Mental Illness (Gonzales, et al., 2015a). An example of such a microaggression would be if a manager implies that a subordinate with a mental illness may be unpredictable, potentially act in a criminal manner, and/or that someone can be contaminated by someone who has a mental illness (Gonzales, et al., 2015b). This could be communicated by not wanting to be around an individual with mental illness or making statements communicating that they may not be able to be completely trusted. Another way this can be communicated is through statements about their unpredictability. For example, if an individual with a mental illness communicates in an emotional manner they may be told that it is because of their mental illness and their actual feelings may be dismissed as just part of their unpredictability, even if the emotion expressed would be considered normal if demonstrated by a person without a mental illness (Gonzales, et al., 2015b).

As leaders or superiors have more real and perceived power than subordinates in an organization, additional pressure and expectations are placed on the leader or superior to be self-reflective and understand their own biases while working to develop inclusive, positive, and effective relationships with their subordinates. The next section will explore the leader's dyadic relationship with each subordinate with respect to LMX, mental illness, and to help students think about how they would work through respecting and supporting a co-worker or subordinate with a mental illness.

LEADER–MEMBER EXCHANGE THEORY

Leader–member exchange theory (LMX) emerged from the vertical dyad linkage theory focusing on the unique interpersonal dyadic relationship between leader or superior and follower or subordinate (Dansereau et al., 1975; Graen et al., 1982; Graen & Scandura, 1987). LMX is focused on the quality of dyadic interactions and, thus, the individual relationship between a superior and subordinate. It is one of the few leadership theories in organizational communication that focuses on the quality of the communication between a subordinate and superior as central to their relationship (Northouse, 2021). The theory postulates that those with a high-quality exchange with their superior would also experience a high-LMX quality relationship and be part of the in-group in an organization. Those with lower-quality exchanges and, thus, lower-LMX quality relationships with their superior would end up in the out-group (Graen & Uhl-Bien, 1995). Those in a high-LMX quality relationship, or in-group, will often experience mutual trust with their superior and more concern, information, loyalty, support, guidance, and respect from that leader (Colella & Varma, 2001; Haynie et al., 2019; Northouse, 2021). In return, the subordinate is motivated to do more discretionary work, or work which "goes above and beyond" a typical workload (Haynie et al., 2019).

Ironically, often it is assumed that those out-group members are not good at their jobs, but that is not always the case (Northouse, 2021). The out-group members experience a different type of communication than in-group members. Out-group members do not experience the same quality of communication from their superior, and often do only what is required in their job (Northouse, 2021). They just may not be as likely as an in-group member to go beyond what is expected.

The quality of the communication is the focus of much research as there is a continuum, and subordinates are not always clearly part of an "in" or "out" group. Instead, they may experience varying levels of quality communication with their supervisor. Looking at the quality of exchange and disabilities as a broad category, Dwertmann and Boehm (2015) used LMX to examine the impacts of disability and status (i.e., supervisor or subordinate) on the quality of exchanges. They found that when the superior or subordinate in these dyads had a disability, they were more likely to report lower quality exchanges between the two individuals. This was more pronounced when the leader was the individual with the disability. Those individuals who did not have disabilities in the study reported significantly higher quality communication in their supervisor–subordinate dyads. However, the one variable that changed this dynamic was an inclusive work climate (Dwertmann & Boem, 2015). In inclusive climate was defined as a "nonthreatening environment" where one "can reveal their true selves" and "employee insights" are considered for "rethinking or redefining work practices" (Dwertmann & Boem, 2015, p. 51). In inclusive climate workplaces, those in non-congruent relationships (where either the supervisor or subordinate had a disability) experienced more quality exchanges within the supervisor–subordinate dyad than in the non-inclusive workplaces.

LMX has been one of the leadership theories most used to understand mental illness in the workplace and how leaders interact and motivate those with disabilities and/or mental illness (e.g., Colella & Varma, 2001; Haynie et al., 2019; Zwingmann & Boehm, 2013). It has been found that subordinates with disabilities who ingratiate themselves to their superiors tend to be more likely to experience being in the in-group than those who have disabilities and do not use ingratiation with their superiors (Zwingmann & Boehm, 2013). In addition, self-efficacy was crucial for those who have a mental health diagnosis or illness to whether they experienced high-LMX quality relationships with their leaders. Those who perceived they had a higher internal ability (self-efficacy) to do well at their work responsibilities reported the highest quality LMX relationships with their supervisors, even higher than those with physical disabilities and high perceived self-efficacy. Where those with mental illness had lower self-efficacy (they felt less able to complete their work responsibilities), however, they perceived having the lowest quality relationship with their supervisor. Only those in this study with a mental illness as a disability experienced extreme shifts in the quality of the relationship with their superior based on their perceived self-efficacy.

Along with building an inclusive work environment and improving a subordinate's self-efficacy, empathic concern on the part of a leader has been shown to positively impact LMX exchanges (Haynie et al., 2019). *Empathic concern*, as demonstrated by a leader, is when a leader cares about their subordinates and invests an appropriate amount of time and effort into getting to know and understand them (Humphrey et al., 2008) and in so doing, create "an atmosphere of concern so relationships with subordinates are more likely to materialize" (Haynie et al., 2019, p. 6). Research has demonstrated that working with leaders who demonstrate empathic concern leads to subordinates perceiving a higher quality exchange with their manager and being more likely to do more than expected at work (Haynie et al., 2019).

Although additional research is needed, these studies indicate that more inclusive work climates and promoting self-efficacy among employees will benefit those relationships between subordinates and their leaders, which are the fundamental and most important relationships in an organization. Addressing microaggressions is one way to begin this process. Through less discriminatory communication in the workplace, an individual with a mental illness may perceive that others see them as able to do their job and are needed and valued as who they are in their workplace. This, in turn, could help in increasing their belief in their ability to do their job well. The case which is the focus of this chapter will focus on how microaggressions within a leader-member exchange will either create or not create an inclusive workplace for an individual struggling with GAD.

THE CASE

Organizational Background

The organization is fictitious and given the name Skymad International. Skymad International is a company that produces cybersecurity software for organizational and personal use. It has a marketing department with seven employees tasked with completing a marketing plan for a new product, Zamz, which will protect clients' personal data from identity theft. Zamz will be marketed for personal use. The company needs the anticipated revenue for the continued development of new software and business expansion.

Setting the Stage

Chris is the manager of a six-person team for the marketing department at Skymad International; they are responsible for developing a marketing plan to launch the new product, Zamz. Jo is one of the marketing team members, and they have been out sick for several days. This is causing much stress for Chris and the other five members of the team. Chris is trying to understand the situation and manage the work that needs to be done for the launch of Zamz. Jo, however, is experiencing panic attacks and shares this with Chris but not the other members of the team. The team is frustrated with Jo as they seem "fine" but are not coming back to work to help the team complete the marketing plan on time. The last email sent to Jo from one of their colleagues asked Jo if they were ever coming back to work. Emails like this and Jo's struggle with their anxiety is frustrating to Jo. Then in conversations with Chris, has communicated several microaggressions, making Jo and Chris' relationship much more strained. Chris is not a bad person or leader; they just do not understand how to avoid mental health microaggressions and better support Jo.

Case Description

Chris is the department manager of the marketing department at Skymad International. Chris has six employees eager to launch a new product that is crucial to protecting personal data from identity thieves. The product, Zamz, will be launched in three months, so the marketing team has much work to prepare. All six members of the team and Chris are experiencing high levels of stress over getting the marketing plan together for the product launch.

One of the employees in the marketing department, Jo, has been out sick for several days before finally showing up at Chris' door late one afternoon. Chris is an empathetic and kind person but is still a little irritated that Jo has been out of the office for so long during such a critical time. Jo explains that they have been experiencing a lot of anxiety over the launch and want to talk about it.

Chris maintains their irritation and asks, "What exactly is causing the anxiety for you? What can I do to help?"

To which Jo sighs, sits down, and starts to tell Chris about their diagnosis. They have generalized anxiety disorder and have been experiencing panic attacks. Jo also has not slept in several days. By Chris expressing an interest, Jo thinks to themself, "I am glad Chris is open to talking about this, it has bothered me that I haven't told Chris about what I have been going through."

To Chris, Jo states, "I appreciate you being open to talking about this. Because I have a Generalized Anxiety Disorder (GAD), sometimes I have panic attacks or times when I lose sleep and become very stressed, more than someone who does not have an anxiety disorder. It is hard to explain but usually I am just fine but this project has been one that I have had panic attacks over and I wanted to see if we could work with the timeline at all. I want to stay on the project but just need a little more time."

Chris pauses and responds with, "I totally understand, sometimes deadlines stress me out too."

Jo feels a little dismissed by Chris' statement. It is normal to feel stress when there is a deadline and often deadlines do not cause undue stress for Jo. This time, though, as they communicated to Chris, they are struggling more than usual due to their anxiety disorder and uncontrollable panic attacks.

Jo decides to continue to try to explain, "Usually I just experience some stress when there is a deadline, this time it is more. I am having panic attacks, mostly in the middle of the night, and I can't sleep. This makes it hard for me to concentrate on the project. I think with just a few more days on the deadline, or maybe a week, I can work through this and do a great job on the launch. Is there any way we can ask for a little more time? I know we have before."

Chris thinks about Jo's request but knows that they have already asked for extensions and frankly, they just want to get the launch ready so they can focus on other projects that need attention. To communicate this, Chris tells Jo, "Jo, why don't you take a few days off and not worry about the launch. The team and I can take care of this. We have been working on it while you have been off anyway and are making good progress on it. We can make the deadline, no problem. You are a good employee but we can get this done, no worries."

Chris' intentions are to be supportive but without realizing it, they have communicated to Jo that Jo is not needed. Jo thinks, "Chris doesn't think I am needed, that I can do the job, because I haven't been around as much as usual. And, what does Chris they mean when they say I am a 'good employee,' it sounds like a compliment but why am I just 'good' and an 'employee' and not a member of the team?" From Chris' statement, Jo is beginning to believe that Chris does not think they are capable or wanted at the Skymad International anymore.

Jo has also been receiving emails from the other team members asking when Jo would return. The latest one asked Jo if they would ever return to work and stated that no one could figure out what was wrong with Jo as Jo seems fine, and not sick. Jo tells Chris about the emails and the guilt they feel over not being there for Chris and the team.

To which Chris responds with, "You do look fine, but they don't know what you are experiencing so they don't know any better. Don't worry about it, just relax, get some rest, and then come back."

Jo hangs their head and then looks up at Chris. Jo has tears in their eyes which confuses Chris who thinks the conversation is going well. Chris asks, "Does the anxiety make you feel sad or more sensitive? What can I say to help you?" This attempt at potential compassion, though, further isolates Jo. By stating that an expression of emotion is related to their mental illness, when anyone as frustrated as Jo would express some form of emotion, Jo feels that now any time they express emotion it will be considered because they have a mental illness, not because the emotion is "normal" for the situation.

The conversation goes on for some time. Jo knows that they have much to contribute to the marketing plan, and Chris continues to try to develop solutions to the problem. Jo does not seem receptive to the solutions Chris suggests. Chris finally gets frustrated and again tells Jo, "Don't worry, I've got this. You can work on something else. You are a good employee but we can handle the launch."

Without saying more than a weak "thank you" and leaving Chris' office, Jo goes to clean off their desk and leaves. The next day Chris finds a letter of resignation from Jo on their desk. Chris is baffled. There was no mention of Jo leaving, no mention of that being the issue. Chris does not understand where the conversation went wrong. Was this about the way other team members treated Jo? Was it about the anxiety? It is not a big deal. Sometimes Chris gets anxious or worried, too. Why did Jo leave? Chris now has a team of five and has lost one of the most valued team members. However, Chris is not a bad boss and really cares about those on the team. Chris is confused and now very worried about the marketing plan for the launch of Zamz, will they be able to get the plan for the launch ready in time?

CURRENT CHALLENGES FACING THE ORGANIZATION

Identifying implicit biases is extremely difficult and is the first and most crucial part of any training focused on eliminating discriminatory behaviors like microaggressions. Identifying such biases is difficult because they are part of someone's upbringing; they have learned it through their own lived experiences, and often they cannot access their biases just by reflecting on them (Luc, n.d.). Many training programs in organizations also focus more on compliance training as opposed to integrity training (Bezrukova et al., 2012). Compliance training focuses on telling employees what behaviors are unacceptable in an organization and are usually regulatory. This type of training is necessary for an organization but does not help employees address their biases, of which they may not even be aware. Integrity training focuses on understanding ourselves and others and how to better address the training needs and compliance training in organizations. Still, it can take more time and effort on the organization's part.

In this case, Skymad International only provided compliance training to all employees. The training was all online and included several modules, requiring every employee to review and complete online quizzes—a quiz grade of 80% was necessary for each unit to be completed. The Inclusion and Diversity module included definitions of discrimination, explained that discrimination was not tolerated by the company, and explained what a marginalized group was. This was followed by some case studies with situations that actually occurred at Skymad International at some point in the organization's history. People with disabilities were included as one sizeable, marginalized group, but no mention of mental health was included. One slide in one module had an example of a microaggression toward a person of color. The statement that was an example of this microaggression was, "I didn't think you would do so well on that task!" The implied microaggression was that a person of color could not do well on some organizational tasks.

So, at Skymad International, they have not ever had employees or managers trained on implicit bias and the microaggressions that can result. They also do not make strong efforts to have an inclusive organizational climate. Individuals are encouraged to have opinions about their work but not encouraged to openly communicate about who they are and be open about their issues, like working through a generalized anxiety disorder and being productive at work.

In the recommendations and solutions section below, integrity training could be used by Skymad international to better prepare leaders, in particular, for the importance of their communication with subordinates, how to avoid and/or be more aware of potential microaggressions, and how to better understand productivity from the perspective of an employee.

CASE ANALYSIS

This case focused on two of a myriad of aspects within a leader-member conversation: 1) the importance of leader-member exchanges and; 2) the impact of microaggressions on individuals and organizations. LMX was used as a foundation to the case because leaders do not often understand the power they hold in exchanges with subordinates and that in one conversation they can severely damage the quality of the relationship and future exchanges with subordinates. As discussed in the LMX section, the communication of empathic concern is one way in which leaders can create a more inclusive workplace. In the case, when Chris shared that they sometimes had some anxiety, they may have intended to express compassion but to Jo, Chris was dismissing Jo's lived experience with GAD where "some anxiety" could be a normal day and extreme anxiety could be debilitating, something someone with a little, less constant, anxiety could not understand. By communicating this, Chris was not showing empathic concern which is where a leader expresses concern and tries to understand a subordinate's situation but does not attempt to try to take on the same feelings or experiences as that subordinate (Haynie et al., 2019; Humphrey et al., 2008).

This statement by Chris was also a microaggression in that Jo felt their mental illness was dismissed by Chris and that Chris was using a Patronization type of microaggression. Such a microaggression, as discussed above, is when a manager may be attempting to communicate concern but, instead communicates in a dismissive or insincere manner. Another potential patronizing microaggression was when Chris stated that Jo was a "good" employee. The statement could be positive but good, being an ambiguous word, could also mean that Jo was not an "excellent" or "outstanding" employee. Thus, it was a potential compliment that seemed insincere, or patronizing to Jo.

The other two types or categories of microaggressions include: Assumption of Inferiority, and Fear of Mental Illness. An example of the Assumption of Inferiority in the case could be when Chris tells Jo that they do not have to work on the project anymore. Jo interprets this as a microaggression indicating a belief, on Chris' part, that Jo was not needed by the team because of current struggles they were experiencing due to GAD.

An example of Fear of Mental Illness would be much harder to find and may not be a microaggression communicated as clearly as the other two. That is because stating that a person could potentially be a criminal or act like a criminal, or that they could not be trustworthy are serious accusations in organizations and ones that could lead to litigation. Microaggressions, though, that indicate that a person's expression of emotion is, of course, tied to their mental illness, is a microaggression. One that may be more common than we can anticipate in organizations. In the case, Chris asks Jo if the anxiety makes Jo "feel sad or more sensitive" after Jo looks at Chris with tears in their eyes. Such a statement after the expression of emotion by a person with a mental illness would be communicating that the person's feelings were the result of the mental illness and relegating their "normal" feelings, or feelings that could be felt by anyone regardless of their mental illness, as not real or significant.

The case includes many other microaggressions, these are but a few examples. It is important to note that in a few statements by Chris, that there may be more than just one microaggression. Also, some microaggressions may seem more like a patronizing microaggression with some elements of communicating inferiority. Even in an effort to make the microaggressions relatively straightforward and simple, it is important to realize that the reason why these affronts are called microaggressions is because they are small slights which occur in every day conversations (Sue, 2010).

But, why did Jo leave? Did the small microaggressions in one conversation drive them to want to leave Skymad International? Most likely, no, even though the importance of leader-member exchanges are central to the case. The key with thinking about microaggressions is that they occur, again, on a daily basis. In the current case, all the communication between Jo and Chris as well as Jo and their coworkers, did now happen in a vacuum. Jo surely experienced many microaggressions which added up over time making Skymad International and the Marketing department there a hostile work environment. The irony, though, is that Chris did care but did not know how to overcome their own implicit bias toward mental illness. Effective training could have changed the course of the conversation in the case, perhaps the daily communication before this conversation, and Jo could have possibly remained as a productive employee of Skymad.

SOLUTIONS AND RECCOMENDATIONS

The organization's first and most crucial step would be to provide integrity-based training, at least for the leaders in the organization, including Chris. Integrity-based training would not substitute for compliance-based training, as discussed above. Compliance-based training is focused on what organizational members can and cannot do and is usually regulatory, or based on laws which should not be broken in an organization. Integrity-based training, instead focuses more on positive or proactive behaviors. For example, for training for Skymad, integrity-based training could focus on helping leaders and all organizational members understand their own implicit biases. From first understanding one's own biases, the root of microaggressions could be better understood by organizational members as they work toward communicating in a more inclusive manner.

At Skymad International, integrity-based training could focus on helping Skymad employees understand their implicit biases and microaggressions, overall, with a focus on mental health. If we employ the findings from LMX and people with disabilities, including mental health, we can understand the importance of developing an inclusive climate and a subordinate's perceptions of their value in the organization. This can lead to leaders and members enjoying higher quality exchanges and members being more productive members of the organization. Also, leaders, in particular, could receive training on the importance of leader-member exchanges as well as how to better communicate to their subordinates about perceptions of organizational elements like productivity. What one individual perceives as being productive could vary greatly from how another individual perceives productivity.

With regard to understanding and working through implicit biases, there are companies that offer training to organizations on how to understand and start to address implicit bias. The following, however, are some suggestions on how a leader in an LMX dyad, like Chris, can begin to work on their own implicit biases:

1. Work on developing empathic leadership through training on:
    a. Listening
        i. Listening vs. hearing
        ii. Listening to understand
    b. Demonstration of concern, leaders can ask questions like these to better understand and show concern through questions like these:
        i. What is important to each subordinate?
        ii. What are behaviors that make them feel supported (e.g., appreciation and awards)
        iii. Have they felt put down by the organization? Has the leader made them feel this way?

   - iv. What do they need to be successful?
- c. Take action
   - i. Use what is learned to improve communication through better understanding
   - ii. Ask for feedback often in order to keep improving

2. Identifying, understanding, and unlearning an implicit bias (Note: There are many methods to doing this, and organizations may do well to consider hiring an outside organization to run training and workshops):
   - a. Use tests like the Harvard Project Implicit (https://www.projectimplicit.net/) to begin the conversation on potential implicit biases. This does have a section on disabilities but not specifically on mental health or invisible disabilities.
   - b. Steps in identifying, understanding, and unlearning implicit bias (Edgoose et al., 2019):
      - i. Introspection: Taking tests like the test described above to help identify biases
      - ii. Mindfulness: Work toward reducing stress through mindfulness, yoga, and breathing exercises
      - iii. Perspective-taking: Think about the other person's point of view. Talk with them or learn from books or videos. Seek to understand as much as possible.
      - iv. Learn to slow down: Take time before communicating with people with whom there may be a bias. Reflect on ways to communicate in a more respectful manner.
      - v. Individuation: Look at people as individuals, look at their personal characteristics. There may be a way to connect over shared interests.
      - vi. Check your messaging: Use research-based statements that embrace multiculturalism. Reduce the use of microaggressions.
      - vii. Institutional fairness: Work toward equity in organizational procedures
      - viii. Take two: "Practice cultural humility, a lifelong process of critical self-reflection to readdress the power imbalances" (para. 8)
   - c. Learn about mental health and other invisible disabilities—Websites that can help:
      - i. Invisible Disabilities Association (https://invisibledisabilities.org/)
      - ii. National Institute of Mental Health (https://www.nimh.nih.gov/)
3. What to do if the leader is called out for using a microaggression (Knight, 2020):
   - a. Take a breath, do not get defensive
   - b. Do not make it about you. Often there is a history a leader does not know about that may be why the microaggression is hurtful.

c. Listen, make sure the other person feels heard
d. Sincerely apologize and own behavior
e. Do not overdo it; do not make it so that the subordinate needs to take care of you ("I have never been accused of this; I am so upset")
f. The leader needs to realize that they are not a bad person for saying something offensive
g. How to respond if a leader is called out publicly:
    i. This may happen because the person does not feel safe alone with the leader
    ii. The leader should acknowledge what is said but keep response short and non-defensive
    iii. Talk to the person privately
    iv. Seek to understand on your own time, look up why the person may have been offended or upset
    v. Consider following up by communicating concern for the person and about the situation
    vi. Keep working on it

Two other aspects of the training which are missing from what Skymad provides its employees is: 1) an understanding of the importance of leader-member exchanges in the creation of an inclusive environment; and 2) encouragement of discussion between leaders and teams about what productivity looks like for each individual. First, in terms of leader-member exchanges, the emails from colleagues bothered Jo in the case but it was the conversation with Chris that led Jo to wanting to leave the organization. This potentially extreme reaction was put in the case to demonstrate how important even one conversation could be. At Skymad, if leaders received training on how important what they say is, how words can help or hurt, they can be more cognizant in ways to better communicate empathic concern (as discussed above) to create a more inclusive workplace. Second, what may constitute productivity to one individual may not be seen the same way by another. In the case Chris was focused on the timeline for the launch and all that needed to be done, a burden most leaders share. Jo, though, was focused on their contribution, that they wanted to make that contribution, and did not see the timeline for that work in the same way as Chris. Training at Skymad could also encourage leaders to focus conversations on how to accomplish the needed goals and what a team and individuals see as productivity and success. Sometimes a timeline or deadline could be changed, but sometimes not. If Chris and Jo had changed their conversation from almost blaming Jo for not being there to participate in the work to a conversation on how the work could get done, how Jo could contribute, the outcome could have been much different.

CONCLUSION

As stated at the beginning of the case, approximately 51.5 million people in the U.S. experience some form of mental illness (National Institute for Mental Health [NIMH], 2021). Those who experience mental illness, often experience microaggressions which when they come from a leader or manager, may lead to serious organizational outcomes. The goal of this case was to frame the importance of the leader-member exchange and microaggressions within that conversational context using the leader-member exchange theory (LMX). The case did not have a happy ending in order to demonstrate the importance of daily conversation, the power of leader-member exchanges, and what happens when implicit biases unknowingly influence the way a leader communicates with a subordinate, or organizational member. It is with knowledge and continued efforts to learn how to identify one's own implicit biases and communicate more respectfully which could lead to more inclusive organizational environments.

QUESTIONS

1. What is the overall problem presented in this case?
2. What are the factors affecting the problem(s) related to this case?
3. Discuss managerial and organizational issues and resources related to this case. In particular consider the following: 1) what costs/benefits would you see from adding integrity training to what Skymad International already does; and 2) if individuals like Jo leave a company what does a company have to do to recruit a new person? Does this add more cost to the company in the long run if individuals like Jo keep leaving?
4. What examples of Assumption of Inferiority, Patronization, and Fear of Mental Illness types of microaggressions are demonstrated in the case?
5. Consider the gender of Chris and Jo. If Chris was male and Jo was female, how might that influence the perception Jo has of the microaggressions. After you consider this, flip the scenario and think about if Jo was male and Chris female. How do the dynamics of the situation, the microaggressions, and the gender of the leader and subordinate alter the perceptions of microaggressions and/or the potential outcome?
6. How do you respond to the use of the word "subordinate" when referring to people in Jo's organizational role/position? How does the word "subordinate" communicate about the power differential in a leader-member exchange and how can the perception of being a subordinate to another individual lead to potential perceptions of inferiority even without microaggressions and/or amplify the impact of a microaggression?

7. What is the final solution that can be recommended to the management of the organization described in the case? Provide your arguments in support of the recommended solution.

EPILOGUE AND LESSONS LEARNED

Epilogue

The long-range effects of the conversation between Jo and Chris, and Jo leaving Skymad International, was that Chris realized the marketing team needed training to communicate and work better together. Chris took the initiative to seek out a company that specialized in inclusion and diversity training and contracted with them to work with the marketing team. Chris also realized that they could have been more proactive with Jo and other team members by getting to know them better and becoming a more empathic-concern type of leader. Through this, Chris became better able to anticipate potential struggles among the team before they became more serious. The CEO of Skymad International took notice of Chris' work and invited Chris and the marketing team to talk to the Human Resources and Training department at Skymad International. To date, the organization has not rolled out any new training but one department, Marketing, may be able to lead the way in potential future changes. Jo went on to developing their own marketing consulting company which has been successful at developing and implementing marketing campaigns for small and mid-size businesses. Jo's business continues to grow and hire more associates.

Lessons Learned

Lesson 1: Mental Health Is Important for Organizations to Think About

As discussed in the case, mental health diagnoses are prevalent and common among individuals within organizations. As a mental health diagnosis is an illness, it needs to be treated as such. As it also is a protected disability, individuals with such diagnoses must be treated with respect and receive needed accommodations. Mental health diagnoses, however, are invisible disabilities which may make them more challenging for an organization to consider and properly manage. An individual has to choose to disclose their diagnosis(es), as Jo had to consider in the case, and whether they do or not, managers and coworkers need to learn how to communicate in a way that is inclusive and respectful to individuals within a marginalized group, including those with a mental health diagnosis disability. Organizations that become more inclusive in their climate, as discussed in the case, may also demonstrate this inclusive climate through better training and workshops focused on understanding issues like microaggressions and how to encourage better communication, or exchanges, between subordinates and their supervisors.

Lesson 2: Microaggressions, Though Unintentional, Do Major Harm in Organizations

It may seem extreme, that in the case study Jo decided to leave Skymad International. It is important to point out that this is in fact, not extreme. It may be that Jo has experienced many microaggressions in the past. As mentioned in the case, a leader should not think that the way a subordinate responds to a potential microaggression is about the leader. A person with a disability and/or any other marginalized identity, is likely to have experienced discrimination in the form of microaggressions in the past, thus, any one potential microaggression may be just one of many, leading to potential negative impacts on the organization. Such negative impacts can include employees not being as productive, leaving the organization, and potentially even suing the organization for discrimination.

Lesson 3: Organizational Theory, Like Leader-Member Exchange LMX, Can Help Leaders Do Better

As mentioned in the case study, LMX is one of the few organizational theories which has been used to research disabilities in the workplace. It is useful because the focus is on the relational dyad of the superior and subordinate. The theory has much that it can offer to the understanding of how leaders can also be leaders for inclusion in organizations through working to improve the quality of exchanges with their subordinates. The research cited in the case further demonstrated how variables like self-efficacy and empathic-concern also work to improve the communication between a superior and subordinate when the subordinate has a disability, in particular, a mental health diagnosis disability.

Lesson 4: Inclusion and Diversity Training HAS to Be More Than What Not to Do

Organizations tend to focus on providing more regulative training, like Compliance training. Such training is crucial for organizational members to understand the rules and potential laws within which the organization operates. Integrity training in addition to Compliance training may offer more reflection and communication about what topics like implicit bias and microaggressions. In order to communicate and demonstrate a more inclusive organizational climate, organizational members need to identify their own implicit biases so that they can work to understand their biases and work to overcome them. When organizations put the time and effort into these types of training programs, organizational members will understand better what a microaggression is and have the potential to improve the way they communicate with others and reduce the use of microaggressions.

REFERENCES

ACCESS Community Health Network. (2021, November 18). *3 most common mental health disorders in America*. https://www.achn.net/about-access/whats-new/health-resources/3-most-common-mental-health-disorders-in-america/

Anxiety Disorders. (2020). In *WebMD*. Retrieved November 29, 2021, from https://www.webmd.com/anxiety-panic/guide/anxiety-disorders

Basford, T. E., Offermann, L. R., & Behrend, T. S. (2014). Do you see what I see? Perceptions of microaggressions in the workplace. *Psychology of Women Quarterly*, *38*(3), 340–349. doi:10.1177/0361684313511420

Bezrukova, K., Jehn, K. A., & Spell, C. S. (2012). Reviewing diversity training: Where we have been and where we should go. *Academy of Management Learning & Education*, *11*(2), 207–221. doi:10.5465/amle.2008.0090

Campbell, F. K. (2001). Inciting legal fictions: Disability's date with ontology and the ableist body of the law. *Griffith Law Review*, *10*, 42–62. https://research-repository.griffith.edu.au/handle/10072/3714

Center for Social Justice. (2021). *Implicit bias, microaggressions, and stereotypes resources*. National Education Administration. Retrieved November 29, 2021, from https://www.nea.org/resource-library/implicit-bias-microaggressions-and-stereotypes-resources

Colella, A., & Varma, A. (2001). The impact of subordinate disability on leader–member exchange relationships. *Academy of Management Journal*, *44*, 304–315. https://www.researchgate.net/publication/37156513_The_Impact_of_Subordinate_Disability_on_Leader-Member_Exchange_Relationships

Crocker, J., Major, B., & Steele, C. (1998). Social stigma. In D. Gilbert, S. T. Fiske, & G. Lindzey (Eds.), *The handbook of social psychology* (4th ed., Vol. 2, pp. 504–553). McGraw Hill.

Dahnke, G. (1982). Communication between handicapped and nonhandicapped persons: Toward a deductive theory. In M. Burgoon (Ed.), *Communication Yearbook 6* (pp. 92–135). Sage. doi:10.1016/0890-4065(93)90009-9

Dansereau, F. Jr, Graen, G. B., & Haga, W. (1975). A vertical dyad linkage approach to leadership in formal organizations. *Organizational Behavior and Human Performance, 13*(1), 46–78. doi:10.1016/0030-5073(75)90005-7

Dwertmann, D. J. G., & Boehm, S. A. (2015). Supervisor–subordinate disability incongruence and climate for inclusion. *Academy of Management Journal, 59*(1), 44–64. doi:10.5465/amj.2014.0093

Edgoose, J., Quiogue, M., & Sidhar, K. (2019). How to identify, understand, and unlearn implicit bias in patient care. *Family Practice Management, 26*(4), 29–33. https://www.aafp.org/fpm/2019/0700/p29.html PMID:31287266

Elraz, H. (2018). Identity, mental health and work: How employees with mental health conditions recount stigma and the pejorative discourse of mental illness. *Human Relations, 71*(5), 722–741. doi:10.1177/0018726717716752

Gonzales, L., Davidoff, K. C., DeLuca, J. S., & Yanos, P. T. (2015a). The mental illness micro-aggressions scale – perpertrator version (MIMS-P): Reliability and validity. *Psychiatry Research, 221*(1-2), 120–125. doi:10.1016/j.psychres.2015.07.061 PMID:26233830

Gonzales, L., Davidoff, K. C., Nadal, K. L., & Yanos, P. T. (2015b). Microaggressions experienced by persons with mental illnesses: An exploratory study. *Psychiatric Rehabilitation Journal, 38*(3), 234–241. doi:10.1037/prj0000096 PMID:25402611

Graen, G. B., Novak, M., & Sommerkamp, P. (1982). The effects of leader–member exchange and job design on productivity and satisfaction: Testing a dual attachment model. *Organizational Behavior and Human Performance, 30*(1), 109–131. doi:10.1016/0030-5073(82)90236-7

Graen, G. B., & Scandura, T. (1987). Toward a psychology of dyadic organizing. In B. Staw & L. L. Cumming (Eds.), *Research in organizational behavior* (Vol. 9, pp. 175–208). JAI Press.

Graen, G. B., & Uhl-Bien, M. (1995). Relationship-based approach to leadership: Development of leader–member exchange (LMX) theory of leadership over 25 years—Applying a multi-level multi-domain perspective. *The Leadership Quarterly, 6*(2), 219–247. doi:10.1016/1048-9843(95)90036-5

Haynie, J. J., Baur, J., Harris, J. N., Harris, S. G., & Moates, K. N. (2019). When caring leaders are constrained: The impact of LMX differentiation on leader empathic concern in predicting discretionary work behaviors. *Journal of Leadership & Organizational Studies*, *26*(1), 5–17. doi:10.1177/1548051818767394

Humphrey, R. H., Pollack, J. M., & Hawver, T. (2008). Leading with emotional labor. *Journal of Managerial Psychology*, *23*(2), 151–168. doi:10.1108/02683940810850790

Jammaers, E., Zanoni, P., & Hardonk, S. (2016). Constructing positive identities in ableist workplaces: Disabled employee's discursive practices engaging with the discourse of lower productivity. *Human Relations*, *69*(6), 1365–1386. doi:10.1177/0018726715612901

Joachim, G., & Acorn, S. (2000). Stigma of visible and invisible chronic conditions. *Journal of Advanced Nursing*, *32*(1), 1365–2648. doi:10.1046/j.1365-2648.2000.01466.x PMID:10886457

Knight, R. (2020, July 24). You've been called out for a microaggression. What do you do? *Harvard Business Review*. Retrieved December 3, 2021, from https://hbr.org/2020/07/youve-been-called-out-for-a-microaggression-what-do-you-do

Luc, K. (n.d.). Microaggressions at work: Recognizing and overcoming our biases. *Culture Amp*. Retrieved November 29, 2021, from https://www.cultureamp.com/blog/microaggressions-at-work

Lundberg, B., Hansson, L., Wentz, E., & Björkman, T. (2009). Are stigma experiences among persons with mental illness, related to perceptions of self-esteem, empowerment and sense of coherence? *Journal of Psychiatric and Mental Health Nursing*, *16*(6), 516–522. doi:10.1111/j.1365-2850.2009.01418.x PMID:19594673

Miller, C. T., & Kaiser, C. R. (2001). A theoretical perspective on coping with stigma. *The Journal of Social Issues*, *57*(1), 73–92. doi:10.1111/0022-4537.00202

National Institute of Mental Health. (2021, September 20). *Any Anxiety Disorder*. Mental Health Information. https://www.nimh.nih.gov/health/statistics/any-anxiety-disorder

Northouse, P. G. (2021). *Leadership theory and practice* (9th ed.). Sage Publications.

Olkin, R., Hayward, H., Schaff Abbene, M., & VanHeel, G. (2019). The experiences of microaggressions against women with visible and invisible disabilities. *The Journal of Social Issues*, *75*(3), 757–785. doi:10.1111/josi.12342

Rose, D., & Thornicroft, G. (2011). Service user perspectives on the impact of a mental illness diagnosis. *Epidemiology and Psychiatric Sciences*, *19*(2), 140–147. doi:10.1017/S1121189X00000841 PMID:20815298

Substance Abuse and Mental Health Services Administration. (2016). *Impact of the DSM-IV to DSM-5 changes on the National Survey on Drug Use and Health: DSM-IV to DSM-5 generalized anxiety disorder comparison*. https://www.ncbi.nlm.nih.gov/books/NBK519704/table/ch3.t15/

Sue, D. W. (2010). *Microaggressions in everyday life: Race, gender, and sexual orientation*. John Wiley & Sons Inc.

Terlizzi, E. P., & Villarroel, M. A. (2020). *Symptoms of Generalized Anxiety Disorder Among Adults: United Stated, 2019*. NCHA Data Brief, no 378. https://www.cdc.gov/nchs/data/databriefs/db378-H.pdf

Unger, D. (2002). Employers' attitudes toward persons with disabilities in the workforce: Myths or realities? *Developmental Disabilities Research Reviews*, *17*(1), 2–10. doi:10.1177/108835760201700101

Yanos, P. T., Rosenfield, S., & Horwitz, A. V. (2001). Negative and supportive social interactions and quality of life among persons diagnosed with devere mental illness. *Community Mental Health Journal*, *37*(5), 405–419. doi:10.1023/A:1017528029127 PMID:11419518

Zwingmann, I., & Boehm, S. A. (2013). Disability and LMX–the role of self-efficacy, performance, and type of disability. *Proceedings of the Academy of Management Annual Meeting*. 10.5465/ambpp.2013.17261abstract

KEY TERMS AND DEFINITIONS

Ableism: The belief that there is a perfect version of what a human should be. A person is considered "able" if they can meet these expectations.

Empathic-Concern Leadership: A leadership style in which the leader spends an appropriate amount of effort getting to know followers or subordinates and, through knowing them, demonstrates concern for them as individuals.

Generalized Anxiety Disorder: A medical diagnosis characterized by excessive or unrealistic anxiety about two or more aspects of life (work deadlines, work pressures, social relationships, etc.).

Leader-Member Exchange Theory (LMX): LMX is focused on the quality of the interactions and, thus, relationships between leaders and their subordinates.

Mental Health: A person's condition with regard to their psychological and emotional well-being.

Mental Illness: A medical diagnosis pertaining to a mental disorder; when a person has a mental disorder or disability.

Microaggressions: Microaggressions emerge from implicit biases, which come from stereotypical and simplistic views of individuals in marginalized groups. A microaggression is a statement that is considered disrespectful and possibly discriminatory by a person in the marginalized group with whom the microaggression is directed.

National Institute for Mental Health: The lead federal agency for research on mental disorders.

Chapter 3
Concealing Mental Illness in the Workplace:
Applying Communication Privacy Management Theory to Managing Mental Health Privacy in the Workplace

Andrea L. Meluch
The University of Akron, USA

EXECUTIVE SUMMARY

Mental health issues, such as depression, anxiety, and post-traumatic stress disorder, are increasing in the U.S. However, people diagnosed with mental illnesses often experience stigmatization and discrimination in their workplace. The chapter examines how people with mental illness make decisions around revealing and, importantly, concealing their mental illness in the workplace. The concepts stigma and communication privacy management theory are used to examine the challenges associated with living with mental illness in the workplace. A case study is used to illustrate these concepts and provide a pedagogical context in which the factors around concealing mental illness in the workplace are situated. Finally, an analysis of the case study is presented using the conceptual and theoretical frameworks applied in the present chapter.

INTRODUCTION

Roughly one in five U.S. adults, or 51.5 million Americans, are struggling with a mental illness at any given time (National Institute of Mental Health, 2021). According to the CDC, the number of adults with symptoms of anxiety and depression

DOI: 10.4018/978-1-6684-3753-7.ch003

rose sharply between 2020 and 2021, and 11.7% of adults struggling with mental health disorders reported an unmet healthcare need (Vahratian et al., 2021). While mental illness remains a common issue for many Americans, mental illness is also highly stigmatized and individuals struggling with mental illness report increased experiences of discrimination in the workplace (Thornicroft, 2006). Thus, individuals diagnosed with mental illnesses, such as depression, anxiety, post-traumatic stress disorder (PTSD), and bipolar disorders often face immense struggles when they decide to try to conceal their mental illness within their workplace to avoid potential stigmatization and discrimination.

Although individuals' experiences with mental illness vary significantly by diagnosis and access to mental health resources, research examining these differences closely remains limited (Thornicroft, 2006). That is, some mental illnesses have more intense stigmas associated with them than others (e.g., schizophrenia), but research comparing levels of stigma by diagnosis is not well-developed. As such, it can be complicated to understand precisely how individuals make decisions about concealing or revealing mental illness because of the continued lack of community understanding regarding the nature of these lived experiences (Thornicroft, 2006).

This case study examines how individuals struggling with mental illness navigate the challenges of concealing or revealing their mental illness in the workplace. In particular, this case study will highlight the unique challenges associated with managing a mental illness condition in the workplace and how communication theories can be applied to understand the experiences of employees diagnosed with a mental illness.

Mental Illness and the Workplace

Many individuals struggling with mental illness face the challenge of deciding whether they should or should not disclose their diagnosis in the workplace (Wheat et al., 2010). Although some countries have legislation protecting individuals with mental illness (e.g., Americans with Disabilities Act in the U.S; Equality Act 2010 in the U.K.), many of these laws do not cover all mental illness diagnoses and require individuals to disclose their mental health conditions to their employers to receive workplace accommodations. As such, for many individuals living with a mental health condition, revealing their mental health condition in the workplace is a difficult decision that can leave them in the position to be stigmatized and/or discriminated against if their condition is revealed (Thornicroft, 2006). Research indicates that individuals have a variety of motivations for revealing and concealing personal health information in their workplace (Smith & Brunner, 2017; Westerman et al., 2015, 2017). Further, employees diagnosed with mental health conditions often have additional concerns regarding disclosing their mental health condition in the workplace, including fear of not being hired, unfair treatment, loss of credibility, and lack of protection (Brohan et al., 2012). Indeed, in their systematic review of research examining mental illness disclosures in the workplace, Brohan et al. (2012) noted that disclosure and concealment of mental health conditions in the workplace are complex decisions that are informed primarily by "stigma and discrimination" (p. 11).

Stigma

Goffman (1963) defined stigma as an "attribute that is deeply discrediting" (p. 3). Unlike other types of stigmatized identities, mental illness can sometimes be concealed to avoid detection. As such, mental illness is often referred to as an *invisible illness* (Davis, 2005). The stigmatization of mental health issues is a global phenomenon affecting individuals diagnosed with mental illnesses (Sartorius, 2007; Thornicroft, 2006). Mental health stigma is defined as "profoundly negative stereotypes about people living with mental disorders" (Smith & Applegate, 2018, p. 382). Kreps (2020) argues that the social stigma around mental illness continues to promote stereotypes that portray people living with mental illness as dangerous to society. People struggling with mental illnesses often report that they are discriminated against in a variety of contexts (e.g., family, friendships, workplace, healthcare) because of the stigma associated with their condition (Thornicroft, 2006). Further, since individuals may experience self-stigma or the internalization of stigma in society, individuals living with mental health conditions face a variety of challenges (Corrigan & Watson, 2002). Thus, the issue of stigma often informs whether an individual is willing and/or comfortable with disclosing or not disclosing their mental health condition to others.

The stigma surrounding mental health issues is even more problematic when one examines the potential impact that it can have on one's livelihood if it is revealed in the workplace. Research indicates that people diagnosed with mental illnesses often have trouble both finding employment and keeping their positions (Becker & Drake, 2003; Corrigan & Lundin, 2001; Thornicroft, 2006). Although people living with mental illness may experience a variety of challenges associated with finding and keeping one's employment, research indicates that work can have a positive impact on one's mental health as it provides one's livelihood and can further help individuals to feel more valued by society (Warr, 1987). As such, the challenge for many individuals living with mental illness is to decide whether to disclose their mental illness for potential accommodations or to conceal their mental illness. Communication research examining how individuals manage private health information in the workplace offers some explanations regarding decisions surrounding disclosure or non-disclosure of mental illness in the workplace.

Communication Privacy Management Theory

Communication privacy management theory is a theoretical framework used to understand how individuals make decisions about the process of disclosing private information (Petronio, 2002). Research confirms that individuals believe that they have ownership of their personal private information and make decisions about when they reveal or conceal this private information (Petronio, 2002). There are five key components of communication privacy management theory, including the disclosure process, the ownership of private information, privacy boundaries and rules for private information, and privacy turbulence (Petronio, 2013).

The first component of the theory is the disclosure process. Disclosure is the process of sharing our private information with others. Research examining disclosure processes often considers the information that is disclosed and the manner in which it is disclosed (Petronio, 2004). The second component of communication privacy management theory relevant in the present chapter is the concept of private information. Private information is any information that could make an individual feel vulnerable if it were to be revealed to others (Petronio, 2002). Further, individuals believe that they have ownership of their private information (Petronio, 2002). Private information encompasses a variety of issues and beliefs. For example, a personal health diagnosis, such as being diagnosed with clinical depression, can be considered private information. The process of disclosure is important to consider when we look at private information because when individuals make the decision to disclose private information, they are making themselves vulnerable and, thus, sometimes individuals choose not to disclose private information. However, when individuals do disclose private information to others, those confidants become co-owners of the private information.

The third component of communication privacy management theory is the concept of privacy boundaries. Petronio (2002) advanced the boundary metaphor to explain how private information is shared among individuals. That is, a boundary is a protective layer that can protect what lies beneath it. Boundaries are also permeable, which means that private information can pass through the boundaries when shared. In terms of private information boundaries, individuals may choose to allow others within their privacy boundaries when they share private information. Further, individuals may choose to group several individuals within a privacy boundary (e.g., a family) to share private information, whether that is for a short or long duration (Petronio, 2013). Individuals often have privacy rules for their confidants. These rules can be both explicit (i.e., clearly defined) or implicit (i.e., ambiguous) and often focus on the directions we provide to others when we want them to understand how to manage the private information that has been shared with them. The final component of communication privacy management theory is privacy turbulence, which focuses on what happens when a confidant breaks the rules. That is, sometimes someone shares private information with a confidant, and that confidant tells that information to someone else without the permission of the discloser. When there is privacy turbulence, it can cause conflicts between confiders and confidants.

The present chapter focuses on several elements of communication privacy management theory, including disclosure/nondisclosure, ownership of private information, and privacy boundaries. Research on disclosure and non-disclosure of private information demonstrates that individuals have many different motivations for revealing and concealing private information in the workplace (Smith & Brunner, 2017; Westerman et al., 2015, 2017). That is, disclosing one's personal health information in the workplace may be considered risky in terms of how others perceive the individual when they learn this information (Smith & Brunner, 2017). Research shows that decisions to share or not share private information around mental health are often the result of weighing the risks of disclosure with the benefits of disclosing (Meluch & Starcher, 2020). Thus, the decision to share or conceal private health information in the workplace, such as mental health information, is often a complex one that is based on a variety of factors (e.g., one's privacy boundaries, risk-benefit evaluation).

The case study examines how a financial advisor living with bipolar II disorder manages his private information related to his mental health within his workplace. The Mayo Clinic (2021) defines bipolar disorder as "a mental health condition that causes extreme mood swings that include emotional highs (mania or hypomania) and lows (depression)." Bipolar II disorder is distinguished from other types of bipolar disorders by individuals experiencing both hypomania, or periods of over-active behavior, and depressive episodes (Mayo Clinic, 2021).While some individuals believe that bipolar II disorder is less severe than other types of bipolar disorder since individuals diagnosed with bipolar II have not experienced a manic episode, research indicates that the periods of depression that people diagnosed with bipolar II disorder experience are more severe (PsychCentral, 2021). As such, bipolar II is a chronic condition that can be challenging for individuals to manage alongside their daily lives.

The following case study highlights the challenges around concealing private information because of the fear of stigmatization. This case study is informed by a larger qualitative study examining the experiences of individuals living with mental illnesses and working in the U.S. Names and other identifying information have been changed to protect the anonymity of participants in the larger study informing the present case study.

CASE STUDY

Todd reviewed the documents for his 1:00 pm meeting with clients for the third time that morning. He was having problems focusing on the numbers and preparing mentally for the upcoming meeting. After working as a financial advisor for more than ten years, Todd was used to client meetings and always made sure that he was ready to answer any client questions. However, today he was struggling to focus on his work since his mind kept wandering back to the conversation he had with his supervisor, Noland, yesterday afternoon.

Todd had found himself in the break room around 3:30 pm the day before refilling his water bottle and taking a quick break from the spreadsheets and virtual meetings that had occupied the majority of his day. He loved his work as a financial advisor and was happy to have found a career so fulfilling. Not only did he get to work in finance, but he also got to see how he could help his clients to achieve their financial goals. Todd truly felt that this was a career path that had the ability to make a real and long-term difference in the lives of the clients he worked with.

As he stood in the break room looking out the third-floor window at the Canadian geese that were swimming peacefully in the pond that sat adjacent to the office building, he heard Noland wander into the break room. Todd had worked at Lighthouse Financial Services (LFS) for the past two years with his manager Noland and so far, they had gotten along fairly well. Noland always seemed interested in helping his staff and clients as the manager of the Northeast LFS office.

Todd came to LFS after a rather difficult few years, personally and professionally. Todd and his wife struggled with immense grief after losing their infant daughter shortly after her birth to a rare disorder. However, when Todd's depression was not improving, he visited his doctor and was diagnosed with bipolar II disorder several months after his daughter's passing. Todd had never known before he fell into a deep depression following the death of his daughter that his low and high moods were the result of being bipolar and that he needed to get help to manage his mental health better. Todd and his wife had worked together to grieve and on managing his mental health struggles, but he knew that his mental health was still an ongoing challenge that he faced.

When Todd was in the middle of a depressive episode two years ago, he had quit his job of eight years at CalSo Financial as he was just not able to continue to work and manage his condition. As he slowly began to come out of his depressive episode, he felt ready to return to the workplace and to the career that he loved. He was receiving regular therapy and on a medication plan that was working for him. When Todd was interviewed at LFS and they asked him about the gap in his résumé and he explained that he needed to take time off of work after the loss of a child. It was a painful but understandable explanation. However, Todd was careful not to reveal that he was also struggling with bipolar II disorder during the interview process or after he got the job.

One of Todd's greatest fears was his colleagues or his clients feeling like they could not trust his judgment because of his mental health condition. Todd knew that people often acted accepting and understanding when it came to mental health but that they did not always trust people who were diagnosed with a mental health condition. So Todd had kept his secret and felt that it was the best decision for his career.

"Hi Todd, how is your week going?" Noland said, walking toward the coffee machine.

"It has been busy, but good," Todd replied. "What about you?"

"Oh, you know, just trying to keep the ship afloat," Noland said lightly.

As Todd and Noland exchanged pleasantries in the breakroom, he felt that something was bothering Noland.

"Is everything going okay?" Todd asked.

"Well, you know how it goes with family. Olivia has been having a hard time recently, and we are thinking about sending her to see a therapist. I don't know. It just doesn't seem like a ninth-grader needs a therapist. I mean her school counselor is saying she is depressed, but she is just a teenager. Aren't they supposed to be full of angst? It just seems like an awful waste of money for her attention-seeking," Noland sighed heavily.

Todd felt like he should speak up about the benefits of therapy. After all, Todd knew that without his therapist, he would likely have struggled with his depressive episode much longer. Therapy had become an important part of his life and allowed him to really manage his moods and identify why he was feeling high or low.

"That sounds really hard. I don't know what to tell you since our kids are all still pretty young. I am sure that the teenage years are rough," Todd said, trying to be supportive while purposively not commenting on Noland's opinions about therapy.

"Yeah, I get it. How old are your kids now?" Noland asked.

"Five and four," Todd said. He thought about the fact that his daughter would be turning three soon. He knew that mentioning the loss of a child often made people feel uncomfortable, so he didn't talk about it much in the workplace beyond sharing it to explain the gap in his work history.

"Those are great years. Really. Their problems are all small in so many ways. It is just easier when they are at that age. It is true what they say that it just gets harder as they get it older," Noland said.

"I can imagine," Todd replied.

"I just still can't wrap my head around paying $180 a session for some therapist to listen to teenage troubles. I don't think Olivia needs it or needs the stigma that comes along with it. People who need therapy have issues. Olivia is just a teenager; she does not have real problems that require a psychiatrist or something," Noland said.

Todd just nodded and tried to keep a neutral expression. He felt hurt by his manager's comments about therapy. He did not think that Noland was trying to be hurtful and was likely just working through some of his own issues and feelings, but it still stung to know that if the people around Todd knew about his condition that they might think less of him. Todd was a competent financial advisor and a good father. He knew that about himself, but he also knew that he had a mental illness.

"Well, I hate to cut this short, but I should be getting back," Todd said, walking out of the breakroom.

"Yeah, yeah. I get it. Hey, can you maybe not mention this to anyone else around the office?" Noland said. "I would hate anyone to think I have a crazy daughter at home."

"No problem," Todd said, quickening his steps to get back to his office as quickly as possible. Once he was in his office, he shut the door and felt himself choke up.

Next Week's Therapy Session

Todd felt his chest tightening a little as he waited for his therapy appointment to begin. He tried to look at his phone and check updates on his Bloomberg app but could not focus. Todd was really feeling in rough shape since his conversation with Noland. It just seemed like Noland confirmed all of Todd's worst fears. Todd felt like if the world knew that he was a "crazy person," that his entire life would be over. As Todd mulled over everything, he saw his therapist, Dr. Hayes, come out of her office to greet him.

"Hi Todd, you can come on back," Dr. Hayes said cheerfully. Todd walked into her office and sat in the usual blue upholstered chair across from Dr. Hayes.

"So, how have you been doing this week?" Dr. Hayes started.

"Not so great," Todd said. He knew he needed to open up more, but it was sometimes hard to talk about everything that was bothering him, especially when he felt like it might seem inconsequential. After all, it was just a quick breakroom chat with his manager and about his manager's daughter. Todd did not understand why it should be throwing him off so much.

Dr. Hayes gave him a minute to continue before she asked another question. When it was clear that she was going to need to prompt Todd a little further, she said, "Why don't we talk about what is bothering you? Is it the upcoming anniversary of Halle's passing?"

It was really hard coming up on that anniversary, and Todd would be lying if he said that he was not struggling with it, but that was not the only thing.

"Yes, I mean that is hard, and I have been thinking about it a lot. But I actually have been more bothered by something my manager said at work. Noland is usually a pretty great guy, but I guess his daughter is having some issues and is going to therapy and he was really talking down therapy. He was acting like only insane people need help and I just felt really defeated. I mean it is so hard to hide this part of me from my job and I know that I need to hide it because honestly who would want to take financial advice from someone who is bipolar? But it still stings to have it confirmed. For it to be thrown in my face." Todd took a deep breath.

"I see," Dr. Hayes said. "That does sound really frustrating that Noland said those things. Unfortunately, it is hard for a lot of people to understand the value of therapy even today. But I'm more interested in your reaction to his comments. You said that people would not want to take financial advice from someone who is bipolar. Is that what worries you?"

"Yes," Todd said. "I already had my career go off the rails once because of my bipolar disorder."

"But you were able to recover your career," Dr. Hayes interjected.

"Only because I was able to use my daughter's death as an excuse, and honestly, I hate myself for doing that. It feels like a cop-out."

"I don't think the death of a child could ever be called a 'cop-out,'" Dr. Hayes said.

"I know. I know," Todd said. "It is just hard at times to have to hide this part of myself from the world. For me to have to pretend like I constantly have all of my shit together when honestly it does not feel that way most days."

"I think that the stigma in society around mental health and bipolar disorder, in particular, is a very real issue that you are working through. I don't know what it is like to give financial advice, but I would imagine that you feel the need to project an image of perfectionism," Dr. Hayes said.

"Yes, I do feel that way a lot. I do feel like I need to be someone who my clients can look up to if they are going to trust me with their retirement planning or their investments. How can I ask them to feel that their assets are safe if they question whether or not I am sane?"

"I think that is a really hard issue to deal with, and I know that you are not alone in the struggle with the stigma," Dr. Hayes said.

"I think the thing is that before I was diagnosed, I guess I was a lot like Noland. I did not really understand therapy. Maybe I did not really even care. I probably also called someone crazy or bipolar because I did not like them or thought that they were being annoying. But now those comments seem so mean. I feel this constant fear and guilt. I am afraid of being found out and I feel guilty that I used to act like Noland and that I still can't speak up and say, 'Hey, it is not okay to call someone crazy for going to therapy.' I suppose it just hits home hard," Todd said.

"Yes, yes, I can see that," Dr. Hayes said. "But you seem to be identifying what is bothering you really well. You know why you are feeling the way you are feeling about this situation and even though you are struggling with those feelings, you are confronting them."

Todd thought about what Dr. Hayes said and realized that she was right. He was doing a good job and understanding what the problem was.

Back at Work

The following Monday, Todd found himself back in the office and feeling a little bit better since his therapy session last week. He was still avoiding Noland since he really did not want to get cornered again and listen to Noland's opinions about therapy, but otherwise, things were going well. He was working his way through his email inbox when he heard a knock on his office door. It was Noland. The exact person he was trying to avoid.

"Hey, got a minute?" Noland said.

"Of course!" Todd said, trying to sound as enthusiastic as he could muster under the circumstances.

"I feel like you have been avoiding me," Noland started. Todd felt his stomach drop. This was the exact kind of conversation he did not want to have with Noland. He cleared his throat.

"I don't know why you would think that," Todd said. Noland looked unconvinced.

"I've just been really busy," Todd added quickly.

"Oh, I don't want to distract you. I guess I just got a little heavy last week, and I didn't want you to think I was being unprofessional or anything," Noland said.

"No, no, it is nothing like that. Like I said, I've just been really busy and haven't had a ton of time to chat," Todd said.

Noland nodded, seeming to understand that the conversation was not going to go much further. "Okay, then. I guess I will be going." Noland began to walk out of Todd's office, and suddenly, Todd felt the urge to speak up.

"Hey, Noland," Todd said. Noland turned around. Todd realized he had to say it.

"Um . . . I think you should encourage your daughter to get the help she needs. I hope it works out for your family," Todd said.

"Thanks, buddy. I appreciate it," Noland said. "Okay, I'll let you get back to work." Noland left, and Todd felt a moment of reprieve. Maybe he could not tell Noland about his bipolar disorder. Maybe he could not tell anyone about his bipolar disorder, but he could say that he believed in people getting the help they need. He could try to make a difference. At least he hoped he could. But he still worried.

CASE ANALYSIS AND DISCUSSION

Applying communication privacy management theory and stigma to the present case study demonstrates the challenges that individuals living with a mental illness face in the workplace. In the case study, Todd faces the challenge of living with bipolar II disorder and navigating a stressful career as a financial advisor. *Communication privacy management theory* can be used to understand the factors that informed

Todd's decision not to disclose his mental illness to colleagues or clients. Specifically, Todd clearly was not willing to share his *private information* related to his bipolar disorder within his workplace. Todd explained that he feared being stigmatized and losing credibility in his workplace if his colleagues or clients found out about his condition. Brohan et al. (2012) note that fear of losing credibility in the workplace is a key factor informing the decision to conceal a mental health condition within the workplace for many individuals. Todd is clearly concerned that if anyone finds out about his bipolar disorder that he will not be seen as a competent individual to provide financial advice. Thus, he works to hide his diagnosis so as not to experience *stigma*.

Todd's fears of the stigma surrounding mental illness are confirmed when his manager Noland discusses his feelings about therapy and mental illness in conversation with Todd. While Noland is not aware of Todd's condition, Noland describes how therapy can be stigmatizing and, thus, worries about his own daughter seeking mental health treatment because of the stigma that surrounds mental illness. As such, Noland's comments in many ways highlight Todd's worst fears about his own mental illness and treatment being revealed in the workplace. While Todd is able to keep his mental illness concealed from his colleagues and clients, he is clearly concerned about what would happen if he were outed in the workplace.

Todd's therapy session with Dr. Hayes further demonstrates that Todd is constantly living in fear of losing his credibility and potentially his livelihood if anyone in his workplace was to find out about his mental illness. Research indicates that individuals often find concealing their mental health issues to be stressful (Wheat et al., 2010). Todd's conversation with Dr. Hayes shows the everyday struggle that he faces when choosing to conceal his mental illness in the workplace. Namely, he must constantly be on guard to make sure that he protects his private information. As such, Todd feels guilty that he is unable to speak up when mental illness is stigmatized by those around him. Todd struggles with making sense of his feelings after Noland shares his negative views toward mental illness and therapy and sees these comments as an attack on his own identity as an individual who receives therapy and is living with bipolar II disorder.

Notably, this case study highlights the challenges associated with concealing one's identity in the workplace. Organizational communication scholars have explored our decisions around disclosing and not disclosing personal health issues in the workplace (Smith & Brunner, 2017; Westerman et al., 2015, 2017). Importantly, the issue of the *risk* associated with disclosure is often a key factor in the decision to conceal an aspect of one's identity in the workplace (Smith & Brunner, 2017). In the context of the present case study, Todd believed that his bipolar II diagnosis presented a clear perceived risk to both his credibility and, subsequently, his relationships with his colleagues and clients. Thus, an important implication of this case study is that employees struggling with mental illness may find that the risk of disclosing their mental illness in the workplace is too high and, thus, may feel resigned to conceal their condition. While Todd ends the case study choosing to continue to conceal his mental illness from his colleagues and clients, he does choose to be more open about his beliefs regarding the value of seeking treatment to manage mental illness. This choice provides Todd with the opportunity to share his own beliefs surrounding therapy with his colleague to help raise awareness and even remove the stigma associated with mental illness.

The case study in this chapter illustrates the complex challenge of revealing or concealing mental illness in the workplace. Although there is a robust body of literature dedicated to the nature of mental health disclosures in the workplace (see Brohan et al., 2012), there remains little understanding regarding the nature of these decisions from an organizational communication perspective. That is, few scholars have examined how broader organizational processes, structures, and systems impede or facilitate accessibility and inclusion for individuals living with mental illness. Thus, future research is needed to more closely address this matter and understand the lived experiences of employees who have a mental health condition.

DISCUSSION QUESTIONS

1. How does Todd protect his private information in the workplace? What private information does he choose to disclose? What private information does he choose to conceal?
2. Todd struggles with the stigma surrounding mental illness. What types of stigmatizing language does Noland use to reinforce Todd's beliefs regarding the stigma associated with mental illness?
3. What risks does Todd associate with disclosing his mental illness in the workplace? Do you believe his fears surrounding the stigma of mental illness are justifiable?
4. How does Todd's profession as a financial advisor add complexity to the case? Does one's profession significantly impact the risk associated with disclosing a mental illness in the workplace?
5. If you had a friend managing a mental illness who was considering disclosing it within their workplace, what advice would you give that friend? What concerns would you have if your friend's mental illness was known to their colleagues/clients? What benefits do you believe your friend might experience as a result of disclosing?

REFERENCES

Americans With Disabilities Act of 1990, 42 U.S.C. § 12101 et seq. (1990). https://www.ada.gov/pubs/adastatute08.htm

Becker, D. R., & Drake, R. E. (2003). *A working life for people with severe mental illness*. Oxford University Press. doi:10.1093/acprof:oso/9780195131215.001.0001

Brohan, E., Henderson, C., Wheat, K., Malcolm, E., Clement, S., Barley, E. A., Slade, M., & Thornicroft, G. (2012). Systematic review of beliefs, behaviours and influencing factors associated with disclosure of a mental health problem in the workplace. *BMC Psychiatry*, *12*(1), 1–14. doi:10.1186/1471-244X-12-11 PMID:22339944

Corrigan, P., & Lundin, R. (2001). *Don't call me nuts*. Recovery Press.

Corrigan, P. W., & Watson, A. C. (2002). The paradox of self-stigma and mental illness. *Clinical Psychology: Science and Practice*, *9*(1), 35–53. doi:10.1093/clipsy.9.1.35

Davis, N. A. (2005). Invisible disability. *Ethics*, *116*(1), 153–213. doi:10.1086/453151 PMID:16578955

Equality Act. 2010, Chapter 15 § Part 2 (2010). https://www.legislation.gov.uk/ukpga/2010/15/pdfs/ukpga_20100015_en.pdf

Goffman, E. (1963). *Stigma; notes on the management of spoiled identity*. Prentice-Hall.

Kreps, G. L. (2020). The chilling influences of social stigma on mental health communication: Implications for promoting health equity. In L. R. Lippert, R. D. Hall., A. E. Miller-Ott, & D. C. Davis (Eds.), Communicating mental health: History, contexts, and perspectives (pp. 11–26). Lexington Books.

Mayo Clinic. (2021). *Bipolar disorder*. https://www.mayoclinic.org/diseases-conditions/bipolar-disorder/symptoms-causes/syc-20355955

Meluch, A. L., & Starcher, S. (2020). College student concealment and disclosure of mental health issues in the classroom: Students' perceptions of risk and use of contextual criteria. *Communication Studies*, *75*(5), 768–782. doi:10.1080/10510974.2020.1771392

National Institute of Mental Health. (2021). *Mental illness*. https://www.nimh.nih.gov/health/statistics/mental-illness#part_2539

Petronio, S. (2002). *Boundaries of privacy: Dialectics of disclosure*. State University of New York Press.

Petronio, S. (2004). Road to developing communication privacy management theory: Narrative in progress, please stand by. *Journal of Family Communication*, *4*(3&4), 193–207. doi:10.120715327698jfc0403&4_6

Petronio, S. (2013). Brief status report on communication privacy management theory. *Journal of Family Communication*, *13*(1), 6–14. doi:10.1080/15267431.2013.743426

PsychCentral. (2021, May). *What bipolar II disorder really looks & feels like*. https://psychcentral.com/bipolar/what-bipolar-ii-disorder-really-looks-feels-like

Sartorius, N. (2007). The health crisis of mental health stigma. *Lancet*, *387*, 1027–1028. PMID:27025171

Smith, R. A., & Applegate, A. (2018). Mental health stigma and communication and their intersections with education. *Communication Education*, *67*(3), 382–408. doi:10.1080/03634523.2018.1465988 PMID:31354181

Smith, S. A., & Brunner, S. R. (2017). To reveal or conceal: Using communication privacy management theory to understand disclosures in the workplace. *Management Communication Quarterly*, *31*(3), 429–446. doi:10.1177/0893318917692896

Thornicroft, G. (2006). *Shunned: Discrimination against people with mental illness*. Oxford University Press.

Vahratian, A., Blumberg, S. J., Terlizzi, E. P., & Schiller, J. S. (2021). *Symptoms of anxiety or depressive disorder and use of mental health care among adults during the COVID-19 pandemic – United States, August 2020 – February 2021*. Centers for Disease Control and Prevention. https://www.cdc.gov/mmwr/volumes/70/wr/mm7013e2.htm

Warr, P. (1987). *Work: Unemployment and mental health*. Oxford University Press.

Westerman, C. Y. K., Currie-Mueller, J. L., Motto, J. S., & Curti, L. C. (2017). How supervisor relationships and protection rules affect employees' attempts to manage health information at work. *Health Communication*, *32*(12), 1520–1528. doi:10.1080/10410236.2016.1234538 PMID:27819516

Westerman, C. Y. K., Miller, L. E., Reno, K. M., & Spates, S. A. (2015). Sharing personal health information at work: What is appropriate and expected within organizations. *Communication Studies*, *66*(3), 378–397. doi:10.1080/10510974.2015.1019157

Wheat, K., Brohan, E., Henderson, C., & Thornicroft, G. (2010). Mental illness and the workplace: Conceal or reveal? *Journal of the Royal Society of Medicine*, *103*(3), 83–86. doi:10.1258/jrsm.2009.090317 PMID:20200178

ADDITIONAL READING

Corrigan, P. W. (2000). Mental health stigma as social attribution: Implications for research methods and attitude change. *Clinical Psychology: Science and Practice*, *7*(1), 48–67. doi:10.1093/clipsy.7.1.48

Hall, R. D., & Miller-Ott, A. E. (2020). Communicating about mental health: What we know, what we need, and what we give. In L. R. Lippert, R. D. Hall., A. E. Miller-Ott, & D. C. Davis (Eds.), Communicating mental health: History, contexts, and perspectives (pp. 3–10). Lexington Books.

KEY TERMS AND DEFINITIONS

Disclosure: The act of revealing private information to another individual.

Discrimination: Unfair treatment of individuals based on an aspect of one's identity (e.g., race, gender, mental health diagnosis).

Invisible illness: A health condition in which the individual does not visibly exhibit symptoms.

Mental illness: A variety of conditions that impact one's mental health and wellbeing, often by influencing one's mood, emotions, and/or behaviors.

Private Information: Any information that can make an individual feel vulnerable if it is revealed to another individual.

Stigma: Any attribute that leads others to regard one as being lesser or disgraced in society.

Chapter 4
"Stop Trying So Hard!" Disclosing ADHD in the Workplace

Jessica A. Kahlow
https://orcid.org/0000-0002-6174-5351
University of Wisconsin, Milwaukee, USA

EXECUTIVE SUMMARY

In college, people who have learning differences or ADHD are provided an array of different resources (e.g., notetakers, tutoring, additional test time, counseling, etc.). People with these differences learn ways to manage them, but these strategies do not directly translate to the workplace. Resources are often not available in the workplace, leaving people with learning differences to manage on their own. The case study follows Suzie—a young professional diagnosed with ADHD at an early age—through a day in her new role as a communication coordinator. Suzie has accepted ADHD as a part of her identity, but she often questions the accuracy of her notes, has difficulty interpreting her notes, and finds it difficult to remember conversations. The case begins with Suzie in a meeting with her supervisor. After the meeting, she goes back to her desk to interpret her notes. In doing so, she attracts attention from her coworkers. The case provides opportunities to discuss concepts such as minority stress, stigma, self-disclosure, invisible disabilities, and workplace accommodations.

DOI: 10.4018/978-1-6684-3753-7.ch004

INTRODUCTION

ADHD and the Workplace

People who have invisible disabilities refer to people burdened by conditions that cannot be seen by looking at them; this includes chronic pain or fatigue, learning differences, brain injuries, cognitive dysfunctions, mental health disorders, hearing impairments, and vision impairments (Syma, 2018). One such invisible disability is Attention-Deficit Disorder or Attention-Deficit/Hyperactivity Disorder (ADHD). ADHD is considered a chronic, lifelong condition that affects attention, hyperactivity, and impulsiveness. Individuals often assume that the symptoms of ADHD simply go away once an individual reaches adulthood; however, more than eight million adults in the United States are diagnosed with ADHD (Fayyad et al., 2017). So, there are millions of adults trying to manage their ADHD in the workplace with very few accommodations readily available to them.

ADHD is a protected disability by the Americans with Disabilities Act. The Act entitles some individuals to organizational support in the form of workplace accommodations. Organizational support for individuals with ADHD can include informal steps from managers such as dividing large assignments into multiple smaller tasks, providing assignment checklists, using shared calendars to keep the ADHD employee on track, providing organizational tools (e.g., timers, alarms, and color-coded systems), giving precise and clear directions, and setting timelines for projects (Robbins, 2017). More formal and costly interventions include psychotherapy, providing a job coach or counselor, and access to a distraction-free workspace (Nadeau, 2005; Robbins, 2017; Sarkis, 2014).

ADHD Accommodations

For many young adults, college is like their workplace, and their assignments are their work. Accordingly, students with ADHD are supported throughout college, and they are provided an array of resources and accommodations such as notetakers, tutoring, additional time on tests, and counseling (Sarkis, 2008). Over time, and with the appropriate resources, individuals with ADHD learn how to manage their differences. For example, coaching provided through college accommodations can help students with ADHD develop and learn to manage their executive functions (Parker & Boutelle, 2009; Prevatt, 2016). Unfortunately, many people with ADHD find that the strategies they use in school do not directly transfer to the workplace (Sarkis, 2014). The resources present in educational settings are often not available in the workplace, which leaves people who have ADHD to manage on their own (Robbins, 2017). Accommodations such as notetakers, tutoring, and additional time on tests, which are common in school settings, might look different in the workplace. For example, instead of having a notetaker, individuals may instead ask for written directions, and instead of having additional time for tests, individuals may ask for additional time to complete tasks.

A common accommodation for individuals with ADHD is the ability to work from home, which was proposed as a possible reasonable accommodation in the Americans with Disabilities Act (1992). The ability to work from home in a comfortable environment offers many advantages for individuals with disabilities, including those with ADHD (Das et al., 2021). For example, the flexibility of being able to work from home allows people with ADHD the ability to adjust the times they work to a schedule that works best for them, take more time to respond to messages, and have fewer distractions present. Despite these benefits, employers (pre-pandemic, at least) were reluctant to offer remote work options to people who have disabilities because they thought it would be too difficult to hold employees accountable and monitor their performance when they are remote. With the onset of the pandemic and the increase in the feasibility of remote work, there have been more discussions about how changing traditional work practices, schedules, and locations could benefit individuals with disabilities (Das et al., 2021). Even though this may seem promising, people who have ADHD will likely continue to experience marginalization while at work simply due to issues with accessibility issues and the organization's norms.

However, one major hurdle to receiving accommodations such as these is that people need to choose to disclose the disability to their employer.

Self-disclosure

Individuals with ADHD often feel anxious, depressed, overwhelmed, and out of control (Nadeau, 2005; Smyth et al., 2015); however, these setbacks and negative feelings can be alleviated when individuals with ADHD disclose and receive accommodations. Self-disclosure refers to the process of revealing personal information to another person (Choi & Bazarova, 2014). Tichon and Shapiro (2003) noted that "self-disclosure among group members may help them 'make sense of distressing experiences" (p. 169). Seeking support in a distressing situation suggests some level of resiliency and commitment, which may be particularly true for individuals with ADHD who are navigating the workplace.

Thus, the experience of having ADHD influences workplace communication. For some, this means having careful conversations with their coworkers and supervisors about their ADHD to figure out how they can help manage their productivity and efficiency (Robbins, 2017). If an employee chooses not to share that they have ADHD, this means that they need to silently find solutions to manage their ADHD on their own. Therefore, a person's decision to disclose is an important one. For an employee, disclosure could mean the employer takes steps to make sure the employee can be successful in the workplace, or disclosure could mean that the employee is viewed as less capable of doing their job. For instance, Nadeau (2005) explains that individuals with ADHD can have organizational problems that lead to missed deadlines, lateness, and difficulty prioritizing tasks. Given these differences and relational challenges, it is not surprising that individuals with ADHD might struggle when it comes to navigating the workplace.

Stigma

Specifically, people with ADHD may struggle to manage their executive functions, struggle with cognitive skills like problem-solving, and struggle with sustaining attention (Parker & Boutelle, 2009; Prevatt, 2016). In the workplace, poorly managing executive functions is associated with poor time management, misplaced work, missed deadlines, trouble scheduling, and difficulty prioritizing tasks (Nadeau, 2005). As a result, adults with ADHD have trouble handling work that involves multiple complex steps and working independently. Because of this, people with ADHD are often stigmatized as being inattentive or as being underachievers; this is even more so the case with women, who are more quickly labeled as lazy, unorganized, and incapable (Smyth et al., 2015). These symptoms of ADHD can contribute to workplace stress.

Minority Stress

LeBlanc et al. (2015) note that stigmatized groups become exposed to stressors such as "stigma or expectations of rejection, experiences of discrimination (both acute events and chronic everyday mistreatment), internalization of negative social beliefs about one's social groups or social identities, and stressors related to the concealment or management of a stigmatized identity" (p. 43). Minority stress theory (MST) argues that as a result of marginalization, people experience unique stressors that affect their relational quality and well-being (Meyer, 2003) and will use specific maintenance strategies to manage the added stress (Ogolsky et al., 2017). The symptoms consistent with ADHD contribute to relational stress, and "individuals who experience different forms of marginalization as a function of their identities or relationship composition may use maintenance strategies to navigate the added social stress" (Ogolsky et al., 2017, p. 290). The theory assumes that stress is chronic and is "embedded in the broader social context" (Ogolsky et al., 2017, p. 290).

While researchers typically apply MST to same-sex, age-gap, and interracial relationships, it also applies to individuals with learning differences; recently,

Geiger (2019) used MST to connect stigma associated with learning differences to individual distress. Provided that individuals with ADHD deal with many similar challenges regarding stigma, MST can also be applied to individuals with ADHD. However, Kahlow (2021) found that individuals with ADHD do not necessarily feel discriminated against. So, even though people who have ADHD experience various relational challenges, these challenges may be somewhat unrelated to perceived discrimination. This finding implies that having ADHD, or being neurodiverse in general, is simply another type of individual difference.

The subsequent case study follows Suzie—a young professional diagnosed with ADHD at an early age—through a day in her new role as a communication coordinator.

CASE STUDY

Suzie frantically scribbles down notes about what her boss, Kathy, is saying. "For your next role, you'll be responsible for hiring new freelance copyeditors, so you'll be recruiting…" Kathy continues talking, but Suzie's mind wanders. She is suddenly wondering how her friend Gemma from her last job—where she was a recruiter—is managing without her. "… so, you'll need to collect all of that paperwork…" *Oh no, what paperwork?* Suzie looks at her notes. *A W-9? That can't be right.* She was almost certain it was supposed to say W-4.

Then, Suzie hears Kathy say, "Oh, and there's also a test." Kathy must have picked up on the fear in her eyes as she paused to explain. "We ask all potential freelance copyeditors to complete a single-page test."

Suzie breathes a sigh of relief as she realizes she'll be administering the test—not taking the test. She hates tests. But Kathy continues, "When they return the test, you'll just need to compare their edited page to our master page. If they find at least 180 of the possible 200 errors, they pass. Simple as that." Suzie thinks to herself, *180 errors on a single page? How is that even possible?* She recalls the papers she wrote in college and the red marks she received from her professors and understood.

Kathy says, "Yeah, so I think that's pretty much everything. Do you have any questions?"

Suzie thinks, *"Yes, so many questions, starting with, can you write that down?"* but she doesn't want to seem like she wasn't paying attention, so instead, she says, "No, I think I got everything, thank you." Suzie did not get everything. Her mind was still circling around the W-9 issue.

When she gets back to her desk, she struggles to make sense of her notes. While legible, they seem disconnected and fragmented. She reads, "check online submission site, send test with content expertise,"—*What even is content expertise?* — "count errors to see if they pass,"— *wait, count errors?* — "send W-9,"— *that can't possibly be right?* — "contract and info to get started." She suddenly becomes overwhelmed with stress and anxiety as she recalls how helpful notetakers were for her in college. At least with a notetaker, she knew the notes would be accurate and would not need to spend time doubting her own. *I can't believe how much I relied on them. These notes don't even seem to make sense.* At least with a notetaker, she knew the notes would be accurate and would not need to spend time doubting her own. *What am I going to do? I have no idea how to fulfill this role. I don't even know where to start. Why aren't there notetakers for the workplace? Maybe I could ask Kathy if it would be okay to record our meetings. But then I'd have to tell her I have ADHD, and I don't want her to think I'm incompetent or that I can't do the job.* She begins to doubt whether she can handle this new position. *I'm not sure how I'll be able to learn three more roles and keep the responsibilities for each role separate from one another.* She begins to doubt whether she can handle this new position. She opens Indeed on her computer to look for a new job, then quickly closes it.

This morning, Suzie couldn't wait to get started on the second role in her new job rotation schedule. After college, Suzie floated from job to job, quickly and easily becoming bored with each new position. She was so excited to find a job with a rotating schedule because it meant she would not have to do the same thing each week. Her new job included five positions where she and four other people would rotate roles each week. The five roles included (1) responding to customer service inquiries, (2) hiring new freelancers, (3) assigning assignments to freelancers, (4) returning assignments to authors, and (5) processing invoices from freelancers. Her first week was a breeze. She got to learn more about the company by responding to clients and potential clients' questions and concerns. She had to constantly manage the phone, chat window, and email. Learning this role was pretty straightforward. The high volume of quick chats with customers was great for her ADHD. She did not need to remember who was who or even what was going on in the conversation. This role was also great because each new question or concern was different, so she did not get bored.

She thought the job rotation schedule would keep her from getting bored at work since she would not be doing the same tasks every day. She is right about that; she definitely is not bored. She is, however, frustrated and overwhelmed. But so far, the new job has proved to be a challenge for Suzie, as the work environment does not seem very inclusive or very organized; the only training provided is face-to-face with other employees, which isn't great for people with ADHD or other types of learning differences. Even if organizations do not acknowledge or try to help individuals who have ADHD specifically, they could help all employees learn the training materials by providing training information in multiple formats, similar to how teachers try to engage students with materials in a variety of ways (i.e., through reading, activities, videos, etc.).

She sees a text message from her mom on her phone, "hope your first day is going well!" She closes out of the message without responding, genuinely unsure of how the first day is going.

Okay, Suzie, you got this, she thinks to herself. Suzie looks around as she tries to compose herself. She sees the Google homepage screaming at her as if it's going to call her out for her last search—*what if they find out the first thing I searched for was Indeed? That'd be unfortunate*. She takes a deep breath. She sees the dry-erase calendar pinned to the cubicle wall to her left. Without even thinking about it, she finds some markers and begins making the calendar. She begins by filling in the days and then fills in which weeks she'll have what role. *Oh no, what order did the roles go in? Kathy mentioned it, but it looks like I didn't write it down. Maybe it's in an email.* She grabs her notes from her meeting with Kathy this morning. She assigns each sub-task to a day of the week... *Is that everything*, she wonders. *It can't be. What's missing*. Suzie remembers the test. *Who is taking the test? When? Where?* She sits back and then signs into the online submission site to see if she can fill in any of the gaps with information from it. She doesn't find any helpful clues. *Okay, this seems right. Maybe I should ask someone to double-check. But then they might think I'm incompetent. This must be right.*

She sees that Jared (her coworker in front of her in the rotation) had started—but not finished—four applications that were all at different stages, so she decides to finish them. The first person, Courtney, had just returned her copy-editing test. Suzie sees that she doesn't need to deal with scoring the copy-editing tests (a task she is still dreading) until Wednesday. It's Monday, so she skips that one for now. The next person, Steve, just submitted his application. A checked box indicated that Kathy gave the go-ahead to move forward with his application. So, she sends him the test and some form about content expertise. When she does that, she sees an email in the inbox from Courtney, who is wondering if she passed the copy-editing test. She sends her an email to say that she'll get back to her on Wednesday. She moves onto the third person, Kaitlyn. It looks like she hasn't sent her paperwork in yet, so she sends her a reminder email.

Suzie realizes that her current calendar system isn't going to cut it, given all the moving pieces of this role. She instead pins a piece of copy paper to her cubicle (below her newly minted calendar) for a step in the hiring process. She writes each applicant's name on a post-it note and sticks the notes to the page that reflects where they're at in the process. She plans to move them from page to page as they advance through the process.

Kathy appears in the entryway to her cubicle, knocks, and says, "Wow, I never would have thought to do that! What a cool idea!"

Jared overhears the compliment and waits for Kathy to get out of earshot before commenting: "Stop trying so hard! You're making the rest of us look bad". Suzie thinks to herself, *If you only knew the half of it. I wish I didn't have to try so hard all the time. I wonder if I should just tell them I have ADHD and deal with the repercussions later.*

She replies, "I was just having a hard time keeping track of the different stages that all of the applicants were at."

"Oh yeah, I guess that *can* be kind of hard to keep track of," says Jared in a sarcastic tone.

After lunch, it's time for the weekly team meeting. Suzie was meeting with human resources during the team meeting last week, so this is her first. The meeting room is a small interior room, with room for about sixteen people at the conference table. Suzie heads over early since she had never been in that room before. She's surprised to see that she is not the first person there.

"Hi, I'm Suzie. I think I'm in the right place… I'm here for the team meeting at 1:00 PM with Kathy. I think I'm a little early…"

"Hi, Suzie! Yes, you're in the right place. I'm Veronica. It's okay! I'm always early too. It's just easier to get situated into this small room before everyone gets here." Veronica gestures at her chair.

"Oh, okay. That makes sense. I don't think I saw you around at all last week" Suzie says.

Veronica replies, "No, I was on vacation."

"Oh, did you go anywhere fun?"

"No, I just stayed home. I had a yearly checkup on Monday, and that's always hard for me, so I stayed home to mentally recover from that." *How am I supposed to respond to that? Does she want me to ask? I don't want to pry.*

"Oh, well, that's okay too."

"How are you liking it here so far?"

"It's okay here. I think I like having multiple roles. It's a lot to manage at first—there are so many different roles and things to learn." *I wish I could tell Veronica that I have ADHD, but I don't want her to think I'm trying to compare myself to her. I just want her to know that I understand how she feels. At least with her disability, people don't question her competence. With mine, I have to try to act and appear normal, when really, I couldn't be more stressed. Maybe if people knew, they would do things to help me, but I would probably still be signing up for a lifetime of comments and people talking about me behind my back. Maybe I could just tell them I have anxiety. There's less stigma with that, and it might help them understand why I need to keep my tasks so organized and compartmentalized.*

"Yeah, it is a lot and is a bit confusing at first with all of the moving parts. What is your task this week?"

"I'm managing the hiring process for the new freelancers. What do you do?"

"Oh, that's one of the fun jobs! This week, I'm processing invoices from the freelancers. It's so boring." *That's not super reassuring*, thinks Suzie.

"I'm sorry, I need to go grab my notebook—I must have left it on my desk. Do you need me to grab anything for you?"

Veronic says, "You probably don't need to take notes… It's really just a progress update…"

"I understand, but I like to write things down. It helps me stay more focused on the meeting." *And it keeps my mind from wandering off to other tasks*, Suzie thinks. Suzie leaves to go grab her notebook. When she returns, Kathy and her other coworkers (Jared, Monica, Cindy, and Keith) have joined Veronica in the room.

As Suzie re-enters the room, Kathy asks, "Veronica, could you run down to the printer and pick up the agenda for the meeting? I think I left it on the printer…" Jared scoffs at Kathy's unfortunate choice of words. Veronica is in a wheelchair. No one ever says anything about it, and people just seem to ignore Veronica's visible disability. Still, everyone in the room glares at Jared. Surely, Kathy meant well. Suzie thinks, *What would be more appropriate, though? Can you roll down to the printer? Somehow that option seems worse.*

Cindy says, "No, that's not necessary; I can go and grab them." *Ah, yes, 'go' is much better. It seems like Cindy has made this correction before.*

"Thank you, Cindy," says Veronica.

"Yes, thank you," adds Kathy. Kathy looks at Veronica like she should have anticipated the need for the meeting agenda and that they would be on the printer. *Oh, good, there will be an agenda*, Suzie thinks. Cindy returns with the agenda. There are two items, "This week" and "Suzie." *Oh, no, what did I mess up?* Suzie thinks. *Why did Kathy even bother with the agenda if there were only two—very short—items on it? And why did she ask Veronica—the person who has the hardest time leaving and returning—to go get it? The whole interaction just seemed weird. Was it because of Veronica's chair? It must be. There's no way I can tell anyone about my ADHD now.* Suzie sighs.

Kathy calls the meeting to order. Kathy asks everyone to talk about where they left off in their role from last week, so the next person knows where to pick up. *But I spent all morning trying to figure that out. Why didn't anyone tell me? Ugh.*

It's Jared's turn. He says, "I hired two people and started the process for three more." *Okay, so that's not really helpful anyway.*

After everyone else finishes, Kathy comments, "Suzie, wow, you took a lot of notes!"

Jared adds, "Yeah, she does that." Everyone glares at Jared again.

After she closes the meeting, Kathy asks, "Suzie, could you stay after the meeting? I'd just like to talk to you about how things are going."

"Yes, of course." They wait for everyone to leave the room. Jared closes the door in front of Veronica, and she looks to the ceiling in disgust. She sighs.

"I noticed that Jared has been giving you a bit of trouble. I heard a comment he made this afternoon about you supposedly 'trying too hard.' Is everything okay?"

"With Jared, no. He's fine." *It's the messiness of everything else that's the problem... It's so hard to focus with so many moving pieces. Well, I guess Jared is a problem too. But every workplace has a Jared,* Suzie thinks.

Kathy replies, "Okay, well, for what it's worth, you can relax a bit more... you don't need to take so many notes. It's really not a big deal." *But I need the notes.*

"Yeah, I guess I just like to keep them. I can try to stop taking so many." *So, I guess I can't ask her about recording our meetings...*

Kathy responds, "Well, is there anything else I can help with? To help you adjust? *Oh no, did she hear me? Does she know about my ADHD? How could she? Did I say those things out loud? I hope not. How could I possibly ask now?* Kathy continues, "I know it can all be just a little overwhelming at first. I'm just not sure what or how to make it better." *Okay, here's my chance,* thinks Suzie. *It's now or never. Tell her you have ADHD. She'll understand. She's trying to help.*

CASE ANALYSIS AND DISCUSSION

Suzie's case highlights several communication phenomena discussed earlier, including self-disclosure, stigma, minority stress, and accommodations. If the reader were unaware that Suzie had ADHD, the case would seem relatively uneventful since her day consisted of things that were typical of most workdays—going to meetings, taking notes, etc.

Suzie has ADHD, which is considered a cognitive (and invisible) disability. More than four million working adults have ADHD in the United States ("ADHD Statistics," 2016). As people with ADHD age, the symptoms shift in such a way that hyperactivity decreases while problems with inattention and distractibility persist (Nadeau, 2005). These problems with executive functioning lead to potential problems in the workplace, which Nadeau (2005) reports may include poor time management skills resulting in frequent lateness and missed deadlines, organizational problems leading to cluttered desks, misplaced paperwork, and difficulty in scheduling and prioritizing tasks. In addition, individuals with ADHD store and recall information differently, so it can also be difficult for them to quickly access the information they know. Further, adults with ADHD can experience problems with self-regulation, and their need for structure can make it difficult for them to work independently on complex, multi-step tasks (Nadeau, 2005). Given this array of potential workplace problems for adults with ADHD, Robbins (2017) suggests the following ways that organizations can accommodate employees with ADHD and improve productivity:

- Divide large assignments into several small tasks,
- Set a timer to make an alarm after assigning ample time to complete a task,
- Provide a checklist of assignments,
- Supply an electronic or handheld organizer,
- Use a wall calendar to emphasize due dates, and
- Develop a color-coded system where each color represents a task, event, or level of importance. (p. 8)

It is also worth noting that these are easy measures to implement and would help the individual with ADHD and the organization. In cases where the organization does not already make such accommodations, individuals with ADHD may try to create or implement them on their own, or they may not think to and simply continue struggling to stay afloat.

The case ends with Suzie considering disclosing her ADHD essentially as an act of desperation. This feeling is not particularly uncommon. A recent study found that for people with ADHD, communication apprehension essentially promotes the disclosure of ADHD in the workplace. This is problematic because employees should not feel obligated to disclose out of desperation; while disclosing may provide a sense of relief, that same study also found that having high anxiety is also a prerequisite of disclosures, and this is likely what Suzie is experiencing.

Somewhat paradoxically, accommodations are only granted if and when a disclosure is actually made. Robbins (2017) noted that peer support or coaching could help individuals manage their ADHD, which may help build relationships and comfort disclosing. Ideally, such interventions would help employees with ADHD feel comfortable disclosing before they feel the need to disclose out of desperation. As Das et al. (2021) note, working from home may offer several advantages for individuals with disabilities. In Suzie's case, the flexibility of being able to work from home, adjust her schedule, take more time to respond to messages, and have fewer distractions would all be advantageous. Moreover, since Suzie often questions the accuracy of her notes, and she finds it difficult to remember conversations, working from creates an environment where it is normalized to record meetings and share notes, which would help her feel more comfortable in her new role.

However, Suzie is also wary about disclosing because of the stigma associated with people who have ADHD. Since stigmatized groups are often exposed to additional stressors such as stigma and discrimination, they often decide to conceal their differences (LeBlanc et al., 2015). Suzie's coworkers are already calling her out for how she completes tasks—a way that she recognizes as necessary to make sure she gets everything done. Because of this way she manages her ADHD, she's labeled as an overachiever because of the extra effort she has to put in that no one previously had to. It is clear in the case that this—seemingly a compliment—is causing Suzie a good deal of stress. Thus, it is possible that Suzie is also experiencing some of the setbacks associated with MST.

Even though Suzie's coworkers are currently unaware of her ADHD, she still experiences stress associated with having this invisible disability. In other words, because of her ADHD, Suzie is inadvertently being marginalized by her coworkers when they tell her things like "Stop trying so hard!" According to MST, people experience unique stressors that affect their relational quality and well-being as a result of marginalization (Meyer, 2003). Suzie's stressors are unique to her experience as a person with ADHD—someone without ADHD likely would not think twice about such a comment, but for Suzie, she can not stop thinking about it. This unique stressor is a result of marginalization (in the form of having ADHD) that is clearly affecting her well-being as she is clearly starting to dislike her new job that she was initially so excited to start.

The discussion questions to follow further explore Suzie's experiences in relation to self-disclosure, workplace accommodations, stigma, minority stress, and likely many other related concepts.

DISCUSSION QUESTIONS

1. How does Suzie conceptualize herself as being similar or different from her coworkers?
2. Should Suzie tell her coworkers about her ADHD? Should she tell her supervisor, Kathy? What are the pros and cons associated with disclosing her difference?
3. What are some of the things that Suzie does to help manage her ADHD while also benefitting the office and others she works with?
4. What organizational tensions exist that might keep Suzie from disclosing her ADHD?
5. If Jared doesn't know that Suzie has ADHD, is he bullying her or discriminating against her? Would your answer change if Jared did know Suzie had ADHD? Why?
6. If Suzie were to disclose her difference, what kind of accommodations could she ask for?

REFERENCES

Bazarova, N. N., & Choi, Y. H. (2014). Self-disclosure in social media: Extending the functional approach to disclosure motivations and characteristics on social network sites. *Journal of Communication*, *64*(4), 635–657. doi:10.1111/jcom.12106

Bora, E., & Pantelis, C. (2016). Meta-analysis of social cognition in attention-deficit/hyperactivity disorder (ADHD): Comparison with healthy controls and autistic spectrum disorder. *Psychological Medicine*, *46*(4), 699–716. doi:10.1017/S0033291715002573 PMID:26707895

Das, M., Tang, J., Ringland, K. E., & Piper, A. M. (2021). Towards accessible remote work: Understanding work-from-home practices of neurodivergent professionals. *Proceedings of the ACM on Human-Computer Interaction*, *5*(183), 1–30. doi:10.1145/3449282

Fayyad, J., Sampson, N. A., Hwang, I., Adamowski, T., Aguilar-Gaxiola, S., Al-Hamzawi, A., Andrade, L. H. S. G., Borges, G., de Girolamo, G., Florescu, S., Gureje, O., Haro, J. M., Hu, C., Karam, E. G., Lee, S., Navarro-Mateu, F., O'Neill, S., Pennell, B.-E., Piazza, M., ... Kessler, R. C.WHO World Mental Health Survey Collaborators. (2017). The descriptive epidemiology of DSM-IV Adult ADHD in the World Health Organization World Mental Health Surveys. *Attention Deficit and Hyperactivity Disorders*, *9*(1), 47–65. doi:10.100712402-016-0208-3 PMID:27866355

Geiger, E. F. (2019). *Don't DIS my ABILITY: Expansion of Minority Stress Theory for Adults with Learning Disabilities*. Columbia University. doi:10.7916/d8-bsjg-yq92

Kahlow, J. (2021). *Improving neurodiverse relationships: Comparing relational quality and maintenance channels in individuals with and without ADHD* [Doctoral dissertation, University of Wisconsin–Milwaukee]. https://dc.uwm.edu/etd/2677

LeBlanc, A. J., Frost, D. M., & Wight, R. G. (2015). Minority stress and stress proliferation among same-sex and other marginalized couples. *Journal of Marriage and Family*, *77*(1), 40–59. doi:10.1111/jomf.12160 PMID:25663713

Meyer, I. H. (2003). Prejudice, social stress, and mental health in lesbian, gay, and bisexual populations: Conceptual issues and research evidence. *Psychological Bulletin*, *129*(5), 674–697. doi:10.1037/0033-2909.129.5.674 PMID:12956539

Nadeau, K. G. (2005). Career choices and workplace challenges for individuals with ADHD. *Journal of Clinical Psychology*, *61*(5), 549–563. doi:10.1002/jclp.20119 PMID:15723424

Ogolsky, B. G., Monk, J. K., Rice, T. M., Theisen, J. C., & Maniotes, C. R. (2017). Relationship maintenance: A review of research on romantic relationships. *Journal of Family Theory & Review*, *9*(3), 275–306. doi:10.1111/jftr.12205

Parker, D. R., & Boutelle, K. (2009). Executive function coaching for college students with learning disabilities and ADHD: A new approach for fostering self-determination. *Learning Disabilities Research & Practice*, *24*(4), 204–215. doi:10.1111/j.1540-5826.2009.00294.x

Prevatt, F. (2016). Coaching for College Students with ADHD. *Current Psychiatry Reports*, *18*(110), 1–7. doi:10.100711920-016-0751-9 PMID:27783338

Robbins, C. A. (2005). ADHD couple and family relationships: Enhancing communication and understanding through Imago Relationship Therapy. *Journal of Clinical Psychology*, *61*(5), 565–577. doi:10.1002/jclp.20120 PMID:15723423

Sarkis, E. (2014). Addressing attention-deficit/hyperactivity disorder in the workplace. *Postgraduate Medicine*, *126*(5), 25–30. doi:10.3810/pgm.2014.09.2797 PMID:25295647

Sarkis, S. M. (2008). Success for the ADHD College Student. *The ADHD Report*, *16*(5), 1–5. doi:10.1521/adhd.2008.16.5.1

Smyth, A., Dipeolu, A., Davies, L., Hargrave, S., & Stevenson, A. R. (2015). Living with ADHD: The unique career development challenges facing women with ADHD. *Career Planning and Adult Development Journal, 31*(4), 44–53.

Syma, C. (2018). Invisible disabilities: Perceptions and barriers to reasonable accommodations in the workplace. *Library Management*, *40*(1/2), 113–120. doi:10.1108/LM-10-2017-0101

ADDITIONAL READING

Scott, C. R. (2020). Identity and identification. In A. M. Nicotera (Ed.), Origins and traditions of organizational communication: A comprehensive introduction to the field (pp. 207–227). Routledge.

KEY TERMS AND DEFINITIONS

Attention-Deficit Disorder or Attention-Deficit/Hyperactivity Disorder (ADHD): A chronic, lifelong condition that affects attention, hyperactivity, and impulsiveness.

Invisible Disability: Refers to people burdened by conditions that cannot be seen by looking at them; includes chronic pain or fatigue, learning differences, brain injuries, cognitive dysfunctions, mental health disorders, hearing impairments, and vision impairments.

Minority Stress Theory (MST): Posits that as a result of marginalization, people experience unique stressors that affect their relational quality and well-being and will use specific maintenance strategies to manage the added stress.

Self-Disclosure: The process of revealing personal information to another person.

Stigma: Typically a negative connotation associated with a particular circumstance or quality; people with ADHD are often stigmatized as being inattentive or as being underachievers.

Chapter 5
Seeing (Speaking) Through Her Eyes (Brain):
Louisa's Journey

Courtney D. Fallon
Missouri State University, USA

EXECUTIVE SUMMARY

This case study examines the experience of Louisa, a new employee at a conflict resolution consulting firm, as she navigates her ADHD and the workplace. She faces ableist biases in the organizational culture at her job that cause her to question her own abilities. Louisa's Journey follows Louisa's interactions with her team as she struggles with her skills as a professional in her field and as a neurodivergent person who needs accommodations to function and prosper in her daily life. Louisa soon finds that the nuances of disclosure and workplace inclusivity are incredibly challenging for her, especially as someone with an invisible disability. She struggles to balance her ambitions in the company, her needs as a neurodivergent person, and the complexities of her identity. This case study challenges readers to consider how organizational culture can contribute to ableism, especially toward neurodivergent people and others with invisible disabilities.

INTRODUCTION

In the quest to understand organizations, it is tempting to treat them as independent entities sheltered from the whims of humanity. In this state, they are predictable, stable, and innocuous; people can join them or leave them as it serves their individual interests without consequence. However, as Bisel (2010) reflects, organizations are

DOI: 10.4018/978-1-6684-3753-7.ch005

as much a part of us as we are a part of them: "Organization is an emergent reality that is constantly in a state of becoming, word by word, message by message, and turn by turn" (p. 126). How we communicate about our membership in organizations in turn impacts how we invite organizations to communicate about us.

Organizational communication does not exist in a vacuum. Organizations are subject to the pressures of external society in how it treats its members, particularly those who are marginalized and disenfranchised by racism, sexism, homophobia, classism, religious intolerance, and ableism. Regardless of how organizations try to negate the mistreatment of minority members through antidiscrimination policies, organizations often perpetuate the social norms of dominant groups in society. Even when organizations do not intend to discriminate against anyone, organizational practices can harm members who do not fit the norms of dominant groups in society. Organizational members with disabilities are often among those unintentionally harmed by societal norms that infiltrate their workplaces.

Disability protections in organizations, particularly the workplace, are upheld by law in the United States (Americans with Disabilities Act, 1990). Even so, accessibility does not look the same for all people with disabilities. Some people with disabilities need mobility aids such as wheelchairs or canes, which organizations must legally accommodate with features such as accessible parking. Other people with disabilities need access to assistive technology like text-to-speech or magnification software. However, people with invisible disabilities (disabilities that are not immediately apparent to onlookers), have different barriers to accessibility in organizations. An example of one such group are people who are neurodivergent.

Neurodiversity is defined by the Stanford Neurodiversity Project as "a concept that regards individuals with differences in brain function and behavioral traits as part of normal variation in the human population. The movement of Neurodiversity is about uncovering the strengths of neurodiverse individuals" (Stanford University, n.d.). The use of the term indicates the desire to increase inclusivity of those diagnosed with neurodevelopmental disorders, such as autism spectrum disorder (ASD), attention deficit hyperactivity disorder (ADHD), Tourette's syndrome, intellectual disabilities, and others. These conditions are not always considered disabilities, but many people who are neurodivergent are disabled.

To explore how neurodivergent people and others with invisible disabilities (such as chronic pain) experience organizations, we must examine the lived experiences of those who are harmed by ableism in their organizations. This chapter will begin with a review of existing literature on organizational culture and neurodiversity. Next, it will proceed with case study following Louisa, an organization member who has ADHD, in the following sections: organization background, setting the stage, case description, and current challenges. The chapter will conclude with possible solutions and recommendations.

LITERATURE REVIEW

Structuration and Organizational Culture

Organizations are ongoing social phenomena. Since people create and maintain organizations through communication, organization members bring in their own ideas about what behaviors are "normal" to that organization. In turn, that organization then applies social rules to its members. This ongoing process can be conceptualized through structuration theory, which was originally developed by sociologist Anthony Giddens (e.g., Giddens, 1984). In their explanation of structuration, Kirby and Krone (2002) explain that "the reproduction of social systems lies in the routinized, day-to-day interactions" of organization members (p. 55). Since individuals bring their own experiences into organizations via communication, organizations reflect norms that align with dominant identities among organization members. The norms adopted by the organization from its members' communication are often called "organizational culture."

Keyton (2005) defines organizational culture as "the set(s) of artifacts, values, and assumptions that emerge from the interactions of various members" (p. 28). Though artifacts and values are crucial elements of organizational culture, assumptions about normal behaviors within an organization have the most impact when considering how people with disabilities might be disadvantaged in the workplace. For example, an assumption in a competitive work environment might be that all new employees take on extra shifts to "earn their keep" in the organization. However, a person with a disability might have an accommodation that includes a flexible work schedule and prevents the organization from scheduling them for overtime shifts. Even though taking on extra work is not required in this example, violating the cultural assumption that new employees work overtime could prevent that person from gaining a competitive edge and opening opportunities for upward mobility in the organization.

Structuration theory and organizational culture were intricately intertwined in the study of family leave policies by Kirby and Krone (2002): "coworker discourse and communication processes have shaped...perceptions of what is valued by their 'team members' in the organization, and the policies did not always mesh with these values" (p. 71). Similarly, organizational values about disability are constructed through member communication. "Good" and "bad" member behaviors might have nothing to do with the written policy. People with disabilities have legal protection to request reasonable workplace accommodations, but their coworkers may communicate negativc attitudes about certain accommodations, like the ability to work from home, because organizational norms say that people who do not come into work every day are lazy or a burden, for instance. These situations are where people with invisible disabilities fall through the cracks of an organization, particularly neurodivergent people who are disabled.

Neurodiversity and Invisible Disabilities

Though disability advocates are wary of medical standards that pathologize people who are neurodivergent, the medical understanding of neurodevelopmental disorders is at present the most thorough body of neurodiversity research to date. Additionally, for neurodivergent people who are also disabled, documentation for access to workplace accommodations largely comes from medical personnel. In order to educate readers about the experiences of people who are neurodivergent, examining existing symptomology from the field of psychiatry is necessary.

The Diagnostic and Statistical Manual of Mental Disorders (5th ed.; DSM–5; American Psychiatric Association, 2013) explains that the neurodevelopmental disorders that are reflected in neurodivergent individuals as "characterized by developmental deficits that produce impairments of personal, social, academic, or occupational functioning. The range of developmental deficits varies from very specific limitations of learning or control of executive functions to global impairments of social skills or intelligence" (p. 31). Neurodivergent people face a variety of barriers in their social environments with each person experiencing different symptoms with a range of visibility. For example, some people with autism are nonverbal and need access to communication tools other than speech, while others are verbal and can communicate with speech. The person with autism who is verbal does not face the same barrier as the person with autism who is nonverbal, but they are both still neurodivergent and face social challenges in the neurotypical (in other words, not neurodivergent) world. These challenges extend to the communicative environments that are organizations. It is imperative, therefore, to keep in mind the levels of support and visibility that vary widely among people who are neurodivergent, especially when it comes to communication.

Neurodivergent people have measurable differences in their brains and nervous systems that result in many of the traits that they exhibit; their brains do not even run on the same track as their peers when it comes to learning social behaviors (Vargo, 2015). Not only do neurodivergent people have to come to terms with how their own brains "run the race" of social life, but they must also learn the world of neurotypical communication with an outsider's perspective, often without the knowledge that they are, in fact, outsiders. The reality is that we live in a neurotypical world designed to protect communicative structures that benefit neurotypical people. These communicative norms are also prevalent in organizations, which can isolate and disadvantage neurodivergent people in the workplace if those individuals violate the unspoken social rules of that organization's culture.

THE CASE

Organization Background

Established in 1997, Conflict Management Consulting United (CMCU) began as a small business consulting firm. As the firm grew, management became aware of a lack of consulting firms in the industry that specialized in conflict resolution and mediation. Today, they are hired to mediate conflicts within organizations so that disputing parties within the organization might find long-term solutions without involving litigation. The firm also contains specialists in human resources and business law who assist consultants when a situation calls for their expertise. CMCU prides itself on being one of the leading conflict resolution consulting firms in the industry.

When CMCU is hired by a company, a team of consultants is sent to the client. When the consultants arrive on the scene, they gather crucial information about the disputing parties, the client's organization, and the dispute at hand. Once the consultants have been sufficiently educated about various aspects of the dispute, they begin a mediation process. Mediation usually involves a process where consultants rotate among meeting individually with each party and holding full sessions with both parties. Consultants make sure to identify the root problems of the dispute, each party's interests, and possible solutions to the dispute. From there, consultants facilitate mediation between parties until a mutually agreeable solution is reached. If a solution is reached, the consultants bring in their own legal experts to document the terms of the solution. If a solution is not reached, consultants may revert to earlier steps in the mediation process or recommend legal action.

Setting the Stage

Louisa is a new junior consultant at CMCU. When a business hires CMCU, a team of three is sent to consult with the business on its issues: a senior consultant and two junior consultants. A junior consultant is an entry-level worker that is hired to assist senior consultants with a variety of tasks related to working with clients. A senior consultant usually has at least 5 years of experience with the company and has demonstrated their capabilities as a mid-level employee. Senior consultants lead consulting teams when assigned to a client that has hired the firm. CMCU also has an internal management structure where employees can apply for upper-level positions later in their careers.

Due to the limited opportunities for promotion, the organizational culture at CMCU is incredibly competitive. Additionally, working with high-profile clients often lead CMCU consultants to find career opportunities through networking during the mediation process. Though CMCU is supposed to be a neutral entity during the conflict resolution process, consultants often leverage previous connections with clients following the conclusion of a case. For this reason, the competition for high-profile clients and promotions is fierce, especially among junior consultants looking to work their way up the ladder.

Case Description

When she was little, Louisa's cousins used to call her "the rocket scientist who couldn't find her way out of Walmart." She was a talented student growing up and excelled in college. However, Louisa always felt out of place. She had a challenging time catching the meaning behind minute facial expressions or vocal tones that are commonplace in nonverbal communication. Her friends and family considered her gullible and naïve, and they liked to play tricks on her because she always believed them so easily. They did not mean any harm, but that did not change how Louisa felt about their remarks and tricks. Though she never said anything to them about it, Louisa felt stupid when her friends and family made these jokes at her expense. Even so, she liked spending time with her friends and family, but she sometimes felt overwhelmed after being with them and found herself sitting alone at social events.

Though Louisa loved school, she regularly daydreamed and had to teach herself most of the material on her own outside of class. She spent a lot more time on her work outside of class than her peers for this reason. Even with these challenges, Louisa persevered and eventually went to college. Towards the end of her college years, Louisa was diagnosed with attention deficit hyperactivity disorder (ADHD). At first, she was shocked by the diagnosis. (ADHD is something that 8-year-old boys had when they could not sit still in class, right?) However, as Louisa began working with her doctor to learn about her disorder and to find the best treatment option, many of her symptoms, even from her earliest memories of her childhood, began to make sense. Louisa was relieved and nervous at the same time – she was glad that she had an explanation for her challenges but was also about to enter the workforce after the completion of her degree. How was she going to establish herself as a professional and still get the treatment and accommodations that had made things so much less stressful for her in college?

Louisa had spoken to her doctor at length about her anxieties related to her diagnosis and the workplace. Her doctor explained that ableism in modern society often causes people with disabilities harm throughout their entire lives, especially in their jobs. Louisa was confused – she did not have a disability, right? She did not use a wheelchair, need magnification technology, or require the capability to work from home. Louisa's doctor explained that a lot of people have invisible disabilities, and that her own internalized ableism (ableism that we learn to have towards others and ourselves based on our socialization) may have influenced her perception of her own accessibility needs. Also, not everyone who is neurodivergent is considered to have a disability, but the law outlines certain parameters for individuals with conditions like ADHD to be considered disabled under certain circumstances based on their condition's severity and need for accommodations (Americans with Disabilities Act, 1990). As she thought about all this, Louisa wondered how her future in her job might look if she needed workplace accommodations. She had benefited from her accommodations in college, but she assumed that she would not have the same access to accessibility tools and other accommodations at work.

Shortly after beginning treatment, Louisa graduated from college and was looking for work. She received her degree in organizational communication with a certificate in conflict resolution. As much as she struggled with the nuances of communication in her personal life, Louisa was passionate about and talented at conflict resolution. In her college internship, she loved watching the process of figuring out solutions to problems between people in a variety of workplace settings. She saw every consultation at her internship as a new challenge for her to solve by following the procedure of conflict resolution. Even though some consultations were more difficult than others, finding the solution was always exciting for Louisa. She was particularly talented in her internship because she was a very direct communicator. She was always professional, but never shied away from calling things like she saw them. The consultations that she had worked on as an intern were more successful than her peers.' Though. Louisa was proud of her accomplishments, she felt as though they isolated her from the other interns.

Soon after graduation, Louisa's mentor at her internship reached out to her about a position that had opened at Conflict Management Consulting United (CMCU), which was a similar consulting firm to the one that Louisa had interned for in college. After hearing about the opening from her mentor, Louisa applied for a full-time position at CMCU as a junior consultant for the firm. Louisa was hired just a few weeks after finishing college. She was so excited to begin working her dream job, but still had hesitations about integrating into a new organizational culture. Louisa's challenges with her social life as a neurodivergent person added an extra layer of stress for her.

Louisa thought about the challenges she could face as she walked into the office on her first day at CMCU. Her first meeting was with her direct supervisor, Maeve, and with the other junior consultant on their team, Anthony. Maeve had been with CMCU for 15 years, with 7 of those years serving as a senior consultant. She had a track record of being one of the best consultants not only in the company but also in the field. There had been countless opportunities for Maeve to move up in the company, but her true passion was being on the ground working with clients. Anthony had been a junior consultant for the CMCU for 5 years and was an up-and-coming star in the company for his talent and charisma. Clients loved him and were often impressed by his expertise as a junior consultant. Anthony was hoping to be promoted to a senior consultant and gain his own consulting team soon.

"We're so excited to have you join our team, Louisa. We've heard wonderful things about you," Maeve began once they had all introduced themselves.

"Thank you so much, I'm happy to be here," Louisa replied.

"I'm honestly surprised that they put you with us being so new, usually they'd have you start with a... slower paced team," Anthony added.

"Oh...well I think I should be able to keep up, I did pretty well in my internship," Louisa said, missing the slight eyebrow raise from Anthony.

"What Anthony means is that our hiring team thought very highly of you, and we're excited for you to join us," Maeve noted, with a pointed look at Anthony.

Louisa was humbled by Maeve's compliment and considered her interaction with her team a positive one despite all her worries. Once she had chatted with her new team and had received a tour of the office, it was time for her to meet with the human resources office. Due to her complications with ADHD, Louisa discussed multiple accommodation options. She decided to request the following accommodations: a semi-private office in a space with limited distraction and more control of her environment for her sensory needs, access to reading assistance and notetaking software, increased break times, and detailed written instructions from her supervisor regarding her task expectations. Louisa was relieved with how easy it was to set up her accommodations and was confident that she would do well in her new role.

After the first two weeks of work and getting familiar with her role, it was time for Louisa to attend her first meeting with the clients that her team had just been assigned to work with. The day before their offsite meeting, Louisa was in the office break room when she overheard Anthony talking with another junior consultant from another team, Imari.

"I don't understand why she gets all this special treatment. When I first started, I was in the shared office with the rest of the junior consultants. And on top of it, I saw written instructions from Maeve on Louisa's desk. What kind of person can't follow instructions from their boss at the meetings we all go to? Why does Maeve spend extra time holding her hand by writing out everything for her?" Anthony said angrily.

"Do you think Louisa is sucking up to Maeve to try and get a leg up for a senior consulting spot?" Imari replied.

"I don't know how she could think that she'd get it, but maybe she's bitter that we're on the same level and I'm much closer to a promotion. Also, it seems so counterintuitive to try to get a promotion by asking for extra help on things she should already know how to do. Don't get me wrong, she has good ideas and seems like a decent consultant, but she needs to know her place. She just somehow seems really naïve and arrogant at the same time," Anthony said.

"That won't last very long. Isn't she going with you and Maeve to meet with that new client tomorrow?" Imari asked.

"Yeah, she'll learn that she isn't all that when we get there. She won't have her own office on site, that's for sure," Anthony retorted.

Louisa was shocked and upset. She thought that Anthony liked her – he always seemed nice when they had worked together so far. She did not understand how she could have given the impression that she was trying to undermine him. Louisa thought Anthony was incredibly talented and was rooting for him to get promoted. She felt crushed that her accommodations made it seem like she was receiving special treatment. Now Louisa was stuck: should she disclose her condition to her colleague so that he understood why she was allowed to work differently than he had when he first got hired? Should she have to disclose intimate details of her medical status to a coworker for him to treat her well? Would he be angry that she was eavesdropping on her conversation if she told him? There was so little time left for Louisa to worry – she had so much to do before her first meeting with their new client. She felt crushed and conflicted by what she had heard but knew that she needed to handle the situation the right way to avoid making things worse with Anthony.

The time finally arrived for Maeve, Anthony, and Louisa to meet with their new client. They met at the office first thing so that they could travel together to the client's location. On the way there, Anthony and Maeve were eagerly chatting about their client, namely whether the break room would have decent coffee. Louisa listened but remained quiet, still reeling from the conversation she had overheard the day before.

"You're quiet today, Louisa. Is everything okay?" Maeve asked.

"She's probably just nervous for her first real client meeting," Anthony interrupted with a smirk. Normally, Louisa would assert that she had already met with dozens of clients through her college internship, but now that she knew that Anthony perceived her as arrogant, she hesitated then said,

"Yeah, I guess so. I'm just thinking about everything I need to remember for our first meeting."

"The other day, it seemed like you felt pretty good about our meeting. Is there something else you're worried about?" Maeve asked, concerned.

Louisa felt trapped. She knew that Maeve was right – they had gone over everything that Louisa needed to know in detail, and Louisa was excited to start. She did not want to seem incompetent to her supervisor but also did not want to appear arrogant to Anthony, who already thought she was trying to compete with him. She felt a sense of irony that she was engaged in the very type of workplace conflict that they were on their way to professionally advise a business about.

She shrugged and said, "I guess it's just the jitters since we're actually on our way there now."

Maeve did not exactly buy Louisa's claim, as she was familiar with what Louisa's references had said about her performance in her internship. She thought about investigating the issue once they had returned to the office. Maeve's thought ended there – they had arrived at their new client's office. The company that they had been hired to consult for was Imagine Entertainment International (IEI), which was a talent agency that specialized in indie music festivals. This company was unique among competitors because they primarily focused on festivals that featured artists that were new to the industry or produced music that was more niche or on the fringe of genres. Though their festivals were not huge or well-known, IEI was successful due to its emphasis on smaller events for the local scene, which allowed them to work with multiple artists and communities simultaneously. For this reason, IEI faced a unique challenge of balancing artist needs with community interests.

CMCU was hired to mediate multiple disputes between artists and IEI. Artists claimed that they were being limited by IEI policies when they planned performances. Some artists wanted longer set times, other artists contested the order in which they performed, and still others were dissatisfied with the compensation and accommodation by IEI on festival days. IEI asserted that they must adhere to policies regarding how festival events are scheduled and run because of staffing and budget needs. IEI management held the position that since artists consent to the policies put forth by the company and that artists benefit from the exposure of local festivals that they should also consent to the festival conditions. Both IEI and festival artists were interested in avoiding litigation, so they hired CMCU to see if its mediation services could assist the parties in arriving at a mutually beneficial solution.

Maeve, Anthony, and Louisa were directed to IEI offices where they first met with top management in the company. IEI and affiliated artists had already been in communication with CMCU to establish their terms of negotiation. The first task for the CMCU team was to meet with both sides to explain the mediation process. Anthony was tasked with meeting with the artists while Maeve and Louisa met with management. Maeve and Louisa had a productive initial meeting with IEI management and felt confident about the process going forward. IEI management had been cooperative and optimistic about the mediation process, which was helpful to Maeve and Louisa. Maeve noticed that Louisa seemed much more comfortable than she did on the ride to the client's office, which seemed odd to Maeve, but she did not linger on the observation.

Anthony seemed a little bitter about his assignment since he wanted to network with upper-level management, but he ultimately did not object. Even so, his meeting was much more frustrating for him than Maeve and Louisa's meeting was for them. On top of already being disgruntled with his assignment to the group with no networking prospects for him, some of the artists seemed incredibly frustrated and uncooperative. They were clearly unhappy with spending their time in an office building rather than doing what they loved: playing music. Anthony was professional but was overall unenthused by his meeting. He was bitter that Louisa got to work with Maeve and the IEI management, even though he was clearly the junior consultant with more experience.

After their initial meetings, the team travelled back to the CMCU office for a debriefing session and to plan for the next day of the mediation process. Louisa was newly encouraged by her first client meeting alongside Maeve and was in much better spirits than the morning – until they began their discussion with Anthony at the office.

Anthony was clearly frustrated by how his day had gone and by Louisa's success with Maeve and IEI management. During their conversation, he said, "I just don't understand why I'm stuck with these ridiculous artists. I would be much more useful with upper management."

"I'm sorry to hear that your meeting was frustrating, but you know as well as I do that we all need to be involved with both parties throughout the mediation process to ensure equitable treatment of both sides. How about I send Louisa to work with you and the artists tomorrow so that she can get some more experience and so that you have some additional support?" Maeve offered.

"That should work, I suppose," Anthony replied.

Louisa was shocked by Anthony's outburst – surely, he knew that he would be working with both parties eventually. *Perhaps he is just used to working with companies who had disputes where the parties were of equal stature in terms of power distribution*, Louisa wondered. Even though she had a great day with Maeve and IEI management, this conversation and the prospect of working with Anthony the next day crushed Louisa's spirit. What would she do without Maeve's support?

The next day arrived more quickly than Louisa would have liked. The consulting team arrived at the office to travel to the IEI office together as they had the day before. This time, both Anthony and Louisa were quieter than usual on the way there. Maeve was concerned by this but decided to keep her worries to herself for the time being. She knew she would need to find a time to speak with Anthony and Louisa individually to see if something was going on between them, but their day was already filled with IEI meetings. She put her concerns aside as they walked into the IEI office building.

Louisa and Anthony walked silently to the space where the artists were waiting. Before they went in, Anthony turned to Louisa and said, "Look, just let me take the lead here, okay? I have more experience here and this group is kind of difficult."

Louisa was taken aback by his command but nodded in agreement as to avoid making things worse between them. They entered the room and greeted the artists. Anthony briefly introduced Louisa as another junior consultant then gave the group instructions as to how the next stage in mediation would proceed. Louisa silently took notes using her assistive technology and wondered if she should try to get a word in or if she should avoid conflict with Anthony altogether.

When it was time for her break that she was provided with by human resources as a workplace accommodation, Louisa quietly exited the room. She was grateful for the opportunity to take a walk, drink some water, and get some sunshine. Her doctor recommended that she take these steps during her break to help her maintain focus and keep her from feeling restless and distracted during long meetings. She found these breaks incredibly helpful in her ability to be productive at work and was much less exhausted at the end of her workday.

When she returned to the room where Anthony was meeting with the IEI artists, he took her aside and asked in a hushed but pointed tone, "Where have you been?"

"I was just taking my break, is there anything that I can help with that I missed?" Louisa asked.

"Why do you think you can just leave me to do all this work by myself?" Anthony retorted.

Louisa was stunned. She muttered, "I'm sorry, I- I didn't mean to leave you by yourself."

"Whatever. Just get a flip chart ready for the full meeting, will you?" Anthony said sharply.

"Sure thing," Louisa said as Anthony stormed away from her. Louisa felt like she could not do anything right. She had not even had any time to say anything to the group before she took her break, but now Anthony was upset that she was not there. Louisa felt overwhelmed and confused. She was so thrilled by her new job and so grateful for her accommodations, but she could not help but wonder, *will I have to go through this with all my coworkers? Will everyone have to know my diagnosis to take me seriously? Isn't that kind of illegal? I don't want to have to go through dealing with human resources on my first real assignment. What if everything backfires and people think I'm incapable or a crybaby?* She began to question her future at CMCU.

After individual preparations, it was time for the full mediation session with the consulting team to begin between the IEI management team and the IEI artists. As everyone filed into the large conference room, Maeve again noticed the tension between the junior consultants. She thought that they had just had a bad morning, but now she knew that whatever was going on between Anthony and Louisa was starting to interfere with their interactions with the client. Before their clients were settled, Maeve took Anthony and Louisa aside and inquired if something was wrong.

"It's fine, I'm used to working more than my share," Anthony muttered.

"What do you mean by that, Anthony?" Maeve asked.

"Nothing let's just get to the meeting," Anthony retorted and stormed away.

Louisa stared at her feet. Maeve was shocked by Anthony's behavior – she knew he was ambitious, but this comment seemed targeted toward Louisa and bordered on unprofessional. She looked at Louisa and gently asked, "is everything okay?"

Louisa straightened her posture and faked a smile, "sure thing, let's get started."

Maeve sensed that Louisa was not telling her the whole story but did not press the issue further for the time being. Instead, she went back to the conference room and took her seat between the two disputing parties. As they had prepared, Maeve began the mediation session between the parties while the junior consultants took notes to go over with each side at the next breakout meeting. Louisa tried her best to stay focused on the proceedings but often found herself worrying about Anthony and his reaction to her. Surely their clients had also picked up on some of the animosity from him towards Louisa. Would this situation cost Louisa her job when she had only been with CMCU for a few short weeks?

Luckily, negotiations seemed to be going well so far. After she considered Anthony's comment and Louisa's silence, Maeve decided to split them up and have them work with each party separately while Maeve prepared for the next full session the following day. When she looked in on Louisa's meeting with the artists, she seemed like a different person. The group seemed to be reacting to her much more positively than they had to Anthony. They were even smiling and laughing at one point in the meeting, which was unusual during tense negotiations. Louisa seemed to flourish when she was able to lead the meeting and make it her own.

Taking charge of the meeting also allowed Louisa to create an accessible environment. She had the group take breaks when she took hers, she encouraged the group to stand and move around when appropriate, and she used multiple forms of media (a whiteboard, verbal discussion, breakout groups) to help maintain everyone's focus while brainstorming their needs and solutions to their conflict with management. Overall, Maeve thought everyone looked more comfortable, which is key for conflict resolution to be successful.

The following day, negotiations were back in session. Louisa still seemed hesitant around Anthony, but the general atmosphere of the consulting team and both parties at IEI was less tense. This mediation session was one of the best that Maeve had ever facilitated. Both groups communicated their needs and interests with clarity, and they brainstormed multiple innovative solutions to their conflict. Maeve was immensely impressed by the work and professionalism of both junior consultants and the overall mediation process with IEI.

After a few short weeks, Louisa's first consulting project with IEI was complete. IEI management and the group of artists worked out a creative solution that incorporated both sets of interests and left both sides satisfied with the results of mediation by

CMCU. Maeve, Anthony, and Louisa received praise from CMCU upper management for their work with this client. For this reason and the fact that other projects were beginning, Maeve forgot about her concerns with Louisa and Anthony.

Back at the office, Louisa and Anthony were professional when they worked together but largely avoided one another when they could. Over the course of the next few months, Louisa felt like she was isolated from her coworkers. She had a suspicion that Anthony, who was immensely popular among staff at CMCU, had either directly or indirectly rallied his coworker friends against her. Louisa loved her job but felt incredibly lonely, especially since she had moved away from the rest of her college friends. She thought work might be a place to establish a new social network, but that task was already so difficult for Louisa without Anthony turning their peers against her. Nevertheless, she continued to do her job well and eventually gained prestige among upper management at CMCU. She still needed to gain some more experience to be considered for a senior consultant position, but she was identified early on as a standout candidate for upward movement regardless.

However, Louisa's experience with Anthony and her peers had a major impact on her upward mobility in the company. She was already at a disadvantage because she did not always have the ability to detect social nuance in the subtleties of organizational culture. She was also perceived as too blunt and difficult to talk to at times, which was confusing for her since her clients often valued her directness and professionalism. Along with her peers' negative perceptions of her, she just could not compete with her colleagues that had schmoozed with the right people and gotten into the insider groups that gave them the advantage for promotion. Repeatedly, Louisa was passed over for high stakes projects and senior consultant positions. As the years went by, she still loved her job at CMCU, but felt that she was becoming overqualified for her position as she gained more experience. It was an impossible dilemma for Louisa, one that she and countless others face regularly in organizations.

Current Challenges

In this case study, Louisa faced a variety of challenges related to ableism in the workplace. Wehman et al. (2021) found that the framing of people with disabilities as a benefit or a hindrance to an organization was the best predictor for coworker attitude, either positive or negative, towards disability in the workplace. In short, organizational culture has a major impact on the experiences of people with disabilities in the workplace. In terms of Louisa's experience, an added complexity to her struggle was the fact that her disability was invisible. In a competitive work environment, Louisa's coworkers saw her accommodations as special treatment rather than recognizing them as the tools that she needed and deserved according to regulations preventing discrimination of people with disabilities in the workplace. Because Louisa was not considered “disabled enough” by her peers to receive accommodations, she was written off as lazy.

Though there are legal protections against discrimination for people with disabilities in the workplace (Americans with Disabilities Act, 1990), an organizational culture that only tolerates disability rather than celebrates it can make the social dynamics of a workplace much more complicated and difficult for workers with disabilities, especially those with invisible disabilities. People with disabilities might feel as though their coworkers are walking on eggshells around them or even mistreat them if they are not properly educated on the importance of inclusion. Even when coworkers do not intend any harm or discrimination, a workplace that does not acknowledge and confront inherent ableism in its organizational culture can often create harmful circumstances for workers with disabilities.

Louisa experienced firsthand the harms that can be done in the space between tolerance and inclusion. Anthony, though he probably would have reacted very differently had he known the reasons behind Louisa’s accommodations, treated Louisa very poorly because her existence in the workplace was not like his. Herein lies the problem: Anthony should not have to know the intimate details of Louisa’s medical history and diagnoses to treat her with dignity and respect. Anthony’s assumption that Louisa was just like him and only received additional resources because of her personal gain exposed his internalized ableism. To Anthony, success in the professional world only looked one way: the neurotypical way.

Additionally, other members of CMCU like Maeve and Imari contributed heavily to the bystander effect. Namie and Lutgen-Sandvik (2010) found that workplace bullies rarely act alone – they often operate with both active and passive accomplices within the organization. Though Maeve and Imari did not actively participate in direct negative treatment of Louisa, they affirmed the ableism within CMCU’s organizational culture by failing to stop it in its tracks. Like other issues of injustice, bystanders in a workplace are just as responsible for creating a harmful organizational culture as those who actively engage in discriminatory practices.

Lastly, CMCU fell short of creating a positive work environment within their organization by failing to establish its expectations of the treatment of workers with disabilities. Though many organizations mandate training on various kinds of harassment and discrimination in the workplace, rarely do they encourage its members to actively participate in the celebration of diversity and the inclusion of difference in its organizational structure. Ableist social control by organizations highly influences an individual’s organizational identity in comparison to the “ideal” (read: nondisabled) worker (Jammaers & Zanoni, 2021). Also, by fostering a structure of competition within its management structure, CMCU opened the door for people already privileged by societal structures to capitalize on those privileges to get ahead in its organization. Though not everyone with privilege uses it on purpose, organizations are affected by existing biases and power structures in broader society, so if they are not actively working against those oppressive structures, they are leaving room for more contributions to injustice.

SOLUTIONS AND RECOMMENDATIONS

- CMCU should incorporate training for employees that not only prevents discrimination against people with disabilities but also educates the organization about inherent ableism and how to address it. This measure would promote a more actively inclusive understanding of people with disabilities in organizations rather than just a passively non-discriminatory view. Ryan and Briggs (2020) highlight the advantages to both workers and organizations by adopting an intersectional perspective – a lens that does not marginalize diversity issues but rather centers them in the organization's identity. Additionally, CMCU should consider practices such as IBM's recent strategies to educate its employees about communicating with their coworkers who have disabilities: "(1) commitment from top management; (2) respect for the person with a disability; (3) a focus on abilities; (4) providing full access to all aspects of employment; and (5) making accessibility a way of life" (Allen, 2011, p. 157).
- Maeve should have a conversation with Anthony about his treatment of Louisa without disclosing her condition or accommodations. This action would encourage Anthony to consider the effects of his actions on his professional relationships with both Louisa and Maeve.
- Imari should confront Anthony about their conversation about Louisa. This discussion could begin to organically change the social acceptance of ableism in CMCU's organizational culture.
- CMCU should regularly ensure that Louisa's needs are being met and that she is not socially isolated within the organization.
- CMCU should reevaluate its cultural assumptions that could be hindering diversity and inclusion within the organization. Low diversity in an organization is often caused by the rate of employee turnover, diversity of applicants, and organizational bias against diverse applicants upon organizational entrance and departure (O'Brien et al., 2015). By addressing these factors, CMCU could ensure that its organization is diverse and inclusive.
- Louisa has a complicated decision ahead of her. On one hand, she should not feel forced to disclose intimate details about her diagnosis to her peers just to be taken seriously in the organization. On the other hand, speaking up about

how her coworkers treat her might allow her to thrive in her work environment by addressing ableism within the organization. Though each course of action has benefits and drawbacks, Louisa should consider reaching out to human resources or other disability support representatives at CMCU for assistance in navigating her situation.

DISCUSSION QUESTIONS

1. How did the communicative structuration of organizational culture at CMCU contribute to the ableism that Louisa faced?
2. What are some specific examples of messaging that CMCU could implement to change its organizational culture from tolerance to inclusion and celebration of disability?
3. What examples of ableism have you witnessed or experienced in organizational culture?
4. How do stereotypes about different disabilities, especially cognitive or mental disabilities, affect the structuration of organizational culture?
5. How do other aspects of a person with a disability's intersectional identity (race, age, gender, sexuality, education level, professional experience, socioeconomic status) impact their experience in an organizational setting?

QUESTIONS AND ANSWERS

1. What is the overall problem presented in this case?
2. What are the factors affecting the problem(s) related to this case?
3. What are some of the emerging technologies that should be considered in solving the problem(s) related to the case?
4. How do various factors of communication perpetuate ableism in organizations?
5. What is the final solution that can be recommended to the management of the organization described in the case?

EPILOGUE AND LESSONS LEARNED

This case study opens the door for organizational communication scholars to address ableism in the workplace. Vast opportunities exist for communication scholars to explore how organizations might make workplaces more inclusive by fostering discourse among people with and without disabilities to consider how personal biases and organization policies might contribute to an ableist work environment. Additionally, assumptions made about invisible disabilities by nondisabled people impact people's perceptions of workplace accommodations that they are uninformed about. Overall, there are several lessons to be learned by interacting with this case study:

1. Everyone in an organization is responsible for acknowledging and addressing ableism, not just management.
2. Ableism in organizations can manifest in ways that are not detectable to nondisabled people.
3. Inclusion of people with disabilities into organizational culture benefits everyone.

REFERENCES

Allen, B. J. (2011). *Difference matters: Communicating social identity* (2nd ed.). Waveland Press.

American Psychiatric Association. (2013). *Diagnostic and statistical manual of mental disorders* (5th ed.). doi:10.1176/appi.books.9780890425596

Americans with Disabilities Act of 1990, 42 U.S.C. § 12101 et seq. (1990). https://www.ada.gov/pubs/adastatute08.htm

Bisel, R. S. (2010). A communicative ontology of organization? A description, history, and critique of CCO theories for organization science. *Management Communication Quarterly*, *24*(1), 124–131. doi:10.1177/0893318909351582

Jammaers, E., & Zanoni, P. (2021). The identity regulation of disabled employees: Unveiling the "varieties of ableism" in employers' socio-ideological control. *Organization Studies*, *42*(3), 429–452. doi:10.1177/0170840619900292

Keyton, J. (2005). *Communication and organizational culture*. Sage.

Kirby, E. L., & Krone, K. J. (2002). "The policy exists but you can't really use it": Communication and the structuration of work-family policies. *Journal of Applied Communication Research*, *30*(1), 50–77. doi:10.1080/00909880216577

Namie, G., & Lutgen-Sandvik, P. E. (2010). Active and passive accomplices: The communal character of workplace bullying. *International Journal of Communication*, *4*, 343–373. https://ijoc.org/index.php/ijoc/article/view/589

O'Brien, K. R., Scheffer, M., van Nes, E. H., & van der Lee, R. (2015). How to break the cycle of low workforce diversity: A model for change. *PLoS One*, *10*(7), 1–15. doi:10.1371/journal.pone.0133208 PMID:26217957

Ryan, A. M., & Briggs, C. Q. (2020). Improving work-life policy and practice with an intersectionality lens. *Equality, Diversity and Inclusion*, *39*(5), 533–547. doi:10.1108/EDI-01-2019-0049

Stanford University. (n.d.). *About the Stanford Neurodiversity Project*. Retrieved from https://med.stanford.edu/neurodiversity.htm

Vargo, F. E. (2015). *Neurodevelopmental disorders: A definitive guide for educators*. W.W. Norton & Company.

Wehman, P., Sima, A., Iwanaga, K., McDonough, J., Brooke, A., Godwin, J., Junod, P., Ham, W., & Brooke, V. (2021). Organizational factors influencing coworkers' attitudes toward employees with disabilities: A hierarchical regression analysis. *Rehabilitation Research, Policy & Education*, *35*(2), 83–93. https://doi.org/10.1891/RE

ADDITIONAL READING

Beasley, V. B. (2021). In search of good humans, speaking well: Communication's ableism problem. *Rhetoric and Public Affairs, 24*(1–2), 291–306. 2.0291 doi:10.14321/rhetpublaffa.24.1-

den Houting, J. (2019). Neurodiversity: An insider's perspective. *Autism*, *23*(2), 271–273. https://doi.org/10.1177/1362361318820762

Dunn, D. S. (2019). Outsider privileges can lead to insider disadvantages: Some psychosocial aspects of ableism. *The Journal of Social Issues*, *75*(3), 665–682. https://doi.org/10.1111/josi.12331

Heasman, B., & Gillespie, A. (2019). Neurodivergent intersubjectivity: Distinctive features of how autistic people create shared understanding. *Autism*, *23*(4), 910–921. https://doi.org/10.1177/1362361318785172

Ocean, M. (2021). Telework during COVID-19: Exposing ableism in US higher education. *Disability & Society*, *36*(9), 1543–1548. https://doi.org/10.1080/09687599.2021.1919505

Ortiz, L. A. (2020). Reframing neurodiversity as competitive advantage: Opportunities, challenges, and resources for business and professional communication educators. *Business and Professional Communication Quarterly*, *83*(3), 261–284. https://doi.org/10.1177/2329490620944456

Smith, S. A., & Brunner, S. R. (2017). To reveal or conceal: Using communication privacy management theory to understand disclosures in the workplace. *Management Communication Quarterly*, *31*(3), 429–446. https://doi.org/10.1177/0893318917692896

Walker, R. (2021). Communication perspectives on organizational culture and organizational identification. *International Journal of Business Communication*, *58*(2), 147–151. https://doi.org/10.1177/2329488420957073

KEY TERMS AND DEFINITIONS

Ableism: Bias against people with disabilities and their needs; privileging of non-disabled bodies, spaces, attitudes, and policies.

Assistive Technology: Any computer software or hardware that is designed to assist people with a variety of disabilities or conditions; for example, magnifying software for someone who is visually impaired to make documents accessible, or notetaking software for someone with ADHD who has trouble focusing.

Attention Deficit Hyperactivity Disorder (ADHD): A chronic neurodevelopmental condition characterized by inability to focus, restlessness, impulsive behavior, trouble staying organized, lack of motivation to complete tasks, and social difficulty. Some people with ADHD also experience executive dysfunction (variety of issues related to the frontal lobe of the brain; examples include difficulty with task initiation, emotion regulation, and memory) and sensory issues (see "sensory needs" below).

Bystander Effect: Social phenomenon where a group of people who have witnessed an injustice fail to act because each one assumes that someone else will step in, resulting in no intervention from witnesses.

Invisible Disability: Disability that is not immediately apparent to other people (for example, chronic pain is an invisible disability since an onlooker cannot see it); has different challenges than a visible disability (disability that is immediately apparent to other people, like a disability that requires someone to use a wheelchair, for instance).

Neurodivergent: Describes a person with a neurodevelopmental disorder or disability such as autism or ADHD; used as an inclusive term to celebrate neurological differences rather than pathologize them.

Neurotypical: Describes a person without a neurodevelopmental disorder or disability.

Organizational Culture: Social norms and values within an organization.

Sensory Needs: Commonly describes some people's sensitivity to noise or light due to a variety of factors; some neurodivergent people are easily overstimulated by excessive sound or brightness, so they utilize tools such as earplugs or sunglasses to keep from becoming overwhelmed. Other sensory needs include sensitivity to textures (such as clothing or food textures) or smells.

Workplace Accommodations: Tools that organizations are required to provide to people with disabilities use to help them do work-related tasks; for example, someone who uses a wheelchair might be provided with a ground floor office that is easily accessible to them.

Section 2

Non-Traditional and Minority Groups

Chapter 6
Avoiding "Beige Cubicle Hell": Emotions and Work-Life Spillover Among Adventure Workers

Kari J. Pink
https://orcid.org/0000-0002-0228-7709
University of Wisconsin, Milwaukee, USA

Emily A. Godager
https://orcid.org/0000-0003-1236-9983
University of Wisconsin, Milwaukee, USA

EXECUTIVE SUMMARY

Every job has tradeoffs. When choosing an occupation, individuals are faced with choices about pleasure, freedom, security, and financial gain. This case study invites readers to consider how workers manage emotions and work-life spillover by contrasting the experiences of white-collar workers with an example of nontraditional workers—adventure workers, or individuals who have short-term adventurous jobs or perform seasonal work to support an adventurous lifestyle. An understudied group in organizational communication scholarship, nontraditional workers do not fit into the white-collar, ideal worker identities commonly represented in organizational communication research. To examine this understudied group along with a range of different work-related emotions, Amy's story and work-life experiences as a seasonal adventure worker are contrasted with the experiences of her brother and his friend who are employed in what she views as "beige cubicle hell." These characters grapple with what makes work emotionally fulfilling and the tradeoffs they face in balancing security with freedom.

DOI: 10.4018/978-1-6684-3753-7.ch006

BACKGROUND

The experiences of nontraditional workers—an understudied group in organizational communication scholarship (Bochantin, 2016; Bochantin & Cowan, 2016)—contrast considerably with those of traditional workers. We differentiate nontraditional jobs from traditional jobs by the stability inherent for workers (e.g., steady income, benefits, long-term employment, consistent hours). Compared to *traditional workers* who work full-time hours with predictable schedules over the long term, *nontraditional workers* engage in work that is often transient, such as freelancing and contracting (also known as "gigging"; Met Life, 2019). While traditional workers can be fulfilled by their work, nontraditional workers often leave traditional jobs to fulfill higher-order needs such as work-life balance or a sense of self-worth or purpose. (MetLife, 2019). One example of a nontraditional worker is an adventure worker, an individual who has a short-term adventurous job or performs seasonal work to support an adventurous lifestyle.

As Millennials and Generation X workers prioritize flexibility over money as a motivation for work and a source of happiness (MetLife, 2019; Ruder & Riforgiate, 2019), this case study chapter is particularly relevant as it illustrates tensions individuals may face in their professional lives. By critically examining how emotion and work-life spillover shape career choices and work experiences, this case study provides individuals with an opportunity to make connections between communication concepts and future work experiences. This chapter begins with an overview of how emotions in organizational communication intersect with work-life spillover, followed by an introduction of adventure workers, the nontraditional workers highlighted in this case study. The chapter continues with the case study, a discussion of the highlighted concepts, discussion questions, and concludes with a list of references for further reading.

Emotions

Emotions are "a short-term response to a stimulus" (Riforgiate & Sepúlveda, 2021, p. 514) and can range in intensity and direction (Waldron, 2012). Emotions are valenced either negatively (e.g., anger, frustration, stress) or positively (e.g., fulfillment, joy, pride) (Waldron, 2012). Although emotions relate to physiological changes in the body, the ability to express emotions both verbally and nonverbally is learned (Riforgiate & Komarova, 2017). Importantly, the way individuals learn to express and respond to emotions shapes behavior and communication (Waldron, 2012). In this way, emotions are a social phenomenon that facilitates interpersonal connections and relationships (Riforgiate & Komarova, 2017).

Emotions differ from feelings or moods because they are socially constructed. Feelings are internal and reflective of individual experiences, and moods refer to feelings not directed toward anyone or anything specifically; emotions are an outward display toward specific individuals, events, or things (Tracy, 2015). Notably, compared to feelings or moods, emotions are social, and their meanings are "negotiated and constructed through organizational norms" (Tracy, 2015, p. 1). Organizational communication scholars study emotions in the workplace at various levels ranging from the micro (the level of the individual) to the macro (the societal level; Tracy & Malvini Redden, 2020). On a small scale, the study of emotion occurs on an individual, relational, or workgroup level; on a large scale, emotion can be studied on an organizational, occupational, societal, or global scale (Waldron, 2012).

Emotions in Organizational Communication

Examining emotions at the organizational and societal levels provides important insight into how individuals are socialized about and into work (Riforgiate & Sepúlveda, 2021; Scott & Meyers, 2005). On a spectrum of emotionality and rationality, individuals in Western cultures are socialized to associate organizations and professionalism with rationality (Mumby & Putnam, 1992; Tracy, 2015). Organizations perpetuate societal-level and cultural notions of professionalism and rationality when individuals are socialized into a workplace (Riforgiate & Sepúlveda, 2021). From an organizational perspective, emotions "are ways to achieve . . . organizational ends [such] as efficiency, profit, and productivity" (Mumby & Putnam, 1992, p. 471). When organizations co-opt emotions for profit, rationality shapes and binds the emotions workers display (Riforgiate et al., 2021b).

Rationality is also manifested in discourses that reflect "the interests of the organization more than the interests of the individual" (Tracy & Trethewey 2005, p. 176). In the workplace, *managerialism* and *managerialist discourses* privilege rationality over emotionality; however, these discourses are reproduced by all employees, and the effects of socializing workers to be rational rather than emotional influence emotions beyond the workplace (Denker & Dougherty, 2013. The privileging of rationality can be observed, for example, when managerialist discourses from the workplace seep into workers' homes, resulting in individuals' desires to control emotions, reduce conflict, and encourage positivity both in the workplace and at home (e.g., Denker & Dougherty, 2013).

Additionally, organizational- and societal-level socialization about emotional displays perpetuates rational ideologies about being an ideal worker (Kirby, 2017; Riforgiate & Sepúlveda, 2021). The *ideal worker norm* is a belief that professionals should be fully committed to work and rewarded for their commitment; ideal workers sacrifice their time, freedom, and control their emotions for the benefit of an organization in exchange for rewards such as higher pay or climbing the career ladder (Drago, 2007). Thus, when individuals do express emotion in the workplace or about work, it is often in service to an organization, such as when white-collar workers express passion, which demonstrates "a set of underlying cultural beliefs, values, and ideals that work should be meaningful, fulfilling, and stimulating" (Rao & Neely, 2019, p. 2).

Despite societal and organizational expectations for workers to remain rational and professional, emotions seep into the workplace. Miller et al. (2007) proposed five types of organizational emotions, all of which can influence emotional experiences in the workplace and beyond. The first two types of emotion, *emotional labor* and *emotional work*, are performative in nature and relate to the emotion individuals feel compelled to express while conducting their jobs. The last three, *emotion with work*, *emotion at work*, and *emotion toward work*, are backstage emotions that stem from the experiences individuals have both in and out of the workplace.

Emotional labor refers to the paid emotional communication and displays of inauthentic emotion (i.e., surface acting) prescribed for workers to perform on behalf of an employer to increase profits. When a cashier, for example, smiles and interacts cheerfully with a customer despite having a bad day, they are performing emotional labor on behalf of their employer. *Emotional work*, on the other hand, is authentic and internalized emotion (i.e., deep acting) felt by workers who exhibit genuine emotion as part of the job. Although a nurse or caregiver might display certain emotions required for the job, these emotions can be heartfelt and genuine as relationships are formed with patients.

Next, *emotion with work* pertains to emotions that arise from relationships and interpersonal interactions on the job. For instance, working with challenging coworkers can lead to frustration and anger; on the other hand, an individual might feel pride and camaraderie after completing an important project with their work team. *Emotion at work* is especially boundary spanning, "[crossing] the fluid boundaries of organizations" as individuals bring emotions from work into the home and vice versa (Waldron, 2012, p. 8). Just as an argument with a family member might influence one's performance in the workplace, a poor evaluation or stressful interaction with a manager can similarly impact one's interactions with their spouse, children, or friends. Finally, *emotion toward work* relates to the feelings individuals have toward or about the tasks or characteristics of a job—there are numerous emotions that individuals can feel toward the work they do, including pride, fulfillment, enjoyment, anger, shame, stress, or frustration.

Work-Life Spillover

Organizational communication scholars study myriad topics relating to the ways in which individuals' paid work and private lives intersect. Research in this area explores how work-life boundaries, balance, and management are influenced and shaped by individuals' identities, gender, and characteristics of their home and work lives (Kirby, 2017). Work-life research pertaining to boundaries, balance, and/or management is characterized by its focus on specific individuals—those who are employed—and specific environments: the home and the workplace (Westman et al., 2009).

A significant portion of work-life research falls under the construct of *work-life balance*, which broadly relates to "the relationship between paid work and the rest of life" (Kirby, 2017, p. 1). Work-life balance is the desirable (and perhaps unachievable; see Kirby & Buzzanell, 2014) opposite of *work-life conflict* (or imbalance; see Westman et al., 2009), characterized by pressures between work and life related to time, energy, physical/psychological strain, and/or behaviors (Kirby, 2017). Work-life conflict creates challenges in both the work and life domains, "as work responsibilities can make it more difficult to fulfill responsibilities in personal life, and personal life responsibilities can make it more difficult to fulfill work responsibilities" (Kirby, 2017, p. 1). A related concept, *work-life spillover*, occurs when there is an imbalance between work and life where "stress experienced in one domain of life [results] in stress in the other domain for the same individual" (Westman et al., 2009, p. 588). Tracy (2015) noted the important intersection between work-life spillover and emotion, calling scholars to further explore how "organizational emotional display expectations, as well as issues of stress, burnout, and bullying, are carried with employees when they go home at night" (p. 6). Ultimately, instances of work-life spillover can affect individuals' ability to perform at home because of work demands and/or individuals' ability to perform at work because of personal demands or obligations (e.g., Riforgiate et al., 2021a).

Emotion at work, discussed above, illustrates the crossing of boundaries that occurs with work-life spillover. For example, an individual might experience work-life spillover when a stressful, time-sensitive project at work requires an employee to bring work home; bringing work into the home domain can result in increased stress and resentment as the employees' time with family members is limited. Similarly, a fight with a spouse or difficulty finding a caretaker for a sick child might result in stress and psychological strain that distract an employee in charge of giving a presentation at work. Finally, technology can exacerbate work-life spillover as many employees are expected to continually be connected and available.

Work-life spillover is related to a similar construct, *work-life crossover*, which refers to "a bi-directional transmission of positive and negative emotions, mood, and dispositions between intimately connected individuals such as spouses or organizational team members" (Westman, 2009, p. 589). Work-life spillover affects the specific individual in both the work and life domains, whereas crossover results in the transference of emotions to others in each domain. In the same scenario as above, work-life crossover would ensue if stress from an employee bringing work home frustrated family members, especially if they felt as though the employees' additional hours working at home were impinging on family life. On the other hand, crossover can occur in the other direction if an employee brings stress or conflict from their personal life into the workplace, and it impacts the employee's team members' ability to focus on the task at hand.

Work-life spillover manifests itself through a range of emotions that span the work-life boundary; not all instances of work-life spillover or crossover are negative. In fact, scholars have been giving increasing attention to instances of *positive emotions* spilling over between work and life. Both Waldron (2012) and Tracy (2015) iterated the importance of examining both negative (e.g., stress, burnout, bullying) *and* positive emotions (e.g., affection, awe, delight) surrounding work. For example, some individuals find work-life spillover positive and productive; while establishing boundaries between work and life is appealing to many workers, some individuals find pleasure in the two domains overlapping almost completely. The borders, or boundaries, individuals establish between work and life can regulate the extent to which both negative and positive emotions can spillover between the two domains.

Boundary theory (Ashforth et al., 2000) and *work-family border theory* (Clark, 2000) explain how work-life boundaries and boundary characteristics can separate the domains of work and life. On a continuum of integration and separation, boundaries between work and life are denoted by flexibility and permeability (Clark, 2000). For some individuals, boundaries between work and life are both flexible and permeable, resulting in an integrated work-life experience. For others, however, work-life boundaries are inflexible and impermeable, resulting in distinctly separate work-life domains (Ashforth et al., 2000; Clark, 2000). Work-life spillover occurs more frequently and to a greater extent when boundaries between home and work erode or become blurred (Ashforth et al., 2000).

Further, research examines how organizational emotions (i.e., *emotional labor*, *emotional work*, *emotion with work*, *emotion at work*, and *emotion toward work*; Miller et al., 2007) relate to spillover between work and life. For example, Denker and Dougherty (2013) demonstrated how individuals performed *emotional labor* both at work and in the home as managerialist values and discourses pertaining to managing emotional displays spilled into the home sphere. Similarly, Sanz-Vergel et al. (2012)

found that emotional labor performed in the workplace related to performing emotional labor at home with employees' spouses. Performing *emotional work* can also result in work-life spillover; Krouse and Afifi (2007) examined how women working in caregiving professions carried stress from the home into the workplace and found that participants needed to manage their own stress in the workplace (*spillover*) and cope with personal stress collectively as a group with coworkers (*crossover*). These are just a few examples of how emotions can spill between employees' work and private lives. *Emotion with work*, *emotion at work*, and *emotion toward work* are particularly relevant to work-life spillover as they illustrate how emotions—both positive and negative—exemplify the messiness that can occur when individuals experience spillover between work and life (Miller et al., 2007). This complexity is magnified even further when we consider how nontraditional workers manage the spillover of emotions between work and life.

Nontraditional Workers: The Adventure Worker

Work-life scholarship has traditionally privileged the experiences and voices of white-collar professionals (Bochantin, 2016). However, nontraditional workers make up a significant—and increasing—portion of the United States workforce (e.g., Uber/Lyft drivers, gig workers, freelancers, independent contractors/consultants; MetLife, 2019). In fact, 49% of full-time employees are planning to quit their jobs in the next five years (MetLife, 2019). "The great resignation" is an example of how traditional workers are quitting their jobs to gain flexibility regarding how, where, and when they work (Hsu, 2021). Thus, examining nontraditional workers illuminates the flexible and perhaps more fulfilling work experiences many individuals crave.

Exploring communication that occurs as emotion and work-life spillover intersect is especially valuable for understudied groups, like nontraditional workers. Organizational communication scholars have begun exploring alternative experiences to those of professional, white-collar workers, including blue-collar workers (Bochantin, 2016; Bochantin & Cowan, 2014) and individuals who perform dirty work (e.g., Blithe & Wolfe, 2016; Rivera & Tracy, 2014; Tracy, 2004). Studying nontraditional workers illuminates how some employees resist the organizational- and societal-level socialization that privileges notions of managerialism and rationality to which many traditional workers ascribe.

Adventure workers are an example of nontraditional workers and are an understudied group of people who experience both negative *and* positive worker emotions. The case study below focuses on adventure workers, defined as individuals who work short-term adventurous jobs or perform work on a seasonal basis to support an adventurous lifestyle. Often, adventure workers piece together two or more seasonal and/or part-time jobs to create year-round, full-time employment (Ciulla, 2000; Duncan, 2007; Landes, 2005). For example, an adventure worker might work as a whitewater rafting guide in summer and install holiday decorations in winter.

Adventure workers refer to themselves in a variety of ways. While some identify as tour guides (Alrawadieh et al., 2020) or adventure guides (Carnicelli-Filho, 2013; Sharpe, 2005), many adventure workers simply refer to themselves as adventurers (Sharpe, 2005) or seasonal workers (Duncan, 2007). Some, with affection, refer to themselves as "bums" (Landes, 2005) or "dirtbags" (Mathis, 2019). The term "lifestyler" accurately represents the spillover between work and life that is common in adventure workers' careers (Carnicelli-Filho, 2011). Adventure workers are representative of nontraditional workers, as they opt out of traditional year-round employment and agentively resist the 9-to-5 career-driven professional lifestyle of so traditional many workers.

Adventure workers present a unique opportunity to examine work-life spillover and the five types of organizational emotions (*emotional labor*, *emotional work*, *emotion with work*, *emotion at work*, and *emotion toward work*; Miller et al., 2007). Like those who work in the service industry (e.g., tourism, hospitality, adventure guiding), adventure workers are paid to engage in high levels of *emotional labor* (Carnicelli-Filho, 2011; Hochschild, 2012; Mumby & Putnam, 1992; Sharpe, 2005). Expressing positive emotions is a part of the job, as "emotional abilities such as friendliness and cheerfulness are largely sought-after assets" (Alrawadieh et al., 2020, p. 51).

However, unlike other service industry workers, adventure workers' encounters with clients often last significantly longer, requiring an all-encompassing persona to display emotions on the job (Sharpe, 2005). Like the caregivers interviewed by Krouse and Afifi (2007), mentioned above, adventure workers perform *emotional work* when they experience and express genuine emotions when working with clients. Additionally, for adventure workers, work can look very much like leisure (Ciulla, 2000; Landes, 2005), and their lifestyle is intertwined with their personality and behavior (Carnicelli-Filho, 2011).

Adventure workers manage *emotions with work* when pursuing adventure activities during their time off, socializing with their coworkers, or becoming friends with clients (Carnicelli-Filho, 2013). Ultimately, adventure workers experience *emotion at work* when the boundaries between work, life, and leisure become blurred as adventure workers' careers align with their passions (Sharpe, 2005). Finally, the fulfillment and enjoyment that adventure workers feel performing their work illustrate their *emotion toward* work.

Taken together, adventure workers experience a spectrum of emotions related to work-life spillover that differs greatly from traditional workers, who might experience spillover as frustration at always being virtually connected to the office while at home or overwhelm at having to be a caregiver to family members while performing their jobs. Instead, the nature of adventure work causes work-life spillover to result in both positive and negative emotions that both complicate and complete the lives of these workers. For example, adventure workers' sense of fulfillment from blending work and play or pride over the courage required to sustain a unique work-life situation might be contrasted with uncertainty about the future, tensions with family members who express concerns about an adventurous lifestyle, or loneliness from parting with coworkers who have become close friends.

CASE STUDY: AVOIDING "BEIGE CUBICLE HELL"

Perched atop Winder Mountain, Amy gazes down Devil's Run, the path she'll take in just a moment. The snow falls gently, resting on her jacket and slowly hiding the tracks of the last skier. It is a perfect day to ski. She takes off, flying down the slope at a breakneck speed. *This is what freedom feels like*, she thinks, as she often does when rushing down the mountain.

At the bottom, her friend and coworker Dana looks ready for another run. Amy and Dana have become intimately familiar with all the trails on Winder Mountain from working as ski instructors at Snowvale Resort. Though they were strangers just two months before, they have become fast friends, spending much of their time off on the hills where they work. Today the pair are joined by Everett, a man Amy was teaching on the slopes just the day before. He whooshes in behind them, joining the two friends at the bottom of the hill.

"That was awesome, Everett! You've made so much progress!" Amy praises him as he lifts his goggles and smiles.

"I had a good teacher!" he exclaims, returning her compliments. "I can't believe I've come this far. Just a couple of days ago, I didn't know what I was doing, and now I'm keeping up with you two on Devil's Run! This has been an amazing vacation. So, what are you two doing when the season ends? Do you go back to your 'real jobs'?"

"I'll substitute teach in the spring," Dana says. "Then, in the summer, I'll work concessions at the sports arena in the city during baseball season. When that's over, I'll have a few weeks off, and then, if the snow starts flying when it should, I'll be back on the slopes by December."

"Sounds like you have the year all planned out. How about you, Amy? Will you be teaching and serving popcorn the rest of the year?"

"No, Dana's the planner. Me? I'm more of a fly-by-the-seat-of-my-pants kind of gal. I don't do well with a super predictable schedule. This summer, I'll be giving wilderness tours up in Alaska. I've done that before, and I love it. But between now and then, who knows?"

"Alaska sounds amazing!" Everett responds. "When does the season start there?"

"It usually picks up in June, and then it gets real intense through August. By September, Alaska pretty much rolls up the sidewalks, so to speak. The tourism season tapers off after Labor Day, so I'm done with that job around that time. Then I'll have a break before I head back here—if they'll have me again and if I don't find a better offer."

"Amy, I've got a great idea." Everett's eyes light up as he goes on excitedly. "I own Sunshine Potato Farm in North Dakota, and I'm always looking for great people to help me run the place, especially during planting and harvesting seasons. We'd be done planting in plenty of time for you to make it up to Alaska, and then harvest season really gets swinging in the middle of September. I could use someone sharp like you to help me keep the operation going. I always need folks whose lives are flexible enough for seasonal work, so if you know of anybody else, let me know."

"Well, I've never been to North Dakota before, and I'm always up for a new adventure. Thanks for the offer, Everett. I'll definitely think about it."

"You do that. I'll see you in the Snowvale lodge tonight, and we can talk about it some more."

"Oh, speaking of the lodge, I'd better get over there," Amy says, glancing at her watch.

"Come on—one more run?" asks Dana, hopefully.

"Nah, I better not," Amy replies. "My brother Beau is supposed to be here soon. It's been ages since I've seen him, and I don't want to miss the big arrival when he checks into his room at Snowvale!"

"It's great that he's coming to see you here," Dana says.

"Yeah, I'm not quite sure how great it'll be. I mean, I've missed him, and I love seeing him, but I have a feeling he's going to give me flack for my lifestyle choices. He can't understand why anyone would want to make a career out of doing seasonal work like we do."

"Maybe he doesn't understand how refreshing it is to work outside and to meet new people every day. I swear this job never gets old."

"I think being here will help him see how awesome it is. The good news is that Beau is bringing a friend with him— he can be our buffer! His name's Craig, and he loves skiing. You might like him," Amy suggests.

"I'm sure I will, but don't get any big ideas, Amy. You know there's not much room in my life for a relationship," Dana answers. "But I'll be around tonight if you want to hang out in the lodge."

Amy treks off, swiftly covering the short distance from the ski slope to her van, which is not only her transportation but also her home. Seeing she still has a few minutes before Beau's arrival, Amy steps inside the van to make herself a cup of coffee. While the hotplate warms the kettle, she thinks about how this vehicle was the perfect choice for her nomadic life. *I took a leap of faith three years ago, and it's paid off,* she thinks, not for the first time. *I would have gone crazy if I'd stayed in that call center job any longer. I enjoy taking life one day at a time. Now I just have to get my brother to realize that.*

Meanwhile, Beau drives the rental car as Craig navigates their way to the resort. "This'll be so great to get some time off," Craig says. "I don't think I've had a day off from A1 Strategies in three weeks. I can't wait until Franny hires more staff."

"Yeah, well, working hard is what you do if you want to get ahead. It's called being a grownup," Beau says. "Hey, I hear something buzzing. Is that your phone or mine?"

"Speak of the devil," Craig says as he sees Franny's number pop up on his phone screen. He taps "accept" and uses his most cheerful voice to greet their boss. "Hey Franny, how's it going? . . . No, I thought the report was due next week . . . Yes, I know the Thompson job is important . . . Yes, and I appreciate you letting me take off a few days . . . I understand. I'll send you the report in a couple of hours. I should be able to finish it by then. I'm sure Snowvale will have Wi-Fi . . . OK I'll— "

Craig shakes his head and returns his phone to his jacket pocket.

"Ha! Let me guess: She hung up on you?" Beau ventured.

"How'd you know?"

"I've been there. Whatever it is she wants, you better get it done, or it won't end well."

"Yeah, she told me if I don't have the Thompson report in today, I can take as much time off as I want because I won't have a job at A1 Strategies to come back to. Seriously?"

"Hey, just hammer it out, and then we'll meet up for drinks before dinner."

"Dammit! I know she told me that the report was due next week. I have it written down somewhere."

"Doesn't matter, bro. The report is due when the boss says it's due. It's OK, Amy will be disappointed that you can't ski with us today, but she'll be fine."

"Yeah, but I'm not sure I will be," Craig answered dejectedly.

As Beau pulls the car into the Snowvale parking lot, they see Amy walking toward them. "Beau!" she exclaims and runs to meet them, giving both Beau and Craig a cheerful hug.

"Looks like you found the place OK," she says.

"It wasn't hard—just followed the signs," Beau answers. "Must be nice living at a ski resort all winter."

"I can't complain!" Amy says.

"Hey, we need to check in," Beau says, lifting the bags out of the trunk. "Where are your staff quarters?

We'll come find you once we get settled."

"Well, you'll find me right here. See that van? That's my humble abode." Amy says with a cheerful smile.

"What do you mean?" Beau asks, concerned. Beau waits for a response, but Amy just keeps smiling.

"You're not serious. Amy, it's 10 degrees out, and it's supposed to drop below zero tonight, and you're what, living out of a van like a homeless person?"

"Beau, I'm not homeless," Amy says. "This *is* my home. I can live anywhere I want with this thing. It's all I need, and it's plenty warm. Don't worry about that. And besides, I need to get to my next job somehow."

"And what might that be?" Beau asks her.

"I'm not sure yet, but one of my clients just offered me a job to help him run his potato farm, so I might be in North Dakota for the planting and harvest seasons. Then in the summer, I'll probably head up to Alaska to give tours like I did last year. We'll see."

Beau looks to the sky and shakes his head. A few moments later, the three enter the Snowvale lobby, and before they head to the main desk to check in, they stop by the roaring fire near the lodge's bar.

"Doesn't living with all this uncertainty bother you?" Craig asks Amy.

"Nah. I actually like it, despite how horrible my brother makes my life sound. To live this lifestyle, you have to be comfortable having a lot of uncertainty in your life. Like when I'm on the road, I don't know where I might end up boondocking for the night, but it always works out."

"Yeah, it works out until your van breaks down, or God forbid you get seriously sick," Beau comments.

"Then what? You can't keep living in your car, Amy. I'm worried about you. You're a grown woman. You should have a real job with benefits, like health insurance and a retirement account."

"Here we go," Amy replies and rolls her eyes. "I wondered how long it would take to get to the subject of a retirement account, and you might have broken the record. It's the same old thing: 'Oh no! Amy doesn't have a retirement account! What will we do?'"

"It's important, Amy! You can't just live on a wing and a prayer. You have to save for the future, so you'll be financially secure. Look at me. I own my own home. I have a new car in the garage, and I can afford a vacation where I sleep in a four-star hotel room instead of a van. I'm one of the top salespeople at our company, and I'm guessing that just my bonus last year was more than you'll make this whole ski season."

"But why should money be the measure of a successful life, Beau? Why isn't it enough to be living a life I love? I'm outdoors, meeting new people, doing what I want to do. Do you know how much that is worth to me? Do you know that I'm not on that anxiety medication anymore? *This* is my medication," she says as she points to the mountains framed in the picture window.

"This view is gorgeous," Craig interjects. "I can't imagine waking up and looking at this every single day. You're so lucky!"

"I *am* lucky!"

"Yeah, lucky is what you have to be to make this 'lifestyle,' as you call it, work," says Beau. "I'm glad you're doing what you love, but seriously, Amy. It might be time for you to reconsider your path. There's a position open at A1 Strategies, and you'd be perfect for it. It's a sales job, so you'd still get to talk to people. You'd like that."

"Oh wow." Amy chuckles. "You mean I could spend all day, every day, in a beige cubicle hell, talking politely on the phone to people who don't even want to take my call, while I get to see the same officemates each day and wait for my two weeks off a year so I can finally do what I want? Sounds like a dream, Beau."

"It's not perfect, but we like it," Beau says earnestly while Craig stands gazing at the mountain. "Life is about tradeoffs. I'm sure you don't like everyone you meet on the ski hill or on the Alaska rivers, Amy."

"You'd be surprised," Amy responds. "When I'm in Alaska, I spend all day with folks out on the rapids. Yes, I have to be nice to them and put on a happy face when the other guides and I have a little too much fun the nights before we go out on the rafts, but it's more than that. Many of them become my friends."

"They become friends for a day, and then they're gone. These aren't normal friendships, Amy. Hell, you can't even have a dog, let alone a boyfriend, with the way you live. I know you're a 'free spirit,' but you've got to have some security in your life."

Amy looks at Beau and smiles. "Big brother, I know you mean well, but let's not talk about 401Ks or career paths anymore today. You two came here to have fun, so let's focus on that."

Beau shakes his head but reluctantly smiles back. "OK, you win. Let's call a truce, so I can race you down Winder Mountain. You know I'm a better skier!"

"You mean you *were* the better skier. I've been practicing, you know!" Amy laughs as Beau heads over to the check-in desk. She turns to look at Craig, who is still gazing out the window.

"I used to love skiing," he says quietly. "It's all I ever wanted to do as a kid. I even taught skiing in college."

"Really? We're looking for another instructor at Snowvale," Amy says. "Craig, you should think about coming here to teach skiing."

"You mean this season? Now?"

"Yeah! You could get a van like me or even a little camper to pull behind your vehicle, and you'd be all set. You could be my neighbor. If you want to live a life that's full of rich experiences and time to do what you want, then you should try this, Craig. What are you waiting for?"

DISCUSSION

This case study exemplifies *emotion* and the accompanying *work-life spillover* in the context of adventure work. By contrasting an adventure worker's lifestyle with the lives of traditional office workers, this case illuminates the spectrum of emotionality and rationality workers must navigate. Amy's character is the foil to the traditional worker embodied by Beau and Craig. Whereas Beau and Craig are professionals that represent the *ideal worker ideology* (Kirby, 2017; Riforgiate & Sepúlveda, 2021), Amy finds fulfillment in her transient, adventurous lifestyle. Compared to the emotion Beau and Craig perform in service of their organization, Amy's emotional experiences surrounding work are not shaped by organizational- or societal-level influences. Further, whereas Amy is in control of her seasonal work and chooses jobs that make her happy, Beau reproduces *managerialist discourses* that privilege rationality when he reasons with Craig about doing work while on vacation and with Amy about getting a "real" job to save for retirement. Taken together, this case demonstrates that organizational emotion can be both positive and negative depending on how individuals make sense of their experiences.

Examples of all five of Miller et al.'s (2007) types of organizational emotion (*emotional labor*, *emotional work*, *emotion with work*, *emotion at work*, and *emotion toward work*) are embedded in this case study. On an individual level, Amy expresses joy and fulfillment as she takes pleasure in how her work so closely aligns with her passions in life. Amy and Craig both perform *emotional labor*; Amy "puts on a happy face" when interacting with the clients she guides in Alaska, and Craig manages his negative emotions when interacting with his manager despite being asked to do work while taking time off work. Compared to the seemingly mundane office work performed by Beau and Craig, Amy engages in *emotional work*—her feelings about both her work and adventurous lifestyle are positive and authentic rather than prescribed by an employer. On a relational level, *emotion with work* is illustrated through the friendships among Amy, Dana, and Everett, as well as between Beau and Craig. Amy exhibits *emotion at work* when her anxiety about Beau's visit foreshadows her conversation with Dana. Her *emotion toward work* is in stark contrast to Craig's, who grapples with negative emotions on a relational level when speaking with his manager and ultimately needing to work while on the ski trip.

Additionally, this case sheds light on emotion as it pertains to *work-life spillover*. Examining this case through the lenses of *boundary* and *work-family border theories* (Ashforth et al., 2000; Clark, 2000), the boundary between work and life is permeable—if it exists at all—for nearly all the characters. For Amy, this permeability is a positive aspect of her job, and she enjoys that the domains of work and life almost completely overlap. In contrast, Craig struggles with the work-life spillover he experiences when his boss requires him to do work on his vacation. For instance, the phone call Craig takes from his boss extends work into his life in negative ways. Further, unlike Amy, who lives a spontaneous and carefree life, both Craig and Beau's lives are scheduled in such a way that work is prioritized above leisure and "off" time. This is evident in how Craig spends time working on a project on his vacation and in the way his boss does not honor his schedule.

Similarly, Beau illustrates how many traditional workers view the work and life domains as separate even though overlap clearly exists. This is seen in his argument for why Amy should get a "real" job and save for the future; from Beau's perspective, a job (work) is a means of preparing for the future (Blithe & Wolfe, 2016; Tracy & Trethewey, 2005) and money earned in the work domain provides the means to enjoy material possessions, like a home and new car in the life domain. Further, whereas Amy's lifestyle is centered on fulfillment and pleasure, Beau and Craig represent *ideal workers* who put work first above all else.

Finally, this case study exemplifies how emotions span the *work-life boundary*. Emotions related to family flow into Amy's work life, just as Beau's concern for his sister flows into his. During their conversation, Beau's worries over Amy's financial stability lead him to offer her a job where he and Craig both work. Conversely, the characters' attitudes about their work color their personal lives and emerge in their statements. Amy tries to convey her positive feelings about work to her brother and Craig, while Craig and Beau manage their emotions related to a demanding boss who has broken into their long-awaited vacation time. Everett, a minor character, is happy to leverage the connections he has made with Amy to advance his potato farm staffing. By contrasting an adventure worker's lifestyle with the life of a traditional office worker, it is evident that work-life spillover can result in both positive and negative emotions, based on how an individual interprets their circumstances.

DISCUSSION QUESTIONS

1. What emotions are evident in this case study? How do the emotions vary among the characters?
2. In terms of Miller et al.'s (2007) five types of organizational emotions (*emotional labor*, *emotional work*, *emotion with work*, *emotion at work*, and *emotion toward work*), which types are evident in this case study? Discuss examples.
3. How is work-life spillover illustrated through positive and negative emotions in this case study? Using specific examples from the case study, what are some benefits and drawbacks of work-life spillover?
4. What choices are the characters facing, and how do those choices relate to emotions and work-life spillover? What do you think they should choose?
5. How do the concepts of organizational emotion and work-life spillover apply in your own life? Discuss examples.

REFERENCES

Alrawadieh, Z., Cetin, G., Dincer, M. Z., & Dincer, F. I. (2020). The impact of emotional dissonance on quality of work life and life satisfaction of tour guides. *Service Industries Journal*, *40*(1–2), 50–64. doi:10.1080/02642069.2019.1590554

Ashforth, B. E., Kreiner, G. E., & Fugate, M. (2000). All in a day's work: Boundaries and micro role transitions. *Academy of Management Review*, *25*(3), 472–491. doi:10.2307/259305

Blithe, S. J., & Wolfe, A. W. (2016). Work-life management in legal prostitution: Stigma and lockdown in Nevada's brothels. *Human Relations*, *70*(6), 725–750. doi:10.1177/0018726716674262

Bochantin, J. E. (2016). "Morning fog, spider webs, and escaping from Alcatraz": Examining metaphors used by public safety employees and their families to help understand the relationship between work and family. *Communication Monographs*, *83*(2), 214–238. doi:10.1080/03637751.2015.1073853

Bochantin, J. E., & Cowan, R. L. (2016). Acting and reacting: Work/life accommodation and blue-collar workers. *International Journal of Business Communication*, *53*(3), 306–325. doi:10.1177/2329488414525457

Carnicelli-Filho, S. (2011). *Managing emotions: White-water rafting guides and the emotional labor theory* [Doctoral dissertation, University of Otago, Dunedin]. University of Otago OUR Archive. http://hdl.handle.net/10523/1705

Carnicelli-Filho, S. (2013). The emotional life of adventure guides. *Annals of Tourism Research*, *43*, 192–209. doi:10.1016/j.annals.2013.05.003

Ciulla, J. B. (2000). *The working life: The promise and betrayal of modern work.* Crown Business.

Clark, S. C. (2000). Work/family border theory: A new theory of work/family balance. *Human Relations*, *53*(6), 747–770. doi:10.1177/0018726700536001

Denker, K. J., & Dougherty, D. (2013). Corporate colonization of couples' work-life negotiations: Rationalization, emotion management and silencing conflict. *Journal of Family Communication*, *13*(3), 242–262. doi:10.1080/15267431.2013.796946

Drago, R. W. (2007). Striking a balance: Work, family, life. *Dollars and Sense.*

Duncan, T. J. C. (2007). *Working tourists: Identity formation in a leisure space* (Order No. U591950). Available from ProQuest Dissertations & Theses Global. (1427349259). https://ezproxy.lib.uwm.edu/login?url=https://www.proquest.com/dissertations-theses/working-tourists-identity-formation-leisure-space/docview/1427349259/se-2?accountid=15078

Hochschild, A. R. (2012). *The managed heart: Commercialization of human feeling*. University of California Press. doi:10.1525/9780520951853

Hsu, A. (2021). As the pandemic recedes, millions of workers are saying "I quit". In *The Great Resignation: Why Millions of Workers Are Quitting Their Jobs*. NPR.

Kirby, E. L. (2017) Work-life balance. In C. R. Scott & L. Lewis (Eds.), The International Encyclopedia of Organizational Communication (pp. 1–21). John Wiley & Sons, Inc. doi:10.1002/9781118955567.wbieoc219

Kirby, E. L., & Buzzanell, P. M. (2014). Communicating work–life issues: Policies, practices, and opportunities. In L. Putnam & D. Mumby (Eds.), Handbook of organizational communication (3rd ed., pp. 351–373). Sage.

Krouse, S. S., & Afifi, T. D. (2007). Family-to-work spillover stress: Coping communicatively in the workplace. *Journal of Family Communication*, *7*(2), 85–122. doi:10.1080/15267430701221537

Landes, M. (2005). *The back door guide to short-term job adventures: Internships, summer jobs, seasonal work, volunteer vacations, and transitions abroad* (4th ed.). Ten Speed Press.

Mathis, T. (2019). *The dirtbag's guide to life: Eternal truth for hiker trash, ski bums, and vagabonds*. Boldly Went, LLC.

MetLife. (2019). *The gig economy: Opportunities, challenges, and employer strategies: A report based on MetLife's 17th annual U.S. employee benefit trends study 2019*. https://www.metlife.com/employee-benefit-trends/ebts-gig-economy-2019/

Miller, K. I., Considine, J., & Garner, J. (2007). "Let me tell you about my job": Exploring the terrain of emotion in the workplace. *Management Communication Quarterly*, *20*(3), 231–260. doi:10.1177/0893318906293589

Mumby, D. K., & Putnam, L. L. (1992). The politics of emotion: A feminist reading of bounded rationality. *Academy of Management Review*, *17*(3), 465–486. doi:10.5465/amr.1992.4281983

Rao, A. H., & Neely, M. T. (2019). What's love got to do with it? Passion and inequality in white-collar work. *Sociology Compass*, *13*(12), 1–14. doi:10.1111oc4.12744

Riforgiate, S. E., Gattoni, A., & Kahlow, J. A. (2021). "Shhhhh, I'm working!": Working from home and struggling to manage relationships. In C. Lieberman & K. Wright (Eds.), *Casing mediated communication*. Kendall Hunt.

Riforgiate, S. E., Howes, S. S., & Simmons, M. (2021). The impact of daily emotional labor on health and well-being. *Management Communication Quarterly*, *0*(0), 1–27. doi:10.1177/08933189211041352

Riforgiate, S. E., & Komarova, M. (2017). *Emotion and work. The International Encyclopedia of Organizational Communication*. John Wiley and Sons, Inc. doi:10.1002/9781118955567.wbieoc068

Riforgiate, S. E., & Sepúlveda, S. (2021). Managing and being managed by emotions. In F. Cooren & P. Stücheli-Herlach (Eds.), *Handbook of management communication* (pp. 511–528). De Gruyter Mouton. doi:10.1515/9781501508059-028

Rivera, K. D., & Tracy, S. J. (2014). Embodying emotional dirty work: A messy text of patrolling the border. *Qualitative Research in Organizations and Management*, *9*(3), 201–222. doi:10.1108/QROM-01-2013-1135

Ruder, E. M., & Riforgiate, S. E. (2019). Organizational socialization of millennial nonprofit workers. In M. Z. Ashlock & A. Atay (Eds.), Examining millennials reshaping organizational cultures (pp. 33–50). Academic Press.

Sanz-Vergel, A. I., Rodrigues-Muñoz, A., Bakker, A. B., & Demerouti, E. (2012). The daily spillover and crossover of emotional labor: Faking emotions at work and at home. *Journal of Vocational Behavior*, *81*(2), 209–217. doi:10.1016/j.jvb.2012.07.003

Scott, C., & Myers, K. K. (2005). The socialization of emotion: Learning emotion management at the fire station. *Journal of Applied Communication Research*, *33*(1), 67–92. doi:10.1080/0090988042000318521

Sharpe, E. K. (2005). "Going above and beyond:" The emotional labor of adventure guides. *Journal of Leisure Research*, *37*(1), 29–50. doi:10.1080/00222216.2005.11950039

Tracy, S. J. (2004). The construction of correctional officers: Layers of emotionality behind bars. *Qualitative Inquiry*, *10*(4), 509–533. doi:10.1177/1077800403259716

Tracy, S. J. (2015). *Emotions and communication in organizations. In International Encyclopedia of Communication*. John Wiley and Sons, Ltd., doi:10.1002/9781405186407.wbiece020.pub2

Tracy, S. J., & Malvini Redden, S. (2020). The structuration of emotion. In A. M. Nicotera (Ed.), *Origins and traditions of organizational communication: A comprehensive introduction to the field* (pp. 348–369). Routledge.

Tracy, S. J., & Trethewey, A. (2005). Fracturing the real-self—fake-self dichotomy: Moving toward "crystallized" organizational discourses and identities. *Communication Theory, 15*(2), 168–195. doi:10.1111/j.1468-2885.2005.tb00331.x

Waldron, V. R. (2012). *Communicating emotion at work*. Polity Press.

Westman, M., Brough, P., & Kallaith, T. (2009). Expert commentary on work-life balance and crossover of emotions and experiences: Theoretical and practical advancements. *Journal of Organizational Behavior, 30*(5), 587–595. doi:10.1002/job.616

KEY TERMS AND DEFINITIONS

Adventure Workers: Individuals who work short-term adventure jobs or perform work on a seasonal basis to support an adventurous lifestyle.

Emotions: One's temporary reaction to a person, event, or situation.

Negative Emotions: Temporary reaction that causes one to feel upset, sad, angry, fearful, or anxious.

Boundary Theory/Work-Family Border Theory: Theories that explain how boundaries and the characteristics of boundaries influence the degree of separation between an individual's work and the rest of life.

Emotion at Work: Emotion that spans the boundaries of the workplace and home; emotion employees take from work to home and vice versa.

Emotion Toward Work: Emotion employees feel about their organization, job, or tasks they perform at work.

Emotion With Work: Emotion generated from relationships and interpersonal interactions in the workplace.

Emotional Labor: An employee's display of inauthentic emotion performed on behalf on an organization to increase profits.

Emotional Work: An employee's display of authentic emotion that aligns with the organizational expectations.

Ideal Worker Norm: A societal belief that professionals should be fully committed to their work and rewarded for their commitment.

Managerialism: An ideology and social structure in organizations that privileges rationality over emotionality to achieve corporate and managerial values; characterized by control of employees' emotion.

Managerialist Discourses: Language (spoken and written) that supports managerialism.

Nontraditional Worker: Individuals who work transient jobs, such as freelancing or contracting.

Positive Emotions: Temporary reaction that causes one to feel uplifted, happy, joyful, energized, or confident.

Traditional Worker: Individuals who work full-time hours and have predictable schedules over the long-term.

Work-Life Balance: Relates to the tensions individuals feel regarding when managing paid work and life (e.g., time, energy, attention).

Work-Life Conflict: Occurs when an individual does not have adequate work-life balance; responsibilities in the workplace interfere with personal life and vice versa.

Work-Life Crossover: Emotions experienced by an individual *and* their relational partners (e.g., family, friends, coworkers) when work and/or life interfere with the opposite domain.

Work-Life Spillover: Emotions experienced by an individual if responsibilities from work and/or life interfere with the opposite domain.

Chapter 7
Convergence and Divergence at Work:
Cross-Cultural Interactions With a Difficult Co-Worker

Seulgi Park
https://orcid.org/0000-0001-9710-3847
University at Albany, SUNY, USA

Patricia Gettings
University at Albany, SUNY, USA

EXECUTIVE SUMMARY

Communication at work often occurs among people from different power, culture, or language groups. Communicating with a difficult co-worker can become a major source of job dissatisfaction. This chapter introduces communication accommodation theory and the exit, voice, loyalty, and neglect model as theoretical lenses for exploring the case of a recent immigrant healthcare worker experiencing job dissatisfaction because of unsatisfying interactions with a co-worker. This chapter then applies these theoretical frameworks to discuss how tensions between co-workers can arise in communicative forms such as convergence, divergence, and overaccommodation and how an employee responds to a deteriorating work condition stemming from difficult interpersonal communication.

DOI: 10.4018/978-1-6684-3753-7.ch007

INTRODUCTION

The workplace is often a site of communication among people who are from different generations, power groups, and/or cultural or linguistic backgrounds. In this context, work demands and varying interests may escalate tensions that already exist among colleagues from differing backgrounds. Thus, communication at work in general, and communicating with a difficult co-worker more specifically, can become a source of job dissatisfaction (e.g., Ducharme & Martin, 2000). These challenges may give rise to some questions for those interested in organizational communication. For example, how do tensions arise from communication between two organizational members from very different backgrounds? How can an employee respond to a difficult interpersonal issue and address the resulting job dissatisfaction? By considering the case of an immigrant healthcare worker in the intensive healthcare setting, this chapter describes these communicative tensions, the motives behind them, and one employee's response(s) to adverse situations in the workplace.[1] This chapter starts with an overview of immigrants' experiences in the U.S. nursing workforce. Then, Communication Accommodation Theory (CAT; Giles et al., 1987) and the Exit, Voice, Loyalty, and Neglect (EVLN) model (Farrell, 1983; Hirschman, 1970) will be introduced as theoretical lenses for analyzing the case study. Next, the case of a Korean immigrant registered nurse (RN) having difficulties communicating with a co-worker will be presented. In the last section, the theoretical lenses will be applied to the case and the key concepts will be explained with specific examples.

Immigrants in the U.S. Nursing Workforce

Immigrants in the U.S. are overrepresented in healthcare occupations. As of 2018, over 1.5 million immigrants were employed as physicians, RNs, and pharmacists (Batalova, 2020). Nursing, in particular, is one of the fields that has seen an influx of foreign-born healthcare workers. The U.S. has "imported" foreign-born nurses to fill the labor shortage. As a result, foreign-born RNs represent a growing proportion of the nursing workforce. According to the Organization for Economic Co-operation and Development (OECD, 2020), foreign-born nurses account for 16.4% of the total nurses in the U.S. In fact, some states in the U.S. have twice as many foreign-born nurses compared to the national average: Nevada (36%), California (35%), Maryland (30%), and New York (29%). Over 20% of foreign-born nurses are either permanent residents or temporary visa holders. Although their English proficiency is higher than the total foreign-born population, 16% of foreign-born nurses in the U.S. reported speaking English 'less than very well' (Batalova, 2020).

Research on the experiences of foreign-born nurses has pointed out that they struggle with communication barriers, different expectations for nursing roles, discrimination, marginalization, and exploitation (e.g., Connor & Miller, 2014; Ea et al., 2010; Cheng & Liu, 2011, Xu, 2007). Culture-related attributes such as acculturation and language skills are associated with the job satisfaction of immigrant nurses (Ea, 2007; Xu, 2007). Specifically, Kim and colleagues (2017) reported that resilience and culture are significantly associated with job satisfaction in a sample of Korean American nurses. Due to cultural and linguistic barriers, immigrant nurses are likely to face challenges in communicating with not only their patients but also their colleagues, which in turn can influence their job satisfaction.

Communication plays a central role for these immigrant nurses in navigating the challenges they face in the workplace and potentially responding to job dissatisfaction. Communication can be the source of job dissatisfaction for immigrant nurses, but at the same time when they respond to job dissatisfaction, they are likely to employ communication strategies to navigate issues at hand. CAT suggests that communicative strategies are used when immigrant nurses negotiate their social identity and distance with their colleagues in the workplace. Also, although the original EVLN model does not necessarily tease out the communicative aspects of employee responses to job dissatisfaction, EVLN concepts can be applied to make sense of the patterns of responses from immigrant nurses who experience job dissatisfaction. The following section discusses CAT and the EVLN model as the theoretical frameworks for analyzing the case study.

Communication Accommodation Theory

Communication accommodation theory (CAT) proposes that people adjust their verbal and non-verbal communication by converging to or diverging from another to gain social approval and regulate social distance and identity (Giles, 2016). CAT began as a framework to explain how an interlocuter accommodates another's accent in a conversation (Giles et al., 1987). Originally named Speech Accommodation Theory, the theory evolved from a framework focusing on speech accommodations to one that embraces non-verbal communication. It aids scholars in understanding the motivations behind and social outcomes of the communicative adjustments individuals make during social interactions. Drawing from a number of socio-psychological principles such as similarity-attraction, causal attribution, and social identity theory, CAT considers why and how communicative accommodation or non-accommodation occurs based on key ideas such as convergence and divergence for the adjustments people make during interactions (Giles et al., 1987).

CAT has been extensively applied to intergroup communication, especially in intergenerational and intercultural contexts. From the beginning, the theory has focused on the impact of group membership on communication by examining how and why people make adjustments in interactions (Gallois et al., 2018). Thus, many scholars have looked at how different groups demonstrate varying accommodative communication strategies as a way to regulate social identity and distance. For example, CAT has been applied to intergenerational communication (Harwood, 2000), intercultural communication (Imamura et al., 2011), and communication across different power groups (Choi et al., 2019; Watson & Gallois, 1998).

Key Concepts of CAT

Convergence

In CAT, convergence was first conceptualized as a linguistic strategy to adapt to each other's speech. For example, Giles et al. (1973) examined convergence as language switching between bilingual English-speaking Canadians and French-speaking Canadians. When French-Canadians showed convergence to English-speaking listeners by using their non-native language, i.e. English, English-speaking listeners reciprocated convergence by mixing some French words or phrases into their responses.

However, as CAT developed further, convergence has been defined as broadly as any adjustments people make in their communication behaviors to become similar or closer to an interlocutor. Examples could include reducing the physical distance with an interlocuter, mimicking speech patterns such as tone of voice or word choices, or backchanneling. Some later studies have operationalized convergence not only as linguistic behaviors but also as the general perception of the interlocuters about their communication. For example, Harwood (2000) examined accommodative behaviors such as being attentive and supportive, showing respect, and sharing feelings as signs of convergence in a grandparent-grandchild relationship.

CAT suggests that convergence involves positive social evaluation or liking of the converger. In Giles et al.'s (1973) study, the English-Canadians rated French-Canadians who converged to them more positively. Harwood (2000) also found that grandparents perceived more solidarity with their grandchildren when grandchildren show accommodation.

Divergence

Divergence refers to adjustments made to become more dissimilar to one's interlocutor. Giles et al. (1973) pointed out that convergence is not likely to happen in all interactions. If an individual wants to avoid the social approval of the interactant, they hypothesized that the speaker would go the opposite way of converging by becoming dissimilar from them. In terms of speech, divergence was defined as "the way in which speakers accentuate vocal differences between themselves and others" (Giles et al., 1987, p. 14).

Some examples could include physically distancing from an interlocuter, maximizing different speech patterns such as pace or tone of voice, or not responding or ignoring the speaker. However, it can also take the form of highlighting differences in their status, or backgrounds. Though divergence was often evaluated negatively, other scholars also pointed out that divergence may bring about positive outcomes for the diverger, in terms of an enhanced sense of social identity (Giles et al., 1987). For example, Hajek (2015) examined how middle-aged gay men used divergence strategies to regulate their social identity by highlighting differences from that of young gay men. The examples of divergence discussed in Hajek (2015) include "changing conversational tone", "refusing to communicate younger identities", or expressing "seemingly conscious and voluntary dissociation from the gay culture" (p. 51).

Overaccommodation and Underaccommodation

In early work, non-accommodation primarily referred to divergence in the sense that it highlights differences between interactants. However, as the term non-accommodation expanded to embrace the perceptions of the listener, it now includes other constructs including overaccommodation. Overaccommodation refers to the perception of the listener that a speaker is overshooting the accommodative behaviors, whereas underaccommodation refers to the perception that a speaker is not doing enough accommodating to ensure a successful interaction (Gasiorek & Giles, 2015; Giles, 2016). Both overaccommodation and underaccommodation are defined as the relative level of accommodation as perceived by listeners.

Motives for Accommodation or Non-accommodation

CAT focuses on the socio-psychological processes of making adjustments based on individuals' perceptions and motivation, as well as the social outcome(s) of these aspects. Though it postulates that people adapt their communicative styles to their interlocutors either consciously or unconsciously, the theory provides two large categories for the motives of the adjustments: cognitive and affective.

Cognitive Motives

Cognitive motives are defined as a desire to "regulate comprehension and increase communicative efficiency" (Giles, 2016, p. 43). For example, by making language choices to accommodate another person, people can increase communicative efficiency and improve comprehension. On the other hand, an individual may want to diverge in terms of speaking a different language, using jargon, and displaying non-verbal communication to reduce the comprehension of their interlocutor.

Affective Motives

Affective motives refer to the motivations for communicative behaviors to manage social identity and distance. CAT posits that individuals' self-concepts are composed of the personal self and social self. As a way of managing one's social self, the theory contends that people use communication to convey social and relational information about themselves. For example, individuals are motivated by their desire to gain social approval from a certain group or person by demonstrating their similarity to them as a way of developing their social identity. On the other hand, if a person disapproves and avoids association with a certain group of people, then, they are more likely to deploy a divergent communicative adjustment to show dissimilarity, again, as a way of developing a distinct social identity. Affective motives can also involve conscious choices on convergence with the purpose of exploiting the person by highlighting their ingroup membership (Giles, 2016).

The case in this chapter will exemplify how an individual shows these accommodative or non-accommodative communication strategies discussed above, the likely motives behind such communication behaviors, and lastly the consequences.

The following section discusses a second theoretical framework for this case, the EVLN model.

The Exit, Voice, Loyalty, Neglect (EVLN) Model

The Exit, Voice, Loyalty, Neglect (EVLN) model is a typology of employee reactions to job dissatisfaction (Farrell, 1983; Hirschman, 1970). When an employee becomes dissatisfied with their job, this individual has a range of choices as to how to respond to job dissatisfaction. The EVLN discusses that employee response to job dissatisfaction can be conceptualized into four categories: exit, voice, loyalty, and neglect. The model suggests that job dissatisfaction influences individuals, leading to these four responses that can have impact on the employee-organization relationship. As the case of this chapter involves the job dissatisfaction of an immigrant nurse, the EVLN model offers one way to analyze the nurse's experiences.

Exit

According to Hirschman (1970), exit refers to voluntary separation from the dissatisfying job either by transferring within the same organization or by leaving the firm. Rusbult et al. (1988) also suggested that exit could mean not only leaving the organization but also looking for a different job or envisioning an exit from the organization. Exit happens when an employee believes that the situation that is leading them to experience job dissatisfaction is unlikely to improve.

Voice

Voice refers to any attempt to change the dissatisfying situation. Hirschman (1970) provided examples of voice that include appealing to managers and conducting any political actions such as protests. Rusbult et al. (1988) broadened the concept by conceptualizing it as any constructive attempt to improve the situation. Voice is likely to be enacted when an organization has high employee involvement.

In the sense that voice can involve the expression of disagreement or complaint, this concept can be compared to Kassing's (1997, 2011) organizational dissent. Whereas Kassing (1997, 2011) suggests that organizational dissent refers to articulated, latent, and/or displaced dissent, the EVLN model does not seem to make this distinction.

Loyalty

Hirschman (1970) defined loyalty as patiently waiting for the situation to change with expectations that it will improve before attempting any actions. It is suggested that loyalty is a passive reaction from employees who believe that the situation is likely to improve over time.

Neglect

Neglect refers to lax and disregardful behaviors of employees in reaction to job dissatisfaction (Farrell, 1983). Examples include absenteeism, lateness, or increased error rates. Neglect was also suggested as a passive reaction of an employee, but it is often conducted when an employee does not have high expectations that their situation is likely to improve in the future.

Farrell (1983) described these four categories of employee reactions in two conceptual dimensions: active/passive and constructive/destructive. For example, exit is active and destructive, voice is active and constructive, whereas loyalty is passive and slightly destructive, and neglect is passive and destructive.

Predictors of EVLN

Withey and Cooper (1989) suggested predictors for EVLN such as the indirect and direct costs of the action, the perceived efficacy of the action, and the attractiveness of the setting. For example, they argued that the direct costs of the actions are the time and energy spent in pursuing the action while there are more indirect costs for the actions. The indirect cost for exit could include lost income and benefits and lost psychological investment. The indirect costs for voice could include the possibility of retaliation, loss of one's personal reputation, and the emotional costs of raising issues to upper-level managers. The indirect costs of loyalty could include emotional costs of wondering if more actions may be needed. The indirect costs of neglect could include the possibility of discipline, lost career opportunities, and a sense of failure.

When people weigh their options, the efficacy of their response comes into play (Withey & Cooper, 1989). For example, employees' prior satisfaction or assessment of the possibility of improvement can influence their actions. When people have higher prior satisfaction with their job, they are likely to believe that whatever situation that led to job dissatisfaction now could be temporary. By the same token, when people believe that improvement is possible, they may opt for alternatives such as voice or loyalty. Individual belief in the efficacy of the response can also be a predictor because when people believe that their actions matter in terms of actually changing the situation, they are likely to choose active alternatives.

Lastly, Withey and Cooper (1989) argued that one's commitment and alternatives can impact their actions. For example, when people have a strong commitment to their current organization, or when they have no other alternative organizations to join, it is not likely that exit is a preferred course of action for them.

In addition to the above factors that could be seen as internal factors, other factors that have been studied as the predictors of EVLN include external or situational factors such as job security (Berntson et al., 2010), general economic climate (Chia et al., 2000), and role conflict and autonomy (Naus et al., 2007).

This chapter employs two theoretical frameworks to analyze the case: CAT and the EVLN. CAT offers insight into communication strategies used in conversation and their implications for social identity and the EVLN lays out the range of choices for an employee to react to job dissatisfaction. Now that these theoretical frameworks have been discussed, the rest of the chapter offers the case and discussion.

CASE STUDY

As she drove down the driveway, Kim already felt dread about meeting Jennifer at work. Put simply, she was having trouble with Jennifer. It was not the first time that Kim felt disregarded or ignored by her colleagues, but most of the instances seemed so trivial and subtle that Kim was not sure if she could even call it discrimination. Kim was finally starting to feel more comfortable with her co-workers as she was in her third year after her relocation to the U.S. and starting her job at St. Mary's Rehabilitation Hospital.

Moving to the U.S. was not an easy decision for Kim and her family. She was already financially and professionally settled in Korea as a registered nurse (RN) and, previously, had trained in one of the best nursing schools in the country. Nursing was her life's passion. At first, she just wanted to venture into a new environment as a professional. She thought there were more career opportunities for nurses in the U.S. Of course, she also wanted to give a better education and economic environment for her children. Her husband was a big supporter of the idea of moving to the U.S. He received his Master's degree in the U.S. and enjoyed staying in this country before their marriage. Kim's job as a nurse became a convenient avenue for them to pursue permanent residency in this "land of opportunity."

Life in the U.S. as an immigrant was much harder than she thought it would be. Language was a big challenge. Although she learned English in Korea, she did not have much experience speaking it in a professional setting. Not only that, Kim needed to adjust to the unique culture of the healthcare industry here. The hospital system was also very different from what she was used to. If it were in Korea, about half of her patients in this rehabilitation hospital would have been in the ICU. Her part-time employee status did not help either. Because of this work status, she had to cover different patients every time she came to work. After making a few mistakes, she started to feel insecure about her own skills and knowledge as a nurse despite her outstanding training and experience.

As Kim was driving into the hospital parking lot, she groaned. "How am I supposed to handle this?" Kim did not understand why Jennifer was treating her so coldly. She just wanted to be treated as a colleague as professional as her. Without noticing, she began replaying in her mind their shift report[2] from last week.

One Week Earlier...

Kim arrived at St. Mary's before 7 a.m. for her day shift. Kim checked her assignment. Out of 7 patients assigned to her, 4 were new patients that she never had before. She thought she would need a detailed report.

It was Jennifer that Kim was to get the report from. Kim did not like her very much as Jennifer was usually very blunt with her. However, as Jennifer was one of the few full-time RNs who had worked for over 10 years in this hospital and was generally respected by other colleagues, Kim could not express her dislike to others. In fact, Kim wanted to be liked by Jennifer but did not know how to earn her respect. Kim felt nervous about changing shifts with Jennifer but tried to stay calm. "I just need to get her shift report about the patients. That's all," she thought. She went to see Jennifer. But Jennifer was nowhere to be found.

"Good morning," Kim greeted her colleagues in the station. They all seemed to be busy getting ready for the day. "Well, she should be around here somewhere," Kim said to herself and decided to wait for her a few more minutes. In the meantime, Kim was trying to pull up the medical record system for the patients assigned to her. With 7 patients on her plate, she did not have enough time to carefully read their charts. She also wanted to know whether there had been any changes overnight.

When Jennifer finally came back from getting a drink at the vending machine to meet with Kim, it was about 15 minutes after the start of the shift. Kim was already receiving calls from her patients. She was feeling anxious. Jennifer, after working a long shift and experiencing a code blue last night, was already exhausted and eager to go home.

Jennifer looked at Kim and gave a very subtle nod. Kim walked closer to Jennifer.

"How many of them have you had before?" Jennifer asked with her eyes going over her report sheet.

Kim answered, "I know 3 of them from a few days ago, but 4 of them are ...." Before Kim finished her sentence, Jennifer interrupted, "Okay." Then, she started to give report.

Kim started to frantically take notes. She didn't want to miss anything important, but Jennifer was a fast talker. She went on reporting the patients, not looking up to see if Kim was following her.

"Room 360-1. Bernard Baker. 79 year old male. He's full code. He got a traumatic brain injury after a fall at home. He's confused, forgetful, very irritable. He has a history of CHF..."

Kim asked, "What did you say? History of..."

Jennifer sharply answered, "CHF!"

"Okay." Kim wrote it down on her sheet.

"And heart murmur, diabetes. He has irregular heart rates. He has room air. He needs a Hoyer transfer. He's NPO. He has G-tube feeding. He has ABX Ceftin for UTI. He is incontinent bladder/bowel."

Kim asked, "Did you say Ceftin?"

Jennifer answered impatiently, "Yes," checking thc time. She quickly continued, "He has Stage 3 pressure injury in the coccyx. He has video, lap tray.

"You said he has stage 3 pressure injury. Any dressing?" asked Kim.

Jennifer snapped, "You can see the order!"

"Okay, I will check," Kim said.

With a frown, Jennifer asked. "Can I move on to the next?"

After going over 7 patients, Kim wanted to check a few more things but felt hesitant about asking Jennifer more questions who was already about leave. Kim decided to check the patient charts instead when she had time.

Later that day, Kim was reflecting on her negative interaction with Jennifer that morning. In the past, she had asked Jennifer to slow down but to no avail. Jennifer was a fast talker and with a mask on, it was even harder for Kim to hear. She had tried to lean toward Jennifer to hear her more clearly, but it seemed as though Jennifer did not want to be close to Kim.

After a few more attempts to clarify what she heard, Kim thought maybe it is best not to ask any questions during the report. Kim was wondering if it is only her that was having troubles with Jennifer. Kim was not sure if this is because of a language issue, or if she was being treated unfairly.

Fast-forward to This Week...

Kim decided to ask her colleague Chen about Jennifer. As a second-generation immigrant, Chen was generally kind and understanding toward Kim. Chen seemed to be in the know when it came to what's happening in the unit whereas Kim felt she was often the last one to hear about changes. Kim thought that Chen could give her some advice on how to handle the situation.

"Chen, what do you think about Jennifer? Do you guys get along?" Kim asked Chen.

"Jennifer? Yeah. Why?" Chen answered casually, turning to Kim.

Kim stepped closer and told Chen about what happened between her and Jennifer.

"Ohh, it must have been tough. Well, actually, Jennifer once told me that she's frustrated when communicating with you. Not that you are doing anything wrong, but I guess she is just stressed out these days. And you know, she is always in a rush. She rushes when I get a report from her too. So, I have to slow her down."

"Yeah, right? She always rushes. It's so hard to catch up with her."

Kim felt much better finding out that she was not the only one having this issue with Jennifer.

Chen went on, "Yeah, also she misses things, so I have to ask her."

"She does miss things! And she doesn't like it when I ask questions." Kim was glad that Chen understood her situation. At least there was one colleague that could completely understand what she was going through. Kim felt much closer to Chen than before.

Chen lowered her voice and said, "Jennifer actually told me that she'd talk with her supervisor about you. So, you might want to talk with Sophia, too."

Kim was taken aback. "Jennifer talked with Sophia about me?" Kim asked, but in a soft voice.

"Yeah, she said she would. Well, I know you are trying hard. And I think that is great. I just think that Jennifer is so stressed out these days. I'm sure Sophia will understand the situation," Chen added.

"I'm just trying to get my job done! I have to make sure that I understand her report," Kim thought. She felt offended that Jennifer talked with her supervisor without saying anything to her first.

"I know I need to improve my English, although the patients and other colleagues seemed to understand me just fine" she thought to herself, but she also knew that her language skills won't improve overnight. Asking questions was Kim's way to try to better communicate with Jennifer. Kim felt like she was already doing everything she can. "Is there anything I can do to change the situation?" Kim wondered.

Maybe it was time for her to escalate this issue to her supervisor so that they could take whatever actions were needed. Kim also thought that Sophia would understand her and could do something about it as Chen said.

Kim decided to go see Sophia.

"Do you have a minute?" Kim asked Sophia when she saw her in the hall. Sophia and Kim went into an empty room next to the nursing station.

"I am having trouble with Jennifer," Kim told Sophia. "It is so hard for me to keep up with her especially during her report. I asked her to slow down for me, but she does not seem to care."

"I see. Do you have trouble with others too? Or is it just with Jennifer?" Sophia asked Kim.

"I mean, it is sometimes hard for me to understand everything when people speak so fast. But I make sure that I double-check and ask them again to make sure I'm not missing anything. Everyone else is fine answering my questions."

"Okay. I will look into the schedule and see what I can do with you and Jennifer. But I also want you to know that you'll probably want to improve your language skills too. You need to understand that you'll have the same problem with others if you don't work on it. You know what I mean?"

Kim was confused.

Sophia caught her confused look and repeated herself. "I mean, when you find time, it is better for you to continue working on your English." Sophia spoke very slowly and clearly. The way she spoke was almost condescending and it made Kim a little uncomfortable.

Kim was confused again. Not because she did not understand what Sophia said but because she thought she was already doing everything she could. She had taken English as a Second Language (ESL) classes for over 6 months at the same time that she was preparing for the RN license exam. She was already regularly attending English conversation clubs to improve her language skills. She was disappointed to see Sophia assuming that Kim did not understand her.

After her talk with Sophia, Kim considered her options. She could just ignore Jennifer and hope that Sophia does not put her after Jennifer's shift. But as their unit was already understaffed, Kim couldn't expect that she would avoid interacting with her forever. Also, Kim didn't think that Jennifer would magically be nicer to her. Although Jennifer may have asked to move to another unit, Kim wasn't sure when or if that would happen.

Maybe, Kim could just get down whatever she catches from Jennifer's report and then try to wing it from there. But that will mean her patients won't get the best care. "No, no…" Kim shook her head. It was not only unprofessional but unethical to do that.

"Maybe I should request a transfer to outpatient," Kim said to herself. "There I wouldn't need to get reports from colleagues." But she enjoyed the patients in the floor she was on!

CASE ANALYSIS AND DISCUSSION

CAT and the EVLN model apply to this case study as it demonstrates conversations among people from different backgrounds and in different groups interacting with each other in the workplace. Specifically, Kim and Jennifer are having trouble communicating which results in Kim's current job dissatisfaction.

Concepts from CAT such as convergence, divergence, and overaccommodation are illustrated in Kim's interactions with Jennifer, Chen, and Sophia. When Kim interacted with Jennifer, she demonstrated that she tried to converge with her. Her verbal communication such as matching her use of the words and asking questions to confirm understanding ("Did you say Ceftin?", "you said Stage 3 pressure injury…") can be seen as attempts of convergence, although it was mostly one-directional. Kim's non-verbal cues also demonstrated examples of convergence. For instance, Kim walked up to Jennifer to get the report and she frantically took notes to try to keep up with Jennifer's pace. She also leaned toward Jennifer to hear her more clearly. All these non-verbal cues spoke to Kim's efforts to narrow down her physical and psychological distance with Jennifer.

On the other hand, Jennifer demonstrated divergence or non-accommodation in this interaction. Her verbal communication did not accommodate Kim who was having a hard time following her. She spoke so fast that Kim could not catch up with her. She also did not try to check on Kim to see whether Kim is following her. In response to Kim's questions, Jennifer either answered with short phrases or did not answer at all ("You can see the order!"). Her non-verbal cues seemed to show divergence as well. Her lack of eye contact and body position demonstrated that she was not becoming similar or closer to Kim, but instead, keeping distance from her.

In contrast, Kim's conversation with Chen illustrated convergence. When Kim brought up the issue with Jennifer, Chen responded by talking about a similar experience. By saying that she had the same experience, Chen narrowed her distance from Kim. Chen and Kim went back and forth by talking about how Jennifer is a fast speaker and overlooks important details of the reports, and how hard it is for them to follow her. They shared not only the topic of the conversation but also the stance on the issue at hand. Although convergence does not always involve agreement between the people engaging in a conversation, Chen and Kim had a common perspective on the matter, demonstrating convergence. They also showed overlap in their lexical choices ("rushes") and used backchannels. These verbal cues are signals of convergence. Their non-verbal communication cues also illustrated convergence. For example, when Chen lowered her voice toward the end of their conversation, Kim also responded in a softer voice. As Chen physically oriented toward Kim for the conversation, Kim stepped closer to Chen. These non-verbal cues showed that they were reducing the distance between them, achieving convergence in their interaction.

Lastly, the interaction between Kim and Sophia showed an example of overaccommodation. According to Giles (2016), overaccommodation is a failed attempt to accommodate. Overaccommodation is also often based on stereotypes or assumptions about an outgroup member (Giles, 2016). Here, Sophia made an inaccurate assumption that Kim was confused because she did not understand what Sophia said (based on language). Sophia made adjustments to her speech by repeating what she said slowly and clearly to accommodate Kim. However, by making these adjustments, Sophia revealed her assumptions about Kim, which made Kim uncomfortable and ultimately failed at accommodating her.

CAT explains that there are motives behind these adjustments for convergence, divergence, and overaccommodation. Cognitive motives are most evident in the interaction between Kim and Jennifer. Kim needed to make convergent efforts to ensure that she understood Jennifer. When asking questions and confirming what she heard, Kim had clear cognitive motives to improve comprehension and communication efficiency.

However, CAT also suggests that people may make adjustments in their communication for their affective motives. For example, considering Kim's social status in the workplace as a racial and ethnic minority and a part-time employee, Kim sought social approval when she tried to converge with Jennifer ("Kim wanted to be liked by Jennifer but did not know how to earn her respect"). One may argue that Jennifer, being a member of the dominant group in terms of race and ethnicity as well as employment status, would not have felt the need to earn social approval from Kim, hence not converging with Kim.

Affective motives for convergence and divergence also include social identity. In other words, people converge to demonstrate their social identity as ingroup members. When Chen and Kim converged in their interaction, this affective motive was illustrated. For example, Chen and Kim both share backgrounds as immigrants. Their identification as ingroup members (i.e., immigrants) may have affected their use of convergence in this particular interaction. As a matter of fact, Chen and Kim were talking about their shared experience of dealing with a person who did not accommodate them as second-language speakers of English. Their ingroup membership was highlighted by the topic of the conversation, accentuating their close social identity.

Later in the case study, Kim, who was faced with conflicts with a difficult co-worker, demonstrated the potential reactions of employees suggested by the EVLN model. What Kim did first was to meet with her colleague Chen to seek her advice. Although Hirschman's (1970) definition suggests that voice refers to complaining about the situation to upper-level management or taking a political action such as a protest, one could argue that Kim was voicing her concern by asking for advice from Chen who was a co-worker but more integrated with the organization. Kim was consulting with Chen to decide how to approach the situation and was trying to constructively improve it. Thus, applying the definition from Rusbult et al. (1988), Kim's consultation with Chen could be seen as voice. When using concepts from organizational dissent, Kim's conversation with Chen could be interpreted as latent dissent as she discusses with her colleague, who according to the theory is an ineffective audience (Kassing, 1997).

Then, Kim proceeded with talking with her supervisor, Sophia. This voice event fits with the original concept suggested by Hirschman (1970) as Kim was appealing to an upper-level manager in an effort to improve the situation. The EVLN model suggests that voice is an active way to respond to a dissatisfactory situation in the workplace. Before her conversation with Sophia, Kim believed that the situation is likely to improve by actively voicing her dissatisfaction to her supervisor. However, Kim's appeal to Sophia was not very successful. In fact, Kim was disappointed that Sophia assumed that Kim was not trying to improve her communication skills. Considering the indirect costs of talking with a supervisor such as the emotional burden of having to confront them, Kim could have high expectations for her meeting with the supervisor. Unless Kim believed that the supervisor would take an action to improve the situation, she would not have chosen to take this option.

When Kim's assessment of the possibility of improvement was changed after she met with the supervisor, loyalty became a less desirable option for Kim. Although Kim did consider waiting until the situation gets better, she realized that there is a low possibility that she could be able to avoid interacting with Jennifer ("But as their unit was already understaffed, Kim couldn't expect that she would avoid interacting with her forever"). Kim also knew that "her English won't improve overnight," and that "Jennifer would not magically be nicer to her." These reveal why Kim felt that there is not much to be improved unless her supervisor intervenes. Thus, when she felt that Sophia may not do anything about the situation but ask Kim to accommodate Jennifer, her expectation for improvement decreased remarkably. This led her to think about neglect.

Kim briefly considered neglect but quickly dismissed this option. According to Withey and Cooper (1989), her reasons for dismissing the option of neglect may include her commitment to her job, reputational damage, the possibility of discipline, or lost career opportunity. Kim thought about the reputational and ethical consequences of neglect and determined that the costs of neglect (e.g., harming patients) outweigh the efficacy or benefit of that response. While Hirschman (1970) discusses exit, voice, loyalty, and neglect as constructive or destructive in terms of their impact on the employee-organization relationship, this case seems to point out that neglect can be destructive for other stakeholders, or patients in this case, too.

After considering these alternatives, only then did Kim start to think about asking for a transfer. Although Kim did not physically transfer to another organization, according to Rusbult et al. (1988), when Kim began considering a transfer, she was already demonstrating exit. Depending on personality factors such as locus of control or situational factors such as her employability and the labor market climate, her ultimate decision could be different.

All in all, the EVLN offers a valuable theoretical lens for analyzing this case by describing the typology of options for employee to respond to job dissatisfaction. What Kim considered when she weighed her options in the case such as possibility of improvement, the supervisor's reactions, and the nature of the work can also be analyzed under the framework of the EVLN.

DISCUSSION QUESTIONS

1. In what ways did Kim experience convergence, divergence, or overaccommodation with other co-workers?
2. What do you think could be the motives for convergence, divergence, or overaccommodation demonstrated in the case?
3. How do you think convergence, divergence, and overaccommodation in the interactions between Kim and her colleagues/supervisor impacted her relationships with each?
4. If you were in Kim's position, would you respond with exit, voice, loyalty or neglect? Why?
5. Do you think Kim will transfer to another organization? Why? Or why not?
6. Would Kim's decision be different if she had a more positive or negative experience with this organization? What could the organization do to improve Kim's experience?

REFERENCES

Batalova, J. (2020, May 14). *Immigrant Health-Care Workers in the United States.* Migration Policy Institute. https://www.migrationpolicy.org/article/immigrant-health-care-workers-united-states-2018

Berntson, E., Näswall, K., & Sverke, M. (2010). The moderating role of employability in the association between job insecurity and exit, voice, loyalty and neglect. *Economic and Industrial Democracy, 31*(2), 215–230. doi:10.1177/0143831X09358374

Cheng, C. Y., & Liou, S. R. (2011). Intention to leave of Asian nurses in US hospitals: Does cultural orientation matter? *Journal of Clinical Nursing, 20*(13-14), 2033–2042. doi:10.1111/j.1365-2702.2010.03594.x PMID:21401765

Chia, H., Landau, J., & Ong, J. S. (2000). Predictors of Voice: The moderating effect of the general economic climate. *Research and Practice in Human Resource Management, 8*(2), 3–28.

Choi, C., Khajavy, G., Raddawi, R., & Giles, H. (2019). Perceptions of police-civilian encounters: Intergroup and communication dimensions in the United Arab Emirates and the USA. *Journal of International and Intercultural Communication, 12*(1), 82–104. doi:10.1080/17513057.2018.1503317

Connor, J. B., & Miller, A. M. (2014). Occupational stress and adaptation of immigrant nurses from the Philippines. *Journal of Research in Nursing, 19*(6), 504–515. doi:10.1177/1744987114536570

Ducharme, L. J., & Martin, J. K. (2000). Unrewarding work, coworker support, and job satisfaction: A test of the buffering hypothesis. *Work and Occupations, 27*(2), 223–243. doi:10.1177/0730888400027002005

Ea, E. (2007). Facilitating acculturation of foreign-educated nurses. *OJIN: Online Journal of Issues in Nursing, 13*(1). Advance online publication. doi:10.3912/OJIN.Vol13No01PPT03

Ea, E., Itzhaki, M., Ehrenfeld, M., & Fitzpatrick, J. (2010). Acculturation among immigrant nurses in Israel and the United States of America: Acculturation. *International Nursing Review, 57*(4), 443–448. doi:10.1111/j.1466-7657.2010.00812.x PMID:21050195

Farrell, D. (1983). Exit, voice, loyalty, and neglect as responses to job dissatisfaction: A multidimensional scaling Study. *Academy of Management Journal, 26*(4), 596–607. doi:10.2307/255909

Fullwood, C., Orchard, L. J., & Floyd, S. A. (2013). Emoticon convergence in Internet chat rooms. *Social Semiotics*, *23*(5), 648–662. doi:10.1080/10350330.2012.739000

Gallois, C., Watson, B. M., & Giles, H. (2018). Intergroup communication: Identities and effective interactions. *Journal of Communication*, *68*(2), 309–317. doi:10.1093/joc/jqx016

Gasiorek, J., & Giles, H. (2015). The role of inferred motive in processing nonaccommodation: Evaluations of communication and speakers. *Western Journal of Communication*, *79*(4), 456–471. doi:10.1080/10570314.2015.1066030

Giles, H. (Ed.). (2016). *Communication accommodation theory: Negotiating personal relationships and social identities across contexts*. Cambridge University Press. doi:10.1017/CBO9781316226537

Giles, H., Mulac, A., Bradac, J., & Johnson, P. (1987). Speech Accommodation Theory: The first decade and beyond. *Communication Yearbook*, *10*, 13–48.

Giles, H., Taylor, D. M., & Bourhis, R. (1973). Towards a theory of interpersonal accommodation through language: Some canadian data. *Language in Society*, *2*(2), 177–192. doi:10.1017/S0047404500000701

Hajek, C. (2015). Gay men in early midlife: Intergenerational: Accommodation for approval, reclaimed status, and distinctiveness. *Language & Communication*, *41*, 46–56. doi:10.1016/j.langcom.2014.10.003

Harwood, J. (2000). Communicative predictors of solidarity in the grandparent-grandchild relationship. *Journal of Social and Personal Relationships*, *17*(6), 743–766. doi:10.1177/0265407500176003

Hirschman, A. O. (1970). *Exit, voice, and loyalty: Responses to decline in firms, organizations, and states*. Harvard University Press.

Imamura, M., Zhang, Y. B., & Harwood, J. (2011). Japanese sojourners' attitudes toward Americans: Exploring the influences of communication accommodation, linguistic competence, and relational solidarity in intergroup contact. *Journal of Asian Pacific Communication*, *21*(1), 115–132. doi:10.1075/japc.21.1.09ima

Kassing, J. W. (1997). Articulating, antagonizing, and displacing: A model of employee dissent. *Communication Studies*, *48*(4), 311–332. doi:10.1080/10510979709368510

Kassing, J. W. (2011). Dissent in organizations. *Polity*.

Kim, Y. I., Geun, H. G., Choi, S., & Lee, Y. S. (2017). The impact of organizational commitment and nursing organizational culture on job satisfaction in Korean American registered nurses. *Journal of Transcultural Nursing, 28*(6), 590–597. doi:10.1177/1043659616666326 PMID:27589946

Liou, S.-R., & Cheng, C.-Y. (2011). Experiences of a Taiwanese nurse in the United States. *Nursing Forum, 46*(2), 102–109. 10.1111/j.1744-6198.2011.00211.x

Naus, F., van Iterson, A., & Roe, R. (2007). Organizational cynicism: Extending the exit, voice, loyalty, and neglect model of employees' responses to adverse conditions in the workplace. *Human Relations, 60*(5), 683–718. doi:10.1177/0018726707079198

Organization for Economic Co-operation and Development (OECD). (2020, May 13). *Contribution of migrant doctors and nurses to tackling COVID-19 crisis in OECD countries.* https://oecd.org/coronavirus/policy-responses/contribution-of-migrant-doctors-and-nurses-to-tackling-covid-19-crisis-in-oecd-countries-2f7bace2/

Rusbult, C. E., Farrell, D., Rogers, G., & Mainous, A. G. III. (1988). Impact of exchange variables on exit, voice, loyalty, and neglect: An integrative model of responses to declining job satisfaction. *Academy of Management Journal, 31*(3), 599–627. doi:10.5465/256461

Watson, B., & Gallois, C. (1998). Nurturing communication by health professionals toward patients: A communication accommodation theory approach. *Health Communication, 10*(4), 343–355. doi:10.120715327027hc1004_3 PMID:16370979

Withey, M. J., & Cooper, W. H. (1989). Predicting exit, voice, loyalty, and neglect. *Administrative Science Quarterly, 34*(4), 521–539. doi:10.2307/2393565

Xu, Y. (2007). Strangers in strange lands: A metasynthesis of lived experiences of immigrant Asian nurses working in Western countries. *Advances in Nursing Science, 30*(3), 246–265. doi:10.1097/01.ANS.0000286623.84763.e0 PMID:17703124

KEY TERMS AND DEFINITIONS

Convergence: Communicative adjustments to become similar or closer to an interlocutor.

Divergence: Communicative adjustments to become dissimilar from an interlocutor.

Exit: Any attempts for voluntary separation from the organization.

Loyalty: A response to a deteriorating work environment by passively waiting for improvement.

Neglect: Negligent work behaviors in response to a deteriorating work environment.

Overaccommodation: A failed attempt at accommodation that is perceived as demeaning by the listener.

Voice: Constructive actions for improvement of the situation by making it known to management.

ENDNOTES

1. This case is based on the actual experiences of an immigrant nurse. We are very grateful to this individual for sharing her experiences.
2. Shift report, or change-of-shift report, refers to the collection of detailed information about each patient's condition and progress during the previous shift which is handed over from nurses ending their shift to those who are beginning the next shift.

Chapter 8
"You're Very Smart for a Black Woman": A Case of Microaggressive Communication

Eletra Gilchrist-Petty
The University of Alabama in Huntsville, USA

EXECUTIVE SUMMARY

This case study explores an instance of microaggressive communication occurring at an organizational professional meeting. The case examines how "You're very smart for a Black woman" functions as a microinsult. Though intended as a compliment, this chapter illustrates the negative impact of this racially biased and stereotypical communicative act. This case study adds further credence to the everyday slights and indignities experienced by Black women academics, who represent an understudied population within organizational communication.

INTRODUCTION

Professors at research intensive universities generally must excel in teaching, research, and service in order to navigate and tenure and promotion ranks and establish themselves as bona fide scholars. Research not only consists of publishing, but presenting at academic and professional conferences. These research opportunities provide novice and seasoned scholars alike the opportunity to polish their presentation skills, gain feedback on research in progress, and collaborate as a cohort academics. The American Psychological Association adds, "Perhaps one of the important

DOI: 10.4018/978-1-6684-3753-7.ch008

benefits from conference presentations is the ability to advocate for your science" (Dunn, 2007, para. 4). In other words, professional conferences allow academics to inform each other about innovative research generated in particular subfields of inquiry, which increases the visibility and legitimacy of various topics of importance.

Research on the experiences of minorities has historically been regarded as lower status and underappreciated by reviewers in the research world (Gregory, 1995; Thomas & Hollenshead, 2001; Yancey-Bragg, 2021). Research has even determined that proposals submitted by Black applicants were significantly less likely to be funded by the National Institutes of Health because the research topics that Black applicants commonly propose deal with disenfranchised groups, which are perceived as less favored by reviewers (Mervis, 2019). A cohort of Stanford researchers found compelling evidence that women and racial minorities introduce novel research findings at higher rates than White men across all disciplines, but are less likely to reap the career benefits because their work is regularly devalued and discounted (Hofstra et al., 2020). Because the research of minorities is often perceived as subpar, academics who publish within this realm of research have historically had a more difficult time navigating the tenure and promotion processes in academia (Collins, 2000; Gilchrist, 2011; Herbert, 2012; White, 2012). More specifically, the academy has traditionally been labeled a "space of racialized and gendered oppression and domination" (Davis, 1999, p. 370).

Black women professors at Predominately White Institutions (PWIs) have historically been repressed by racialized and gendered hegemonic forces. Thomas and Hollenshead (2001), stated that for Black women and other women of color in the academy, their "research is frequently viewed as insignificant" and "these women often receive little or no support for their intellectual pursuits, especially when their work centers on racial, ethnic, or gender issues" (p. 166-167). Subsequently, White (2012) noted that Black female faculty do not experience the institution in the same way as their counterparts who identify differently. Hence, in order for Black women professors at PWIs to successfully navigate the tenure and promotion processes, they must negotiate the "intersections of race and gender while acting as agents of change within the confines of hegemonic structures" (Herbert, 2012, p. 101). Through the lens of microaggressions, this case study further illuminates the experiences of Black women professors at PWIs, as an understudied population in organizational communication.

Microaggressions

Microaggressions represent a contemporary form of discrimination and emphasize the individual experiences of daily racist and discriminatory practices (Sue, 2010; Sue et al., 2007). As a working definition, microaggressions are "brief and commonplace daily verbal, behavioral, or environmental indignities, whether intentional or unintentional, that communicate hostile, derogatory, or negative racial slights or insults toward the target person or group" (Sue et al., 2007, p. 273). There are many characteristics to unpack from this definition. First, microaggressions are brief and commonplace, which suggests they emerge frequently in everyday interactions (Sue, 2010; Sue et al., 2007; Wang et al, 2011). Second, microaggressions are communicated via a variety of ways based on what people say (i.e., verbal), what people do (i.e., behavioral), and the settings in which people dwell (i.e., environmental; Sue, 2010; Sue et al., 2007). Third, the definition of microaggressions acknowledges that some microaggressive messages are intentionally communicated, whereas others are not. In other words, people are not always cognizant that they have communicated offensive, derogatory, or racist messages and, instead, perceive their statements or actions as well-intentioned and innocent (Davis, 2019; Sue, 2010; Sue et al., 2007; Sue, 2021; Wang et al., 2011). However, regardless of the communicator's intention, per the fourth part of the definition, microaggressions are perceived as offensive to the target. Specifically, microaggressions demean the experiences and identity of the victim based on their group membership and imply that they are a lesser human being (Sue, 2010; Sue et al., 2007).

Researchers have identified three categories of microaggressions: microassaults, microinsults, and microinvalidations. M*icroassaults* are akin to old-fashioned or traditional forms of racism, whereby they are overt and intentional (Sue, 2010; Sue et al., 2007). Microassaults are conscious and explicit derogations that intend to offend and harm the intended victim. Examples of microassaults include yelling racial epithets, physical violence, or defacing property by drawing a swastika on it. While the perpetrator is conscious of their communication or action with microassaults, they may be less aware of the hurt they inflict with the other two forms of microaggressions. *Microinsults*, a second category of microaggressions, are more nuanced and subtle forms of communication that are characterized by rudeness and insensitivity that demean a person's racial heritage or identity. Microinsults are frequently in the form of a compliment, as noted in the following statement: "I had no idea you were from Africa since your skin tone is so light and pretty." While the compliment in the preceding example is intended to be positive, the hidden message is that dark skin is not as attractive, which is insulting and demeaning. The third type of microaggression, *microinvalidations*, is akin to microinsults, whereby they tend to be subtle and invisible to the perpetrator. Microinvalidations represent messages that "exclude, negate, or nullify the psychological thoughts, feelings, or experiential reality of a [member of a particular group]" (Sue et al., 2007, p. 274). An example invalidation is: "I don't see color." While the communicator's intent might be to inform the target that they are not perceived differently based on race, the message is perceived as denying the target's racial identity and ignoring the daily experiential reality of marginalized groups; hence, microinvalidations are offensive.

Microassaults, microinsults, and microinvalidations can all have detrimental effects on the victims. Sue (2021) metaphorically described microaggressions as "death by a thousand cuts" because the daily slights, insults, and offensive behaviors experienced by marginalized groups can result in real psychological harm. Microaggressions are constant and cumulative reminders that the marginalized group members are second-class citizens; hence, microaggressions are energy depleting and lead to battle fatigue (Sue, 2021). Moreover, microaggressions can be detrimental to the victim's physical and psychological well-being by promoting feelings of confusion, anger, anxiety, helplessness, hopelessness, frustration, paranoia, and fear, which can lead to negative coping mechanisms, such as denial, withdrawal, and even substance abuse (Williams, 2020).

Microaggressions can be directed toward a number of different groups, including women, racial and ethnic minorities, members of the lesbian, bisexual, gay, transgender, and queer plus community, and people with disabilities. People can also experience microaggressions based on their nationality, religion, socioeconomic status, age, and basically any other marker of difference that places one in a marginalized group (Sue, 2021). Black women have been identified as a group who experiences microaggressions on a daily basis (Davis, 2019). Moreover, since microaggressions exist in the daily lives of individuals, they can occur in any setting, including work organizations. This study focuses on a case of microaggressive communication experienced by a Black woman professor, who was presenting research at a professional conference in her academic discipline. For confidentiality, all names are pseudonyms.

CASE STUDY

Shawna and about 5,000 other academics gathered in a large U.S.A. city for the annual meeting of their professional organization. Shawna always looked forward to this yearly experience because it not only allowed her to receive useful feedback on her research, but it granted her the opportunity to connect with peers who shared the same professional experiences as she did. Shawna is the only Black woman professor in her academic department that is housed in a PWI. Hence, professional conferences represent some of the rare occasions where she can connect with other faculty who are also the sole woman of color in their department. Shawna finds comfort in connecting with her kindred scholarly sisters, as they share their trials, triumphs, and mentor each other.

Shawna had enjoyed a fulfilled and productive conference, and was currently on day four of the five-day conference. As she was soon to petition her University for tenure and promotion, she had a very busy conference and presented five scholarly works. Her goal was to present and publish as much as possible to strengthen her case before embarking upon the tenure and promotion process. Toward the end of day four, she was down to her last presentation, which she was excited about because she was presenting some of her ethnographic research on the microcultural experiences of Black women faculty at PWIs. Afterwards, she looked forward to enjoying her last night at the conference by having dinner with colleagues and engaging in casual conversation.

There were five speakers on Shawna's last panel, and Shawna was slated to go last. There were about 20 audience members in attendance, who ranged from first-year graduate students to seasoned professors. John was one of the well-established scholars in the audience. He had an impressive resume of scholarship and more than 30 years in the professoriate. His work was known throughout the discipline, and Shawna considered it a privilege to have him in attendance. While John was there to support one of his graduate students, he stayed for the duration of the presentations. For the first four presentations, Shawna noticed that he seemed very engaged and was practicing comprehensive listening. So, she expected he would do the same during her presentation. While all papers on the panel related to the central them of teacher-student communication, Shawna's paper was the sole one that focused on the dynamic interactions of Black women faculty and White students at PWIs.

The conference program gave the title and a brief description of each presentation, so before the speakers began the audience had a general idea of their topic. As Shawna readied herself to begin her presentation, she noticed that John took out his phone, which was something he had not done during the other panel presentations. As she commenced her presentation, John not only continued dabbling on his phone, but he had a very disinterested look on his face. While Shawna expected a more civil and collegial attitude from a veteran scholar, she had been teaching long enough not to be side-tracked by one disinterested audience member. Moreover, speaking was her passion, and she had a gift for engaging an audience. Consequently, the more she spoke, the more John occasionally looked up at her. About mid-way through Shawna's 10-minute presentation, John had completely put down his phone was honed into her every word. By the end of her presentation, it was clear that John was intrigued and had a slight smile on his face. After Shawna's presentation, there were about 15 minutes allotted for questions and answers. While John asked his graduate student a question, he did not ask Shawna anything during the open forum. Instead, he spoke with her one-on-one after the panel concluded, and following conversation ensued:

"Your research is rather interesting," John said to Shawna as she gathered her materials to leave the room.

"Thank you!" Shawna replied with glee. "And, thank you for coming to our panel. I've been a fan of your research since I was a graduate student."

"So what theory do you typically use with your research?" John asked.

"Well, it usually depends on the precise study's objective, but I'm a big fan of otherness, co-cultural theory, muted group theory, and Black feminist thought," Shawna said.

"What is your motivation for researching in this area?" John inquired in a follow-up question.

"My life," Shawna said. "I was educated at a PWI, and now I'm a professor at a PWI. I'm not saying that my experiences have been bad, but they have been different than others in my department, and I resonate with every article and book I have read on the experiences of women of color at PWIs. So my goal is to just add to the conversation."

"I'm impressed," John said with a smile and positive body language. "You're very smart for a Black woman."

"I beg your pardon?" Shawna asked, thinking her ears were deceiving her.

"I mean you're really smart and are doing some good work," John said, attempting to clarify. "You have a bright future ahead."

"But, why did you have to say that I was smart for a Black woman?" Shawna queried in a bewildered tone.

Awkward silence followed for a few seconds.

"What you said was very offensive," Shawna stated in a slightly elevated and vexed voice. "There are plenty of Black women who are smart, and I encourage you to get to know them and their work. It's so unfortunate that in this day and age a scholar of your caliber has such a limited and stereotypical view of people."

Shawna's colleague and friend, Tabitha, who attended the panel and was waiting for Shawna became aware of the conversation, sensed Shawna's frustration, and decided to intervene.

"Hey, let's go," Tabitha said, grabbing Shawna's hand and pulling her toward the door.

"Did you hear what he said to me?" Shawna asked Tabitha.

"Yes, but he's not worth it," Tabitha responded. "As Black women in academia there will always be those who question our legitimacy and credibility. We have to pick our battles, and he simply is not worth it. Let's go."

Shawna left with Tabitha, and they joined other colleagues for dinner, but she could not get the statement "You're very smart for a Black woman" out of her mind. For the rest of the conference, she had a smile on her face, but pain in her heart.

CASE ANALYSIS AND DISCUSSION

According to Long et al. (2016), "microaggressive communication is an everyday interpersonal and organizational event that needs rigorous study and exploration as a negative communicative act" (p. 119). This case study helps answer the call for "rigorous study" of these negative acts of communication by exploring an instance of microaggressive communication occurring at an organization's professional meeting.

Per the widely cited definition provided by Sue et al., (2007), microaggressions are brief indignities. Seven brief words comprise the microaggression addressed in this case study—"You're very smart for a Black woman." While the words may be few in number, the collective impact of them is great and provides further credence to the everyday realities of subtle racism experienced by Black women (Davis, 2019).

Of the three types of microaggressions (i.e., microassaults, microinsults, and microinvalidations), this case study relates to microinsults. As previously defined, microinsults are subtle forms of communication characterized by rudeness and insensitivity that degrade a person's racial heritage or identity (Sue et al., 2007). Moreover, microinsults often contain *metacommunication* or hidden messages that imply the demographic group in question is not respected or valued, but the target of the message is viewed as an exception (Sue, 2021). In relation to this case study, "You're very smart for a Black woman" functions as a subtle way of saying that Black women, at least from a stereotypical perspective, are not viewed as smart. However, John perceived that Shawna contradicted the stereotypical image he held of most Black women, in that she was "smart."

Interestingly, perpetrators of microinsults often do not realize they have insulted the target because of their own unconscious bias or prejudice (Sue, 2010; Sue et al., 2007; Sue, 2021). With this case study, John thought that he was giving Shawna a compliment regarding her research. His affirming nonverbal cues demonstrated that he was impressed with her competence and confidence as a young scholar. Yet, his words communicated a very different message. As noted by Sue (2021), most people who commit microaggressions believe that they are moral and decent human beings who would never consciously discriminate against someone. Yet, they have inherited societal biases that dwell beyond the level of conscious awareness and occasionally seep out. Hence, as an older White male scholar who has taught for nearly four decades at a PWI, it is very likely that John has had limited interactions with Black women scholars, and he only knows them from the stereotypical heuristics that allege research by Black women is insignificant (e.g., Gilchrist, 2011; Thomas & Hollenshead, 2001; Tindall, 2009).

As stated by Long et al. (2016), "Ill-intended micro-communication consequences happen primarily because many individuals have not been socialized to exist in a pluralistic society and their latent privilege standpoint prevails" (p. 119). Hence, sometime people's views are clouded in ignorance simply because they have lived very encapsulated lives. Yet, regardless of the motivation behind the communication breach, it is important to remember that microaggressions "communicate hostile, derogatory, or negative racial slights or insults toward the target person or group" (Sue et al., 2007, p. 273). In other words, microaggressions hurt. Sue (2021) has compared microaggressions to a papercut. While a papercut is generally small, it still hurts. Because microaggressions are painful to the recipients, they can result in significant macro-level consequences (Williams, 2020), with impacts ranging from lower emotional well-being to impaired employee performance (Long et al., 2016; Sue, 2021). The microinsult "You're very smart for a Black woman" took a heavy toll on Shawna. Though she dined and fellowshipped with colleagues afterwards, the smile on Shawna's face could not mask the pain in her heart. Hence, it is clear that the microinsult deeply affected Shawna on an emotional level.

Additionally, microaggressions are cumulative, with different instances of microaggressions coalescing to compound hurt (Sue, 2021). Hence, while a single microaggression might hurt like a papercut, the collective experience of these everyday slights and indignities can seem more like "death by a thousand cuts" (Sue, 2021). Shawna's friend Tabitha acknowledged the frequency that Black women professors experience microaggressions when she told Shawna that "As Black women in academia there will always be those who question our legitimacy and credibility." Tabitha also suggested a coping mechanism for dismantling the potential devastating impact of microaggressions by encouraging Shawna to pick her battles. "We have to pick our battles" implies that microaggressions occur with such frequency that Black women who inhabit the halls of ivy must strategically decide when to address them and when to simply walk away. Yet, this case illustrates that though one may physically separate themselves from the source of microaggressions, the memory and residual effects of microaggressions can endure for a lifetime. Hence, it is important for well-intentioned organizational leaders to understand that microaggressions are much more than benign communication hiccups. Instead, organizations must work to educate their members to recognize, challenge, and diminish racially biased and stereotypical communicative acts.

DISCUSSION QUESTIONS

1. If you were Shawna, how would you have responded to the microaggression?
2. Do you agree with Shawna's friend Tabitha that we have to pick our battles and not respond to every microaggression?
3. If you could speak with John about his comment, what would you tell him?
4. Have you ever been on the receiving end of a microaggression? If so, what type was it, and how did you respond?
5. What can organizers of professional academic conferences do to combat microaggressions?

REFERENCES

Collins, A. C. (2000). Black women in the academy: An historical overview. In R. Mabokela & A. L. Green (Eds.), *Sisters of the academy: Emergent Black scholars in higher education* (pp. 29–41). Stylus.

Davis, O. I. (1999). In the kitchen: Transforming the academy through safe spaces of resistance. *Western Journal of Communication, 63*(3), 364–381. doi:10.1080/10570319909374647

Davis, S. M. (2019). When sistahs support sistahs: A process of supportive communication about racial microaggressions among Black women. *Communication Monographs, 86*(2), 133–157. doi:10.1080/03637751.2018.1548769

Dunn, K. (2007, November). *Why it's important for you to present your data at scientific conferences.* American Psychological Association. https://www.apa.org/science/about/psa/2007/11/student-council-1

Gilchrist, E. S. (2011). "One of These Things Is Not Like The Others": African American women professors' experiences with majority-race students. In M. N. Niles & N. S. Gordon (Eds.), *Still searching for our mothers' gardens: Experiences of new, tenure track faculty of color at 'majority' institutions* (pp. 213–233). University Press of America.

Gregory, S. T. (1995). *Black women in the academy: The secrets to success and achievement.* University Press of America.

Herbert, S. S. (2012). What have you done for me lately? Black female faculty and "Talking Back" to the tenure process at PWIs. *Women & Language, 35*(2), 99–102.

Hofstra, B., Kulkarni, V. V., Galvez, H., Jurafsky, B., & McFarland, D. A. (2020). The diversity-innovation paradox in science. *Proceedings of the National Academy of Sciences, 117*(17), 9284-9291. 10.1073/pnas.1915378117

Long, S. D., Wonznyj, H., Coleman, M. J., Makkawy, A., & Spivey, C. (2016). Microaggressive communication in organizational settings. In E. S. Gilchrist-Petty & S. D. Long (Eds.), *Contexts of the Dark Side of Communication* (pp. 111–120). Peter Lang.

Mervis, J. (2019, October 9). *Study identifies a key reason black scientists are less likely to receive NIH funding.* American Association for the Advancement of Science. https://www.science.org/content/article/study-identifies-key-reason-black-scientists-are-less-likely-receive-nih-funding

Sue, D. W. (2010). *Microaggressions in everyday life: Race, gender, and sexual orientation*. John Wiley & Sons.

Sue, D. W. (2021, March 30). Microaggressions: Death by a thousand cuts. *Scientific American*. https://www.scientificamerican.com/article/microaggressions-death-by-a-thousand-cuts/

Sue, D. W., Capodilupo, C. M., Torino, G. C., Bucceri, J. M., Holder, A., Nadal, K. L., & Esquilin, M. (2007). Racial microaggressions in everyday life: Implications for clinical practice. *The American Psychologist*, *62*(4), 271–286. doi:10.1037/0003-066X.62.4.271 PMID:17516773

Thomas, G. D., & Hollenshead, C. (2001). Resisting from the margins: The coping strategies of Back women and other women of color faculty members at a research university. *The Journal of Negro Education*, *70*(3), 166–175. doi:10.2307/3211208

Tindall, N. (2009). The double bind of race and gender: Understanding the roles and perceptions of Black female public relations faculty. *Southwestern Mass Communication Journal*, *25*(1), 1–16.

Wang, J., Leu, J., & Shoda, Y. (2011). When the seemingly innocuous "stings": Racial microaggressions and their emotional consequences. *Personality and Social Psychology Bulletin*, *37*(12), 1666–1678. doi:10.1177/0146167211416130 PMID:21885859

White, S. B. (2012). "Talking back": The danger of silence and the risk of speaking in Black and White. *Women & Language*, *35*(2), 95–98.

Williams, M. T. (2020). Microaggressions: Clarification, evidence, and impact. *Perspectives on Psychological Science*, *15*(1), 3–26. doi:10.1177/1745691619827499 PMID:31418642

Yancey-Bragg, N. (2021, July 9). It's not just Nikole Hannah-Jones: Black women are underrepresented among tenured faculty. *USA Today*. https://www.usatoday.com/story/news/education/2021/07/09/black-women underrepresented-tenure-university-faculty/7890102002/

KEY TERMS AND DEFINITIONS

Metacommunication: Hidden messages that imply the demographic group in question is not respected or valued, but the target of the message is viewed as an exception (Sue, 2021).

Microaggressions: Microaggressions emerge from implicit biases, which come from stereotypical and simplistic views of individuals in marginalized groups. A microaggression is a statement that is considered disrespectful and possibly discriminatory by a person in the marginalized group with whom the microaggression is directed.

Chapter 9
I Am Me:
Transgender Communication in the Workplace

Victoria L. Bray
University at Albany, SUNY, USA

Patricia Gettings
University at Albany, SUNY, USA

EXECUTIVE SUMMARY

Sam is a transgender individual navigating work and life. Linda, a colleague of Sam's, is an older employee who knows her way around their workplace, Living Life, an organization focused on assisting (dis)abled individuals with a range of life skills. When Linda discovers Sam's gender identity, Linda withdraws and changes the way she interacts with Sam. John attempts to understand both perspectives but is not given enough information to act in one way or the other. The case is explored using transgender standpoint epistemology, social penetration theory, expectancy violations theory, and transgender standpoint epistemology.

INTRODUCTION

Although negotiating identities in the workplace has been a common topic addressed by organizational communication scholars, gender identity—in particular the experiences of transgender individuals—has been largely overlooked. Lesbian, gay, bisexual, transgender, and queer or questioning (LGBTQ) individuals make up a significant portion of employees in the United States, somewhere between 5.4 and 8.2 million employees self-identify as members of the LGBTQ community (U.S. Commission

DOI: 10.4018/978-1-6684-3753-7.ch009

on Civil Rights (USCCR), 2017). One notable exception is the work of Jones (2020) who pointed out that, "The United States has no far-reaching federal legislation that prohibits discrimination against gender and sexual minorities" (p 252). According to the Federal Bureau of Investigation (FBI) hate crimes in the United States based on sexual orientation, gender, and gender identity make up for 17% of incidents in 2020 (FBI, n.d.). Transgender individuals, in particularly, have been overlooked and one study found 44% of participants were overlooked for a job due to their gender identity (USCCR, 2017). This lack of protection and staggering statistics may complicate how transgender individuals interact in the workplace. In addition, members of the LGBTQ community face differing expectations regarding work-life balance compared to those experienced by counterparts from "traditional families" (Dixon & Dougherty, 2014). Understanding how transgender employees negotiate identity in the workplace is important for both individual and organizational success. The Attempts of transgender individuals to integrate into the organization through passing[1] can lead to depression, anxiety, and lowered productivity (Jones, 2020).

Living Life, the organization discussed in this case, assists (dis)abled individuals in living their lives. The aim of the case is to inspire the reader to think about the portrayal of gender in the workplace and the presentation of self in different environments. When negotiating identity at work, factors like gender, age, and ethnicity can impact our journey. Individuals deviating from societal norms may experience workplace identity negotiation differently. The case fosters thinking about the way we negotiate our identities, with a focus on gender, and how these negotiations impact our workplace relationships. In addition, the case will bring light to an understudied group - transgender individuals. To analyze the case, we integrate traditional communication theories (social penetration and expectancy violations) with a more contemporary framework (transgender standpoint epistemology).

Concepts or Theories

Transgender Standpoint Epistemology

Transgender standpoint epistemology focuses on the ways in which "the net realities available to a transgender employee based upon conscious reflections on the nature of oppression and discrimination constituted through cis normative expectations of organizational performance" (Jones, 2020, p. 256). The same way in which oppression and discrimination are reproduced through the societal norms, also reproduces such norms in the organization.

Transgender standpoint epistemology is, as reinforced by the name, rooted in *standpoint epistemology*. Standpoint epistemologies are a family of knowledge theories underscoring the idea of identity and the way in which features of a person's identity that are overlooked in traditional discussions have significant consequences (Toole, 2021). Standpoint epistemologies see *knowledge as a situated* concept, meaning a position one has, such as their gender or class, can change how they understand the knowledge they are given (Toole, 2021). A person may ask themselves "if I were…" and insert any position different from your own. Our identities shape how we see the world, the knowledge we take in, and how we process that knowledge to form meaning.

A similar standpoint theory, feminist standpoint theory, underscores the power structures between men and women and the naturalization of division between the two (Wood, 2005). Transgender standpoint epistemology, similarly, points out the power structures between heteronormative and transgender individuals (Jones, 2020). Five key claims underscore feminist standpoint theory, the first surrounding the aforementioned *power relations* (Wood, 2005). The second involves the accuracy of knowledge, stating individuals in the lower power structure are more likely to see things accurately because those in the higher power structure are interested in maintaining the higher authority (Woods, 2005). The third points out the "*outsider-within*" in which an individual in the nondominated group has access to the privileged groups communication and is able to understand that group better (Woods, 2005). Fourth, standpoints are created through political struggle and requires a more critical understanding of the interplay between social and political contexts and larger discourses (Woods, 2005). The fifth and final key point of feminist standpoint theory involves the *intersectionality* of standpoints created by an individual belonging to more than one membership such as sex and race (Woods, 2005). Theories of standpoint epistemologies look at the way we engage with the world and the activities which shape out identity and therefore out knowledge (Wood, 2005).

Jones (2020) described the negotiation of transgender (trans) identity at work and found agency, or the ability to make decisions, to be an important factor. Individuals felt they had to '*pass*,' or "perform a privileged identity" at work due to traditional rules and resources, which led to anxiety and depression (Jones, 2020, p 262). In Sam's case, their need to pass at work relied on the organization's lack of rules and resources available to transgender employees, and they experienced isolation and anxiety in the process. The need of individuals to develop relationships and navigate the work environment can be seen in a number of communication theories, as demonstrated in the following two sections.

Social Penetration Theory

Social penetration theory describes the trajectory of interpersonal relationships evolving in a path-like manner, progressing from superficial to intimate through the use of *self-disclosure* (Altman & Taylor, 1973; Carpenter & Greene, 2016; Taylor,

1968; West & Turner, 2017). The theory relies on three basic assumptions. The first involves the gradual progression of relationships from non-intimate to intimate (West & Turner, 2017). For example, meeting a co-worker for the first time, your relationship is non-intimate, but the relationship may progress, and you could become close friends. The second assumption is the predictable nature of the progression of relationships. Meeting someone for the first time is usually the first step in the progression of relationships, and one moves forward from there, perhaps with a few bumps in the road. The third assumption pertains to the slow deterioration, or depenetration, of relationships (West & Turner, 2017). Transgressions, or violations of the expectations and rules of particular relationships are often at the start of the depenetration process (West & Turner, 2017). For instance, if a co-worker/friend shares information with others in the workplace that was disclosed in confidence (e.g., dislike for one's boss), this transgression may initiate the *depenetration* of the relationship. Recent scholarship framed using social penetration theory has explored how the theory can be applied to explain relationship development and maintenance in online contexts (e.g., Mason & Carr, 2021; Pennington, 2020).

Often an onion analogy is used to describe the process of social penetration theory disclosures. Moving in from the outermost layer, disclosure happens from the outside, or public image, to the innermost personal matters not visible to the naked eye (West & Turner, 2017). The *reciprocity* of disclosure, or when the same degree of openness is shared between two people, can also impact relational development (West & Turner, 2017). When one person divulges personal information, the other is likely to also disclose personal information (West & Turner, 2017; Taylor, 1968). For example, if one co-worker shares that they dislike the boss's management style, the co-worker/friend is likely to disclose something they dislike about the boss or workplace as well. Sometimes, though, too much disclosure can negatively affect a relationship.

Disclosure can be considered along two dimensions - breadth and depth. *Breadth* refers to the number of topics and amount of time spent on each topic whereas *depth* refers to the level of intimacy in topic discussion (West & Turner, 2017). Breadth is often described as wide or narrow. A wide breadth would include many topics such as work, life, and play. A narrow breadth would be only talking about work while at work (i.e., a small number of topics for a limited time). The information disclosed also matters. Gibbs et al. (2006) found selectively disclosing information in online dating can be beneficial to relationship progression.

Relationships can be regulated by assessing the *reward-cost ratio*, or the balance of positive and negative experiences in a relationship (West & Turner, 2017; Taylor, 1968). If a relationship has more positive benefits than negative, the relationship will be seen as a good one. Too much self-disclosure, although often negatively valenced, can be overlooked because the rewards outweigh the costs (Pennington,

2020). Relationships progress through four stages: orientation, exploratory affective exchange, affective exchange, and stable exchange (West & Turner, 2017). This progression starts with small revelations during the orientation stage to the creation of stable communication where relational partners feel open and honest with each other (West & Turner, 2017). In the middle of the relationship, the exploratory affective stage involves the expression of individual personality while the affective exchange stage involves spontaneity and the use of personal idioms (West & Turner, 2017). For example, a co-worker/friend might have personal idioms like calling one another a "work spouse" (McBride & Mason Bergen, 2015) or other nickname rather than using more formal names. Whereas social penetration theory provides insight into the process of relationship development, expectancy violations theory is a foundational framework that helps us understand the role our expectations play in interactions and relationships.

Expectancy Violations Theory

Expectancy violations theory (EVT) focuses on the behaviors and expectations of individuals situated within interactions and helps to make sense of instances when expectations are violated (Burgoon & Hale, 1988). Key assumptions of EVT are that (a) our *expectations* drive our interactions, (b) expectancies are learned, and (c) we make predictions about the nonverbal behavior of others from our understanding of expectancies (Burgoon, 2016; West & Turner, 2017). For example, considering nonverbal aspects of EVT, our relationships with others and the situational context can determine what physical space is acceptable. There are four *proxemic* zones: intimate, personal, social, and public (Burgoon & Hale, 1988). When talking to a romantic partner, the distance between the two people can often be relatively close (in the intimate space). This would not break our expectations because an intimate partner would be expected to speak to us from a close distance. In the case of a co-worker or supervisor, however, it would not be acceptable for them to be in our intimate space, instead, they would be in our personal or social space. Expectations can be broken if a person is not in the proper proxemic zone. For example, if a co-worker came into a colleague's intimate space, an expectation would be violated. *Violations* may involve social, cultural, and conversational norms, and can lead to loss of idealization and disillusionment with the relational partner (Niehuis et al., 2019). For example, if someone says something hurtful or rude, expectations and impressions of the other person can be negatively impacted. Violations lie on a spectrum from simple rudeness and verbal aggression to lies and physical aggression (Niehuis et al., 2019).

Threat thresholds involve the tolerance a person has for expectancy violations, while *valence* describes the assessment of such violations as positive or negative (Burgoon, 2016). An expectation may have a positive or negative valence, meaning violations can be viewed as either a good or a bad thing (West & Turner, 2017). A violation by a co-worker that you are becoming friendly with, for example, can be viewed as having a positive valence. Indeed, if a co-worker moved from your social to personal space, you may enjoy the expectancy violation because it suggests your relationship is growing closer. The sum of positive and negative valences in conjunction with the potential of the violator to give rewards or punishments is called the *communicator reward valence* (Burgoon, 2016). A supervisor, for example, has the ability to dole out punishments or rewards to employees, effecting the reception of violations. Our expectations of others can be applied to the following case to understand the factors that shape our expectations of others. Individual factors (e.g., gender, age), relational factors (e.g., liking and status differences), and contextual factors (e.g., norms, formality) can be examined through the lens of main characters' experiences.

CASE STUDY

Sam is twenty-four years old and has undergone the transition from female to male prior to beginning their position at Living Life LLC. Sam's job entails bringing individuals with differing degrees of (dis)ability (called "participants" by the organization) on outings in which they volunteer, work, or play in the local community.

Sam often works with Linda as they bring participants around to be more involved in community events and gain new experiences. Remembering the first time they worked together, Sam thinks of Linda's words that day, "I started working here ten years ago after placing my son in the program. He has Autism and I was working at the bank and didn't have much time to care for him. After seeing how happy the program made him, I asked if they were looking for any help and I've been here ever sense" Sam saw how proud Linda was and was found themselves feeling connected with Linda more and more after that day.

One day, Sam and Linda are taking three participants, Pete, Sandy, and Carl to deliver meals for elderly members of the community.

As the group approaches the quaint yellow house with green trim, Pete begins to dance around the path. He smiles and hums to himself as the Sandy and Carl wait patiently. Sandy grins as she watches Pete dance. Carl watches intently and says "We have to work! We are doing important work here! We can't play around Pete!"

Pete continues to dance, and Sandy lets out a loud laugh.

"Alright guys let's bring these meals to the door" Sam announces.

As Sam approaches the house to drop off meals, the owner of the house steps outside. "I don't want these people delivering my meals anymore, they are too slow!"

Taken aback, Sam processes the information, thinking to themselves "What is going on? Why is this lady being so rude? I have to be professional and get the participants out of this situation."

Finally snapping out of thought, Sam decides to act. "I'm very sorry ma'am, we just need a little more time to get everything from the car."

"I don't care!" shouted the woman from her open doorway.

Pete has stopped dancing and is looking from Sam to the woman and back again. Linda approaches from the vehicle and notices Carl staring at the ground with his arms behind his back and Sam's slightly ajar mouth. "What's going on here?" she asks.

"I don't want you people delivering my meals anymore," said the gray-haired lady.

"Why is that?" asked Linda.

"You people are too slow. I don't want to keep my door open forever waiting for my meals to be delivered, it is cold outside."

Linda defends the group saying, "Ma'am, we are volunteering to deliver these meals for free. We are going as fast as we can and shouting will not make us go any faster, we appreciate your understanding as we try our best to provide fast and reliable service. Please do not yell at us, you can keep your door closed until all the meals are on the front porch if that helps keep your heat inside."

Linda and Sam quickly get the participants back to the vehicle and calm them down. As they are driving back to the office after dropping the participants off, Sam turns to Linda "Thanks for defending us back there I was really unsure of what to do and the participants started to see the panic on my face"

"No problem, I was also very unsure of what to do in those situations when I first started ten years ago, but I figured out eventually to just apologize, explain, and move on. There is no need to stay in a difficult situation for more than a few seconds. Some people will never understand the different needs of people with disabilities," Linda replied.

"I don't understand how some people can be like that, we all have different abilities, we should embrace them," Sam said.

"Most people don't think like that. What's important is we take care of our participants and remove them from the situation to deal with the distress it causes, Dear."

They arrive back at the office where their manager, John, has already been informed of what happened. John is a kind manager, who always listens to the needs of his employees. For example, during the annual review, Linda was able to voice concerns over the protocol for accidents and injuries in the field after a company vehicle went off the road in the snow. John encouraged Linda to work with her team to develop a better plan and offered to help change the current protocols. Linda thinks John is a very kind manager and Sam agrees.

John approaches the two and they discuss what happened. "I talked to the food delivery company, heard the viewpoint of woman you were delivering to, and told them we will no longer be delivering for them, my team and our clients are more important, we will find another opportunity for participants" John said.

As they all begin to leave for the night, Linda pulls John aside to say "Hey, I think Sam did a good job handling the situation today, he might just need a bit more conflict training."

"I think you both did a good job today and I told corporate that too, I won't apologize for you guys defending yourselves, but I will take that into account during our monthly training refresh and try to incorporate more training for everyone" John replied, and they both left.

An Unexpected Meeting

Sam often frequents a small cafe with close friends near Living Life on weekends. As the friends sip their coffee and chat about work, Linda comes into the shop unnoticed to order coffee on her way to the grocery store as the group chats.

"How has work been Hailey?" Alex asks.

"It's been a little hectic, cutbacks are really affecting everyone, we don't have enough staff for the night shift, so I had to go into the hospital on my day off," she bemoaned.

"That's awful, it's already so rare we get to hang out. You're so amazing working that many hours," Peter replied.

"Yeah, I just wish I had more time to myself, I had to cancel my last counseling session!"

"Oh no! You need to make sure you are taking care of yourself, work comes second," Alex replied.

Sam is zoning out thinking about what happened at the food delivery the other day and how they could have handled it better while the conversation is going on. "If only I had spoken up sooner or noticed the woman walk out the door" they think.

"Speaking of taking care of yourself, when is your surgery, Sam?" asked Alex. Linda notices Sam and begins to approach the group. Sam continues to stare into the distance. Peter notices Linda approach and becomes noticeably quieter.

"Hello, earth to Sam, are you even listening?" Alex says to the group. Linda reaches the group, standing directly behind Sam with her hands on their seat

Sam snaps out of their daze and looks at Alex. "When is your surgery?" Alex repeats.

"Surgery? What surgery?" Linda asks, startling the group with her seeming intrusion as Sam's friends don't know who Linda is and wonder why she is so close. "Are you okay? Are you going to be out of work, Dear?"

"Oh, umm, Hi Linda" Sam timidly says. Although he is used to them being close to one another, her presence outside of work catches him off guard. "I am having top surgery[2] later this year, John already knows, but it won't be until December."

"Oh okay, I don't know what that is, is it serious, are you okay?" Linda asks with concern.

"Yes, I am fine" Sam replies, feeling Linda right behind them.

They part ways, Sam returns to their conversation and Linda grabs her coffee and heads to the grocery store.

As Linda walks away, Hailey asks Sam with a confused look on her face, "Who was that and why was she standing on top of you asking about your personal business?"

Later that night Linda hops online to do some research about the surgery Sam is having. That's when she learns top surgery is performed, often on transgender individuals, for both physical and psychological reasons. She learns it may help to deal with gender dysphoria, or the discomfort felt by those whose gender identity is different than their assigned sex at birth. Linda is overwhelmed by all the information and realizes that the surgery must mean Sam is transgender and didn't feel comfortable enough to share this with her. Linda feels betrayed by not knowing such important information about someone she thought was her friend.

Changes at Work

The next day at work, Linda is not sure how to act around Sam, and gives them the cold shoulder. Sam is unsure what they did wrong and asks to talk to John about it. He is aware of Sam's transition, as they have had to take time off for medical appointments. When Sam told John, they said to him "I just want to be treated fairly. I need to be able to take time off for medical appointments. I don't want to tell everyone else because I don't want to be treated differently. I want to be treated like myself, for who I am as a person." John is accepting of the change and agrees to keep Sam's situation private until Sam decides to share it with their co-workers.

"Hey Sam, what's up?" John asks.

"Linda hasn't really said a word to me all day" Sam says. "I don't really know what is going on, can you check in on her? I'm worried I've done something wrong."

"Sure thing, I'll look into it" John says, thinking about what Sam said when they first met. "I hope there is nothing bad happening between those two, they always got along before" he thinks to himself.

Sam heads back to their office and spends the day thinking about what could have happened. They think about when they first met Linda and they were unsure of how to talk to her. Sam only knew Linda was older and had much more experience than they did. Then, the two workers got to know a bit more about each other. Linda told Sam about her dog and Sam told Linda about their cat. They learned they both liked crochet and enjoyed helping people with disabilities. Sam thought they knew Linda, but now they had no idea why they were now receiving the cold shoulder.

Later that day John approaches Linda to ask about Sam's concerns. "Hey Linda, what's going on today? Sam said you haven't said much to him today. Tell me what's going on."

"I'm just not feeling it today, Sam must be overreacting" Linda replies.

"You know we value open and honest communication here. Tell me when you feel able and let me know if any changes need to be made, I want you both to be comfortable."

"Thanks John, I'll let you know, you've always been supportive of me."

"I try my best to be supportive of all our employees, but I can only help when help is wanted. Speaking of which, your idea to incorporate more conflict training has been submitted for approval. We will have a weeklong conflict training program in the new year." John expressed with pride. "Thank you for all your hard work."

As Linda dismisses John's worries, saying Sam is just overreacting, John begins to worry about the pairing of the two friends on future outings. The rest of the week continues with Linda giving Sam the cold shoulder. Sam becomes increasingly frustrated and anxious, not knowing what they did wrong. They approach John again and he talks to Linda receiving the same response from her. He begins to send them on community tasks separately. Months go by and Sam's surgery approaches.

Sam thinks about how to talk to Linda, becoming increasingly anxious and depressed. "These past few months have been miserable. I am alone most of the time and don't get invited to group activities. I sit alone at lunch and I'm just plain miserable! I wish Linda would talk to me again. Maybe I should find another Job…"

Sam approached Linda before leaving for two weeks. "Hey Linda, I just wanted to let you know I'm having surgery next week, I'll be out for about two weeks, but I'm still the 'me' you know, I hope you are still the same person I know you are," Sam said. "I hope you have a great holiday vacation." Sam walks out the main office door, wondering what will happen when and if they get back.

CASE ANALYSIS AND DISCUSSION

Social penetration theory, expectancy violations theory, and transgender standpoint epistemology can all be used to analyze the case. To begin, social penetration theory can be applied to explain the development of the relationships among the main characters. Sam experiences different levels of self-disclosure when talking to Linda and they progress through the different stages of the social penetration process together. When Sam and Linda first meet, they begin to disclose information to each other. They disclose information about their age, their likes, and their work. As they progress in their relationship, they disclose more information and move into a new stage of the social penetration process, which is evident in the depth of their disclosures. Sam reveals personal information about their fears and values. The exploratory affective exchange stage of the social penetration process involves the disclosure of personality (West & Turner, 2017). At the same time Linda discloses that she also had trouble negotiating difficult situations when she started the job. She says, "I was also very unsure of what to do in those situations when I first started." When Linda and Sam both share these personal fears, they are engaging in reciprocity (i.e., parallel disclosures). These disclosures facilitate the movement of Linda and Sam's relationship into the effective exchange stage. As Linda and Sam's relationship progresses, more examples of disclosure emerge. Linda reveals close personal information about her family, more close and personal information than she would disclose to someone if they were in the orientation stage. During the affective exchange stage, increased commitment to relational partners emerges and personal idioms may be expressed (West & Turner, 2017). Linda uses the term "Dear" to refer to Sam which is a personal idiom. In addition, the concern Linda has for Sam when first hearing about their surgery is a sign of a deeper relationship. As posited by social penetration theory the relationship between Linda and Sam progresses from non-intimate to more intimate as the two disclose and learn additional information about each other.

In addition, the onion analogy of social penetration theory can be applied to the disclosures in Sam and Linda's case. The onion starts at the outermost layer as the visible disclosures such as gender and age. Sam and Linda first learn about their relative age and outward facing gender when they first meet but, one of the outermost layers, gender, is not as visible as Linda may have thought. Evident in Jones' (2020) study, trans individuals often "pass" as a more privileged identity based on the dominate hegemonic norms. Sam presents themselves differently outside of work then at work. This difference in the self-presentation leads to the start of de-penetration of the relationship. Linda feels betrayed by the lack of disclosure and Sam doesn't know what is going on. As suggested by transgender standpoint epistemology, a transgender employee may try to "pass" at work due to traditional rules present in an organization (Jones, 2020). Although John attempts to foster an open workplace, Sam feels the need to conform to the cis normative expectations developed by the broader society.

Expectancy violations theory posits that the behaviors of individuals and expectations of norms are developed through individual, relational, and contextual factors (Burgoon & Hale, 1988). In the case of Sam and Linda, individual factors such as gender have influenced their expectancies and the violation of those expectancies.

Violations lie on a spectrum from low level violations such as rudeness, to more high-level violations such as lies and aggression (Niehuis et al., 2019). Linda has developed an understanding of Sam's gender and when those expectations are violated Linda sees this as a negative violation, specifically a lie. To Linda, this is a serious violation. As pointed out by Niehuis and colleagues (2019) "severe expectancy violations, even coming from a high-reward-value partner, would likely have an adverse impact on the aggrieved partner's impressions of the violator and of the relationship" (p. 468). This violation causes Linda to act out by ignoring Sam. The threat threshold of Linda for this violation would be relatively low because she immediately shunned Sam. It can be surmised that Linda holds lies as a large offence because of her reaction.

Furthermore, proxemics are exemplified in the case when Linda approaches Sam at the cafe. On one hand, Sam is comfortable with Linda standing right behind their seat – in the personal space zone – as the two are relatively friendly co-workers. On the other hand, though, Linda's presence in Sam's personal space outside of the work context is a bit unsettling (although not a violation). Sam's friends are confused by Linda's proximity to them, however, given that they see her as a stranger who is standing too close to their conversation.

Transgender standpoint epistemology and related standpoint theories can be used to understand Sam's negotiations of work and life in the case. First, Sam is constantly passing at work as they conceal their transgender status. Passing is an act in which individuals of a non-dominant group conceals their membership and blends in with dominant group members (Jones, 2020). Passing is evident in the way that Sam concealed their transgender identity from Linda by asking John not to tell anyone. in addition, the knowledge Sam has their own transgender identity and its relation to their work guides their decisions. according to standpoint theory knowledge is situated and therefore what Sam knows is dependent on their identity (Toole, 2021). what Linda knows is dependent on their own identity as a heterosexual female. The ideas they both share are created and reinforced by broader societal politics (Jones, 2020). key features of standpoint theories can be seen throughout the case.

The power structure can be seen in the way Sam conceals their identity. based on the way society views transgender individuals Sam feels as though their identity must be concealed at work because if the existing power structure. this is a key idea in feminist standpoint theory noting that those power relations exist and create a division between them (Wood, 2005). the second key understanding is that individuals from the lower power structure tend to see things more accurately because those in the more dominant structure want to keep the power society has given them (Woods, 2005). In this case Linda is experiencing conflicting thoughts about her place in society as her knowledge has changed to understand more about Sam and their viewpoint. outsider within can be seen in the case when Sam is working with Linda and John. the concept involves a member of the non-dominant group being able to have access to the privileged group (Woods, 2005). Sam is able to see how Linda and John worked together and how they're power structure worked. the negotiation of Sam's identity is seen from a standpoint perspective as they navigate work and experiencing work relations outside of work. Sam performs a privileged identity at work relying on the lack of rules and resources available to employees who identify as transgender (Jones., 2020). Understanding how Sam navigates work relationships helps to understand how individuals who identify as transgender negotiate the workplace and societal pressures.

As described at the outset of this chapter, transgender individuals face a lack of protections when it comes to negotiating their identities in the workplace and can incur negative consequences when these negotiations go poorly (e.g., depression, anxiety). The use of social penetration theory, expectancy violations theory, and transgender standpoint epistemology provides insight into how and why Sam, Linda, and the others interact in particular ways. This analysis helps us take an important step toward understanding the experiences transgender individuals in the workplace.

DISCUSSION QUESTIONS

1. Have you ever experienced and/or witnessed the development of a close relationship in the workplace? If so, explain how social penetration theory and/or expectancy violations theory can be used to explain the process using key terms.
2. What stage of the social penetration process are Linda and Sam in at the beginning and end of the case?
3. What expectations were violated in the case?
4. What does the future look like for John and Linda?
5. What "layers of the onion" are disclosed throughout the case?
6. How might you handle identity negotiations in the workplace? For example, are there aspects of who you are that you may be (un)comfortable disclosing to everyone in your workplace? How do you think you would respond to certain types of identity disclosures from co-workers (e.g., Sam's identity as in the case)?

REFERENCES

Altman, I., & Taylor, D. A. (1973). *Social penetration: The development of interpersonal relationships*. Holt, Reinhart, and Winston.

Burgoon, J. K. (2016). Expectancy violations theory. In C. R. Berger & M. E. Roloff (Eds.), *The international encyclopedia of interpersonal communication* (pp. 1–9). Wiley. doi:10.1002/9781118540190.wbeic102

Burgoon, J. K., & Hale, J. L. (1988). Nonverbal expectancy violations: Model elaboration and application to immediacy behaviors. *Communication Monographs, 55*(1), 58–79. doi:10.1080/03637758809376158

Carpenter, A., & Greene, K. (2016). Social penetration theory. In C. R. Berger & M. E. Roloff (Eds.), *The international encyclopedia of interpersonal communication* (pp. 1–5). Wiley. doi:10.1002/9781118540190.wbeic160

Dixon, & Dougherty, D. S. (2014). A language convergence/meaning divergence analysis exploring how LGBTQ and single employees manage traditional family expectations in the workplace. *Journal of Applied Communication Research, 42*(1), 1–19. doi:10.1080/00909882.2013.847275

Federal Bureau of Investigation. (n.d.). *Hate Crime in the United States Incident Analysis*. CDE: Hate Crime. Retrieved February 20, 2022, from https://crime-data-explorer.fr.cloud.gov/pages/explorer/crime/hate-crime

Gibbs, J., Ellison, N., & Heino, R. (2006). Self-Presentation in online personals: The role of anticipated future interaction, self-disclosure, and perceived success in internet dating. *Communication Research, 33*(2), 152–177. doi:10.1177/0093650205285368

Johnson, D. I., & Lewis, N. (2010). Perceptions of swearing in the work setting: An Expectancy Violations Theory perspective. *Communication Reports, 23*(2), 106–118. doi:10.1080/08934215.2010.511401

Jones. (2020). Negotiating transgender identity at work: A movement to theorize a transgender standpoint epistemology. *Management Communication Quarterly, 34*(2), 251–278. doi:10.1177/0893318919898170

Mason, A. J., & Carr, C. T. (2021). Toward a theoretical framework of relational maintenance in computer-mediated communication. *Communication Theory*, qtaa035. Advance online publication. doi:10.1093/ct/qtaa035

McBride, M. C., & Bergen, K. M. (2015). Work spouses: Defining and understanding a "new" relationship. *Communication Studies, 66*(5), 487–508. doi:10.1080/10510974.2015.1029640

Niehuis, R., Reifman, A., & Oldham, C. R. (2019). Effects of relational transgressions on idealization of and disillusionment with one's romantic partner: A three-wave longitudinal study. *Personal Relationships*, *26*(3), 466–489. doi:10.1111/pere.12287

Pennington. (2020). An examination of relational maintenance and dissolution through social networking sites. *Computers in Human Behavior, 105*. doi:10.1016/j.chb.2019.106196

Taylor. (1968). The development of interpersonal relationships: Social penetration processes. *The Journal of Social Psychology*, *75*(1), 79–90. doi:10.1080/00224545.1968.9712476

Toole. (2021). Recent work in standpoint epistemology. *Analysis*, *81*(2), 338–350. doi:10.1093/analys/anab026

Top surgery. (n.d.). In *Merriam-Webster.com Dictionary*. Merriam-Webster. https://www.merriam-webster.com/dictionary/top%20surgery

U.S. Commission on Civil Rights. (2017, November 29). *Working for Inclusion: Time for Congress to Enact Federal Legislation to Address Workplace Discrimination against Lesbian, Gay, Bisexual, and Transgender Americans*. Retrieved February 20, 2022, from https://www.usccr.gov/reports/2017/working-inclusion-time-congress-enact-federal-legislation-address-workplace

West, R. L., & Turner, L. H. (2017). *Introducing communication theory: Analysis and Application* (6th ed.). McGraw-Hill.

Wood, J. T. (2005). Feminist Standpoint Theory and Muted Group Theory: Commonalities and Divergences. *Women & Language*, *28*(2), 61–64.

KEY TERMS AND DEFINITIONS

Expectancy Violations Theory: A communication theory focused on the behaviors of individuals and expectations of norms situated within interactions that violate communication norms and rules (Burgoon & Hale, 1988).

Social Penetration Theory: A communication theory positing the trajectory of interpersonal relationships evolving in a path like structure, progressing from superficial to intimate through the use of self-disclosure (West & Turner, 2017).

ENDNOTES

1 Passing can be defined as the performance of "a privileged identity to mask a nonprivileged identity through concealment or discretion, all the while being vigilant about situational markers of "real" identity" (Clair et al., 2002, as cited in Jones, 2020, p 262).

2 Top Surgery is defined as "a type of gender confirmation surgery in which a person's breasts are removed or augmented to match their gender identity" (Merriam-Webster.com Dictionary).

Chapter 10
Workplace Resilience During Cancer Treatment:
An Exploration of Workplace Communication Processes That Lead to Resilience for Female Employees

Donna M. Elkins
https://orcid.org/0000-0002-6266-7332
Spalding University, USA

EXECUTIVE SUMMARY

This case illustrates the communication processes involved in developing resilience when facing cancer diagnosis and treatment in the workplace. Beyond just the initial decision about whether to share the news of cancer, individuals enact ongoing communication behaviors that may enhance or detract from their ability to build resilience when going through this level of hardship, loss, and trauma. The case describes communication choices made and the dialectics faced by two women during breast cancer treatment in two different workplaces. The five communication processes of Patrice Buzzanell's communication theory of resilience are described in some detail and applied to these cases. The goal is for managers and others in workplace settings to gain a better understanding of ways to communicate that help someone going through a hardship, loss, or trauma build higher resilience and to better understand the communal nature of resilience in organizational settings.

DOI: 10.4018/978-1-6684-3753-7.ch010

INTRODUCTION

Facing a cancer diagnosis introduces a significant disruption in the life of patients and those who know them. Couple that diagnosis and the prescribed treatment with a desire or need to continue working throughout, and the stress level rises. This experience often taxes or exceeds any individual's resources. Cancer patients must manage complicated health and treatment information, adapt to changes in body and lifestyle, and figure out how to talk about their cancer with others. When someone is continuing work during this cancer experience, not only must that individual balance the need to seek support and share personal information with those surrounding, but others are also called upon to make decisions about how to talk to the cancer patient (Elkins, 2020; Venetis et al., 2020). The decisions and behaviors of those involved can result in added stress or lessened stress on the individual. This case study intends to explore experiences of two female breast cancer patients in different workplaces to better understand the communication processes that developed their resilience.

Resilience has been the focus of research across multiple disciplines and has been generally viewed as a process of creatively adapting to disruptions and losses in a way that stimulates empowerment to achieve productive outcomes despite adverse circumstances (Buzzanell, 2010). The communication theory of resilience seeks to situate resilience in the face of disruption and hardship not as an individual trait but as a process that is constructed through communication that results in "co-crafting productive narratives, identities, emotions, and networks that enable reintegration and/or transformation after change" (Agarwal, et al. p. 411). The five specific communication processes identified in the theory as building resilience are: (1) crafting normalcy, (2) affirming identity anchors, (3) maintaining and using communication networks, (4) putting alternative logics to work, and (5) legitimizing negative feelings while foregrounding productive action (Buzzanell, 2010).

Concepts or Theories

To properly apply the theory of resilience to communication processes for cancer patients in the workplace, first an explanation of the role of social support and communal coping is necessary.

Social Support and Communal Coping

Social support has been viewed as an interpersonal communication process that ameliorates the harmful effects of stress on an individual experiencing various hardships (Albrecht & Goldsmith, 2003). Social support sees the hardship as a shared problem but maintains management of that problem is delegated to or owned by one specific individual who seeks help from others (Afifi et al., 2006). Social support has been defined specifically as "functions performed for an individual by significant others in various networks, such as family members, friends, and co-workers" (Kim et al., 2013, p. 213).

Early scholarship around the concept of social support focused on efforts to categorize and explain various supportive efforts. James House identified four types of social support: emotional, appraisal, informational, and instrumental (as cited in Braithwaite et al., 1999). Later, House's types were modified into five types falling into two categories (Cutrona & Suhr, 1992). Informational and tangible support described as practical assistance, were categorized as *action-facilitating support* which assists the stressed individual in coping with or eliminating the causes of distress. Esteem, emotional, and social network support were categorized as *nurturant support*, which has as its goal comforting or consoling (Cutrona & Suhr, 1992). Researchers have used typologies of social support to examine the role of support groups for illnesses such as irritable bowel syndrome (Coulson 2005), breast cancer (Wright 2002; Den Oudsten et al., 2010) and lung cancer (Sjolander and Boterö, 2008) and in natural disasters such as earthquakes and floods (Richardson & Maninger, 2016).

Even though social support has been shown in many studies to meet a foundational health need in patients with different types of illnesses (Albrecht et al., 1994; Coulson, 2005; Cutrona & Suhr, 1992; Wright 2002; Zimmermann & Applegate, 1994), support from others is not an unqualified good. Individuals who receive more support have also reported higher levels of stress, distress, conflict, and perceived criticism (Albrecht et al., 1994; Faw, 2014; Ray & Veluscek, 2017). Those who are recipients of support may be plagued by anxiety and uncertainty, finding support to be unhelpful or face threatening. Disaster survivors may perceive that those offering social support, especially close friends or family who are not sharing in the hardships, do not truly understand their suffering (Afifi et al., 2006). They may feel that requesting or receiving support is a sign of weakness or incompetence, that they are under an obligation as overdependent and unable to reciprocate if they receive support, or that they have lost their privacy and that the supporter is overinvolved (Albrecht et al., 1994). Wright (2002) found that individual coping styles, perceptions of supporters, and appraisals of supportive behaviors factored into assessments of support particularly for breast cancer patients.

For instance, though cancer patients benefit from seeking support from communication networks they have established there can be a great deal of effort associated with maintaining these networks (Buzzanell, 2010). Cancer patients particularly have stated that managing the informational needs of close others sometimes interfered with their own ability to cope and characterized communication with others as work because they had to balance meeting others' desire for information with avoiding sharing too much or upsetting others (Elkins, 2020; Lillie et al., 2018) In some cases, avoiding topics, not talking about them was beneficial for patients (Elkins, 2020; Lillie et al., 2018).

The definition of social support and focus on defining discrete supportive actions does not convey the various interpersonal, informational, or emotional dimensions experienced when dealing with hardships and so more recently scholars have shifted to a concept of communal coping to more accurately describe the process of assisting others (Afifi et al., 2006). Communal coping is a situation in which group members see the stressor on one individual as a shared stressor to be acted upon collectively (Afifi et al., 2006). Research has focused on the shifted view of a stressor or hardship suffered by one individual being a shared problem, how survivors share their feelings with others as a form of coping, the material and informational assistance needed to cope with stressful problems, and the shared narratives resulting from this communal coping response (Richardson & Maninger, 2016). This developing view of dealing with hardship, trauma, and loss as a community rather than solely an individual leads into seeing resilience as a process of interaction with others rather than an individual trait.

Communication and Resilience

Resilience has been studied from a variety of different scholarly perspectives. Resilience "reflects an ability to maintain a stable equilibrium" in the face of trauma, loss, or hardship (Bonanno, 2004, p. 20). Resilience has also been defined as "the process of reintegrating from disruptions in life" (Richardson, 2002, p. 309). Resilience is often discussed in terms of protective factors that foster the development of continued or restored healthy levels of psychological and physical function (Bonanno, 2004). Resilience scholarship has focused in three waves: identification of internal and external factors of survivors; processes whereby people attain these qualities; and an innate motivational or spiritual force mobilizing increased energy toward recovery (Richardson, 2002). Much of what psychology knows about how individuals cope with trauma, loss, or hardship is based on those who have sought out treatment or exhibited dysfunctional abilities, therefore, early scholars had not realized how common resilience is and the multiple pathways individuals might take to develop resilience (Bonanno, 2004). From a communication perspective, resilience can be conceptualized as the "effective adjustment to hardship over time through interaction with others" (Lillie et al., 2018, 1516).

In contrast to the waves of resilience study in psychology, communicative theorizing about resilience resides not in the individual but in messages, discourse, and narrative (Buzzanell, 2010). The communication theory of resilience proports that human resilience is "constituted in and through communicative processes that enhance people's abilities to create new normalcies" (Buzzanell, 2010, p. 9).This means resilience is "an ongoing dynamic activated when humans experience distress and disaster" (Buzzanell, 2017, p. 103). Resilience is cultivated and grown through relationships, rituals, shared stories, messages, symbolic gestures, and spending time together. The theory argues that individuals build and maintain resilience through "continuous reintegration of self and others in ways that involve both accepting reality pragmatically and making creative adjustments to adapt to, and potentially change, circumstances" (Agarwal & Buzzanell, p. 412).

The communication theory of resilience situates resilience in interpersonal, family, organizational, health, and mediated communication contexts and argues that our resilience grows over the course of our lives as we take in and make sense of new information. Rather than looking at an inability to 'bounce back' from an individual deficit approach, the theory recognizes that there are "both benefits and costs for the particular ways in which resilience is constituted" (Buzzanell, 2017, p. 99). Rather than conceptualizing communication as a coping strategy engaged by an individual, the theory proposes that resilience is itself grounded in communication (Chernichky-Karcher et al., 2018). Because of its focus on process and relationship, the theory can be used to interpret and explain reactions to hardship, loss, and trauma in work, family, and health settings. "In short, the communication theory of resilience leverages the power of stories, relationships, and creativity, not only to help people survive but (hopefully) to construct a better world" (Buzzanell, 2017, p. 98).

Through research designed to provide exemplars and explicate resilience, the theory has developed five communication processes fundamental to building resilience: (1) crafting normalcy, (2) affirming identity anchors, (3) maintaining and using communication networks, (4) putting alternative logics to work, and (5) legitimizing negative feelings while foregrounding productive action (Buzzanell, 2010). Later research proposes adding a sixth process, that of maintaining dialectics (Wieland, 2020). In order for individuals to build resilience, they must maintain interplay between several opposing discourses and hold conflicting emotions and interpretations in tension. It is a process that is marked by struggle to maintain, rather than deny contradictory experiences, messages, emotions, and interpretations (Wieland, 2020). These processes illuminate how resilience is "developed, shaped or framed, sustained, and grown over the lifespans of individuals, relationships, families, organizations, communities, and nations (Buzzanell & Houston, 2018). The processes are embedded in the everyday life and moments of hardship and loss, as well as extraordinary disruptions of trauma.

It is important to further explain each of the five processes in the communication theory of resilience before applying the theory to cases. First is crafting normalcy, which includes efforts to regain a sense of the lifestyle and routine that existed before the disruption (Buzzanell, 2010). Returning to daily activities, even if modified, is integral in regaining a sense of normalcy following a cancer diagnosis (Walker, Szanton, & Wenzel, 2015). The process of crafting normalcy is integral to cancer survivors' resilience because of the many challenges to daily functioning they face including disruption to routines due to physical challenges and in terms of appearance (Lillie et al., 2018). In research with families, both the discourse and the performance that enabled people to maintain or recover the mundane regularities of life created normalcy. New normalcies developed through talk and maintenance of rituals (Buzzanell, 2010). Following treatment, some couples struggled with discordant desires for returning to a pre-cancer normalcy or continuing the normal the couple had established after diagnosis (Lillie et al., 2018).

Second is the communication process of affirming identity anchors. An identity anchor is defined as a "relatively enduring cluster of identity discourses upon which individuals and their familial, collegial, and/or community members rely when explaining who they are for themselves and in relation to others" (Buzzanell, 2010, p. 4). Affirming identity anchors acknowledges that stressors can alter individuals' sense of self and that interaction with others can be a means of regaining and maintaining a sense of self that existed before the disruption (Buzzanell, 2010). As noted in the discussion of social support, cancer patients have reported rejecting assistance from friends, family members and others in an effort to maintain face and communicate an identity as a well and healthy person (Venetis et al., 2020). Cancer patients report challenges integrating pre-cancer identities with new, post-cancer identities that may often involve being less productive and weaker (Lillie et al., 2018).

The third process identified in the communication theory of resilience is that of maintaining and using communication networks. Using communication networks includes relying on established connections with colleagues, friends, and family to recover from a disruption or stressor. The process of maintaining and using communication networks involves seeking support from these established networks and putting forth the work required to maintain them, particularly through communication that is beneficial (Buzzanell, 2010). Among cancer patients, this process hinges on their willingness to speak with others about their experience, not only the impact it is having on them as an individual but also the impact on others around them (Elkins, 2020; Venetis et al., 2020). However, cancer patients have stated that it interferes with their own ability to cope when they must also manage the informational needs of sharing personal and continual updates with others (Elkins, 2020). Sharing of cancer information has been characterized as 'work,' because the responsibility to balance meeting others' information needs with avoiding upsetting them is placed on the cancer patient creating a dialectical tension of openness and privacy. In some cases, maintaining privacy and not sharing openly was more beneficial for patients (Lillie et al., 2018).

The fourth communication process identified in the communication theory of resilience is putting alternative logics to work. This process involves seemingly contradictory ways of viewing hardship that embrace its negative nature and reframe the situation (Buzzanell, 2010; Lillie et al., 2018). For example, couples managing lung cancer described in one study how talking together about being lucky and more fortunate than other cancer patients served to bolster their relational quality (Venetis et al., 2020) and those going through natural disasters took comfort from feeling they were "in the same boat" as others around them (Richardson & Maninger, 2016, p. 112).

The final communication process in the communication theory of resilience is legitimizing negative feelings while foregrounding productive action. This process involves recognizing that although negative emotion is warranted, it is unproductive (Buzzanell, 2010). Therefore, instead of focusing on negativity, individuals and those around them center on positive aspects of their situation and on making progress. Even when the emphasis is the foregrounding of productive action, there must still be acknowledgement that negative feelings are justified (Lillie et al., 2018). This process can create tension for couples dealing with cancer diagnosis. One study found that during treatment, couples worked to balance the desire to be fully open with the desire to be positive in their communication with one another (Lillie et al., 2018). Breast cancer survivors in this study also acknowledged obstacles to managing cancer but talked about using those obstacles to be strategic in promoting other aspects of family life such as timing chemotherapy around children's schedules (Lillie et al., 2018).

Resilience for Cancer Patients in the Workplace

The communication theory of resilience has been applied in a variety of contexts including couples, families, communities, nationally, and in organizations (Buzzanell & Houston, 2018). However, most of the specific findings have been particular to the context of family and partner communication (Afifi et al., 2006; Bonanno, 2004; Buzzanell, 2010; Chernichky-Karcher et al., 2019; Lillie et al., 2018; Lucas & Buzzanell, 2012; Venetis et al., 2020). Explications of how the theory applies in workplace interactions and among co-workers has been far less prevalent (Wieland, 2020) and application specifically with cancer patients (Chernichky-Karcher et al., 2019; Lillie et al., 2018) has just begun. The cases of two women dealing with cancer diagnosis and treatment in the workplace explored here are a contribution to connecting resilience for health conditions specifically in workplace settings.

CASE STUDY

Case #1 – Fran

Fran, a white woman and an Associate Professor in the College of Education at a small private university, was diagnosed with breast cancer in the same year she turned 60. Her initial reaction was not to tell anybody but her husband.

I was just trying to get through," she said, "but eventually I had to email colleagues and tell them because I had to be out for surgery and there was no way to hide it. They wanted to get me gifts and all of that, but I didn't want anything. I didn't want any big events...I didn't want to tell anyone or have anyone feel sorry for me...I don't need people to feel sorry for me. I don't need people crying for me. I don't even think I cried. I don't even think I cried myself.

After having the surgery, her perspective about talking changed and she began to try to advocate vocally for others who were going through radiation treatment with her healthcare providers. For instance, she was offended that there was not clearer direction about how to best apply preventative medication during her radiation. She was handed a cream to help with radiation burns but not given directions for how to use it.

Nobody told me to put cream all the way around on my back. I told my doctor and the nurse about that. They didn't tell me when or where to put it. I have an advanced degree and I didn't know to put this cream all the way under my arm and around on my back. I told them they need to write that down for people, because if I can't figure that out, I know others can't.

However, Fran never admitted to co-workers or others that she was experiencing burns under her arm and around her back during her treatments. She was determined not to show weakness in her work even though co-workers were cognizant of her situation. In fact, she was also offended and harmed by colleagues trying to assist her and make decisions about her work during this time.

People at work wanted to lighten my load and they tried to force me to take time off. I came back from being out a week for the surgery and they had decided for me that I couldn't do extra work over the summer like I had planned. I need the extra money to pay my $4,000 deductible. So, I called [my supervisor] and told her I could work through, but she said, "No, we already decided this for you." I was mad. I didn't want to be sitting home thinking about the radiation, I wanted *to work…When you come back from surgery, all the people think you're dying. I mean I'm glad they were worried about me and thinking about me, but I didn't want them not to let me work. I think they were more concerned that I wouldn't be able to come back at all…My boss kept telling me to take time off and take care of myself. I think they were worried that if I didn't come back no one else does what I do.*

Fran did eventually convince her supervisor to let her do part of the summer work she had intended to do.

Since her experience with breast cancer, Fran has become an outspoken proponent with every woman she meets for the 3D mammogram. She brings it up in elevators and before meetings, anytime she has opportunity to speak to another woman. She never looked to support groups during her time battling cancer and so she believes speaking to others one-on-one is the best way to reach them. She has also started to live life with more gusto and talks about her change in perspective on the role of her job in her life and the constant fear of cancer recurring. "I still lead a good life," Fran said. "This fall I'm going to Africa. People ask if I'm not afraid, but I'm not. I'm living my life. That is a difference. I do my job, but I take more time for myself. I do the things I want to do. I'm better at taking care of myself."

Case #2 – Tess

Tess, a white 52-year-old Media Writer who works for a large Fortune 500 restaurant corporation, was diagnosed with breast cancer when she was between jobs. She had worked primarily part-time and as a freelance writer leading up to her diagnosis. Just as she found out about the cancer in her body, she also got a full-time job offer and she had no hesitancy telling everyone the news.

Basically, I told everyone right after my diagnosis because that's how I am. My current employer called me two days after my diagnosis to talk with me about a full-time job. I knew legally I didn't have to tell them, but I felt like I had to tell them. I don't know why I said it, but the first thing I said was that I wanted the job and that I could do it despite the treatments and doctor's appointments I would be having. I didn't know if I could of course, but from somewhere I just expressed this confidence.

After discussing this with her new supervisor, the company decided to hire her in a full-time contract position to see if she could do the work. It was not easy to balance.

I had to leave early my first day of work to go to my first oncology appointment. The person who hired me said they hadn't told the team and it was completely up to me what I shared. They had a welcome lunch for me, and I told them all. I couldn't figure out any other way to do it. I didn't want to waste time trying to hide anything. Having people know and talking about it helped. I threw up in the trash can at my desk one day for example. There are things you just can't hide.

Another outlet for Tess to process her experience was to engage in writing poetry and using her normal proclivity to share through words. She was in treatment for ten months and during that time she found herself compelled to write even though she didn't want to. As a writer and reader, she had looked for something to read about cancer she said and found that there was a real shortage.

It was either very morbid or this 'rah rah' stuff. That stuff made me angry… I didn't want to write about it or think about it or be there at all. I wanted to disengage from it. But even when I couldn't raise my head, I would think about it and these phrases would come to me and all I had was a pen and a piece of paper, but I had to write them. Even though I didn't want to, I had to write them down.

She wanted her writing to be real and was very gratified to get attention for her work. She gave a reading with two other poets, and she said her line to sign books afterwards was the longest. "Some area university professors had required their students to come so it was a young audience and afterward I had the longest line, they wanted to talk to me and so many of them said they weren't used to hearing people talking about cancer the way I did."

Tess had to be open about her cancer and needs in part because she relied on friends as her main support. They drove her to chemo and brought her food every day. She had so many chemo appointments that after the first 6 or 7 she didn't want people to sit with her for the three hours they took, so they would just drive her and pick her up. To provide updates on her condition, she also relied on friends to spread the word, "I didn't post on Facebook or anything, I would usually tell only one person and let them share it or send group emails. I had three books come out during this time so I would send group emails with an update and information about the book."

She also found that she ended friendship during this time despite her need for others.

People would call and want me to call them back. I sometimes couldn't even get out of bed and go the ten steps to get in my tub, I couldn't be bothered to call these people I hardly knew back. I would write people off because I just couldn't be bothered…

Say what you want to do and just do it. Don't ask me to call you if I need something. No one likes to ask for help.

She told the story of when she had no food in the house and one friend called and said, "I'm going to the grocery, do you need anything?" Tess said no even though she really did, and the friend said that she was going anyway and bringing her food so she could either tell her what she wanted, or her friend would just try to guess want she wanted and bring it. Tess was clear that this was the kind of support she valued.

Tess also shared frustration with lack of clear information about health procedures and a spirit of advocating for herself. She reached the five-year mark taking inhibitor drugs and expected to be taken off them when she went to her next doctor's appointment. The drugs cause pain and muscle issues and affected her mobility so she was looking forward to not taking them any longer. However, her oncologist cited a recent study that said there were benefits for taking the inhibitors for ten years after treatment rather than just five years. She was frustrated that her doctor did not give her any further information even though she asked, so she decided to go through the trouble of getting a second opinion. The second doctor told her about a genetic test to tell if her tumor was one that was high or low risk for recurrence. Even though she had to pay for the expensive test out-of-pocket Tess said it was worth it to be told that her type of cancer is very low risk for recurrence so she could go off the drug and be less worried about recurrence. "It was a huge weight off," she said because she discontinued the drugs right away, the side effects lessened quickly, and she began to have more stamina at work.

However, she pointed out that her thanks for being one of those who did not have high risk of recurrence was dampened right after she got the news by the death of a close friend from breast cancer and seeing another friend who had breast cancer and was in "terrible" physical condition.

I would like my time talking and thinking about this [breast cancer] to diminish more…I just got back this tremendous news, this big deal, that the genetic testing shows I have a low chance of recurrence and I can go off of the drug. I would like to post that on Facebook and tell everyone about it, but my friend just died from breast cancer this week. It would be in poor taste for me to brag about it on Facebook right now so I'm keeping the news kind of quiet…I just keep thinking about those people who get the message from this test that they are likely to have a recurrence. I told friends at work that if I got back bad test results, I would have to go 'under' for a while, but I realize there are people out there who are getting that message.

CASE ANALYSIS AND DISCUSSION

The cases presented here are designed to provide two examples of how resilience can be developed, shaped, framed, sustained, and grown in the experiences of women who work through a diagnosis and treatment for breast cancer. When their stories are examined through a communication lens, evidence of the communication processes these women used or did not use to develop resilience in the face of this hardship become clear. There are "multiple layers in resilience processes, overlapping and focusing on some processes more so than others" (Buzzanell & Houston, 2018, p. 2) so in each case the processes may be difficult to distinguish clearly from one another. The goal of examining individual cases is not to attach the adjective resilient to a person, network, or organization because "such descriptors do not necessarily mean that everyone can mobilize discursive, interactive, and (network) structural and material resources for resilience in a given moment" (Buzzanell & Houston, 2018) but instead to view the communication processes that may have aided in building resilience.

In the cases of Fran and Tess, we see that both women strived to continue normalcy in their work production despite their physical limitations. Fran crafted normalcy by wanting to continue working in the same way she had before and showing no disruption to her co-workers. She was affronted by being told to take time off and do less than she wanted to do because this conflicted with her goal of maintaining normalcy in her work routine. Tess assured others she could do the new job she was offered even though she was uncertain if she could. Her means of crafting normalcy was to expect the same things from herself in the workplace as she had before the diagnosis even if that expectation was precarious. Both women developed new expectations of normalcy throughout the process. Tess had no choice but to let others at work see some of her physical side effects such as throwing up at her desk. Fran and Tess accepted after their treatments were complete that their new normalcy might involve further bad news about cancer and their health.

One of the most prevalent identity anchors for both women in the workplace was to be seen as competent while going through major cancer treatment disruption. Fran expressed her identity as one who did not cry, did not want others crying for her, and who worked to raise money to meet her own needs. Tess found her identity anchor in writing poetry about her experience. Both women specifically mentioned identity anchors of advocating for their own choices and health care with doctors.

The cases of these two women diverged when it came to maintaining and using communication networks. Fran was extremely reluctant to engage her communication networks in the workplace because she feared their reaction of pity to her. She did not engage with any support groups and only limited friends during her treatment. On the other hand, Tess was immediately open with her new workplace communication network, telling not only her supervisor but her new co-workers right away. Not only did she rely on friends to take her to treatments and provide tangible support during this time, but she also built a new communication network for support by writing and reading her poetry publicly. Tess also culled her communication network, cutting off friends who needed updates too often or offered unspecified support that did not help her. She used her communication network of friends to share information about her condition rather than posting on social media to guard others' feelings. While Fran drew back from her communication networks that could offer support, Tess was active to leverage her new networks as well as existing ones.

Both Fran and Tess developed alternative logistics, or new ways of viewing their experiences. After facing what she felt were unnecessary difficulties and lack of information in her own treatment, Fran became focused on benefiting others who were going through the same. This allowed her to reframe her bad experience into one that could be instructive for others. Tess created rules and boundaries for keeping friendships. She reframed true friends into those who offered specific help without her having to reach out.

Likewise, both women foregrounded positive action while acknowledging their negative emotions. Fran found her positive action in telling other women about the benefits of 3D mammograms and preparing for a trip to Africa once her recovery was complete. Tess foregrounded her gratitude for being one of the women who did not have to continue long-term medication, who did not have the gene that predicted recurrence. Though both women were clear that they had difficult physical and emotional struggles during their treatment, they were able to mitigate these negative effects by focusing on future positive actions they would take.

Managers or supervisors reviewing these cases through the communication theory of resilience can find guidelines for handling situations with employees who are going through major life hardships, losses, or traumas. One thing to note is that interactions that cultivate dignity enable resilience (Wieland, 2020). Being cautious and inquisitive before making determinations about adjusted workload allow the employee to maintain dignity. Secondly, recognizing the mutuality involved in enabling resilience (Richardson & Maninger, 2016) points managers and supervisors to think seriously about the way that co-workers can positively or negatively impact an individual's path to resilience. Promoting connections between individually and organizationally held ideologies around emotional and supportive values can also activate positive communication from team members (Agarwal et al., 2015).

DISCUSSION QUESTIONS

1. What could managers and supervisors do to create a climate where employees are more comfortable to speak about difficulties and thus increase resilience as they go through hardships? Are the long-term benefits of resilient employees worth the short-term interruptions to work?
2. What is the difference between a trait theory of resilience and a communicative theory of resilience? Which theory do you subscribe to? Which do you think most managers subscribe to?
3. In what ways did you see the communication processes of Buzzanell's communication theory of resilience play out in the cases of Fran and Tess? Which individual do you think showed the higher level of resilience and why?
4. How do you think managers should assign work to those employees they know are going through major hardships? What are the positive and negative effects of limiting work for cancer patients?
5. How has your personal view of resilience changed after exploring these cases? How could you employ this new insight in your own work life?

REFERENCES

Afifi, T. D., Hutchinson, S., & Krouse, S. (2006). Toward a theoretical model of communal coping in post-divorce families and other naturally occurring groups. *Communication Theory*, *16*(3), 378–409. doi:10.1111/j.1468-2885.2006.00275.x

Agarwal, V., & Buzzanell, P. M. (2015). Communicative reconstruction of resilience labor: Identity/identification in disaster-relief workers. *Journal of Applied Communication Research*, *43*(4), 408–428. doi:10.1080/00909882.2015.1083602

Albrecht, T. L., Burleson, B., & Goldsmith, D. J. (1994). Supportive communication. In M. L. Knapp & G. R. Miller (Eds.), *Handbook of interpersonal communication* (2nd ed., pp. 419–449). Sage.

Albrecht, T. L., & Goldsmith, D. J. (2003). Social support, social networks, and health. In T. T. Thompson, A. Dorsey, R. Parrott, & K. Miller (Eds.), *The Routledge handbook of health communication* (pp. 263–284). Routledge.

Bonanno, G. A. (2004). Loss, trauma, and human resilience: Have we underestimated the human capacity to thrive after extremely aversive events? *The American Psychologist*, *59*(1), 20–28. doi:10.1037/0003-066X.59.1.20 PMID:14736317

Braithwaite, D. O., Waldron, V. R., & Finn, J. (1999). Communication of social support in computer-mediated groups for people with disabilities. *Health Communication, 11*(2), 123–151. doi:10.120715327027hc1102_2 PMID:16370973

Buzzanell, P. M. (2010). Resilience: Talking, resisting, and imagining new normalcies into being. *Journal of Communication, 60*(1), 1–14. doi:10.1111/j.1460-2466.2009.01469.x

Buzzanell, P. M. (2017). Communication theory of resilience: Enacting adaptive transformative processes when families experience loss and disruption. In D. O. Braithwaithe, E. A. Suter, & K. Floyd (Eds.), *Engaging theories in family communication* (pp. 98–109). Routledge. doi:10.4324/9781315204321-9

Buzzanell, P. M., & Houston, B. (2018). Communication and resilience: Multilevel applications and insights – A *Journal of Application Communication Research* forum. *Journal of Applied Communications, 46*(1), 1–4. doi:10.1080/00909882.2017.1412086

Chernichky-Karcher, S. M., Venetis, M. K., & Lillie, H. (2019). The Dyadic Communicative Resilience Scale (DCRS): Scale development, reliability, and validity. *Supportive Care in Cancer, 27*(12), 4555–4564. Advance online publication. doi:10.100700520-019-04763-8 PMID:30923889

Coulson, N. S. (2005). Receiving social support online: An analysis of a computer-mediated support group for individuals living with irritable bowel syndrome. *Cyberpsychology & Behavior, 8*(6), 580–584. doi:10.1089/cpb.2005.8.580 PMID:16332169

Cutrona, C. E., & Suhr, J. A. (1992). Controllability of stressful events and satisfaction with spouse support behaviors. *Communication Research, 19*(2), 154–174. doi:10.1177/009365092019002002

Den Oudsten, B. L., Van Heck, G. L., Van der Steeg, A., Roukema, J. A., & De Vries, J. (2010). Personality predicts perceived availability of social support and satisfaction with social support in women with early-stage breast cancer. *Supportive Care in Cancer, 18*(4), 499–508. doi:10.100700520-009-0714-3 PMID:19685345

Elkins, D. (2020). How working women navigate communication privacy management boundaries when seeking social support during cancer treatment. *Communication & Medicine: An Interdisciplinary Journal of Healthcare, Ethics and Society, 3*(15), 261–267. doi:10.1558/cam.34969

Faw, M. H. (2014). Young adults' strategies for managing social support during weight-loss attempts. *Qualitative Health Research*, *24*(2), 267–278. doi:10.1177/1049732313520079 PMID:24482423

Kim, S. C., Shah, D. V., Namkoong, K., McTavish, F., & Gustafson, D. H. (2013). Predictors of online health information seeking among women with breast cancer: The role of social support perception and emotional well-being. *Journal of Computer-Mediated Communication*, *18*(2), 98–119. doi:10.1111/jcc4.12002 PMID:24634575

Lillie, H. M., Venetis, M. K., & Chernichky-Karcher, S. M. (2018). "He would never let me just give up": Communicatively constructing dyadic resilience in the experience of breast cancer. *Health Communication*, *33*(12), 1516–1524. doi:10.1080/10410236.2017.1372049 PMID:28952793

Lucas, K., & Buzzanell, P. M. (2012). Memorable messages of hard times: Constructing short-and long-term resiliencies through family communication. *Journal of Family Communication*, *12*(3), 189–208. doi:10.1080/15267431.2012.687196

Ray, C. D., & Veluscek, A. M. (2017). Face threats and additional reasons for perceiving support as unwanted: A study of recently diagnosed cancer patients. *Health Communication*, *32*(11), 1396–1402. doi:10.1080/10410236.2016.1228027 PMID:27767333

Richardson, B. K., & Maninger, L. (2016). "We were all in the same boat": An exploratory study of communal coping in disaster recovery. *The Southern Communication Journal*, *81*(2), 107–122. doi:10.1080/1041794X.2015.1111407

Richardson, G. E. (2002). The metatheory of resilience and resiliency. *Journal of Clinical Psychology*, *58*(3), 307–321. doi:10.1002/jclp.10020 PMID:11836712

Sjolander, C., & Berterö, C. (2008). The significance of social support and social networks among newly diagnosed lung cancer patients in Sweden. *Nursing & Health Sciences*, *10*(3), 182–187. doi:10.1111/j.1442-2018.2008.00395.x PMID:18786059

Venetis, M. K., Chernickhky-Karcher, S. M., & Lillie, H. M. (2020). Communicating resilience: Predictors and outcomes of dyadic communication resilience processes among both cancer patients and cancer partners. *Journal of Applied Communication Research*, *48*(1), 49–69. doi:10.1080/00909882.2019.1706098

Walker, R., Szanton, S. L., & Wenzel, J. (2015). Working toward normalcy post-treatment: A qualitative study of older adult breast and prostate cancer survivors. *Oncology Nursing Forum*, *42*(6), E358–E367. doi:10.1188/15.ONF.E358-E367 PMID:26488842

Wieland, S. M. (2020). Constituting resilience at work: Maintaining dialectics and cultivating dignity throughout a worksite closure. *Management Communication Quarterly*, *34*(4), 463–494. doi:10.1177/0893318920949314

Wright, K. (2002). Social support within an on-line cancer community: An assessment of emotional support, perceptions of advantages and disadvantages, and motives for using the community from a communication perspective. *Journal of Applied Communication Research*, *30*(3), 195–209. doi:10.1080/00909880216586

Zimmermann, S., & Applegate, J. L. (1994). Communicating social support in organizations: A message-centered approach. In B. R. Burleson, T. L. Albrecht, & I. G. Sarason (Eds.), *Communication of social support: Messages, interactions, relationships, and community* (pp. 50–70). Sage Publications.

KEY TERMS AND DEFINITIONS

Communal Coping: Viewing hardship suffered by one person as a stressor to be acted upon collectively.

Communication Networks: Those people around an individual who are in regular communication with that individual and who may hold useful information or other means of support.

Dialectics: Tensions that arise in relationships or within individuals that require balancing two opposing forces.

Resilience: Facing hardship, trauma, or loss in a way that allows for creative adjustment and stimulates empowerment to achieve productive outcomes despite adverse circumstances.

Social Support: An interpersonal communication process that ameliorates the harmful effects of stress on an individual experiencing various hardships. Social support can include both verbal support and tangible, practical support.

Chapter 11
It's Just a Part of Life

Patrice M. Buzzanell
University of South Florida, USA

Suzy D'Enbeau
Kent State University, USA

EXECUTIVE SUMMARY

"It's Just a Part of Life" focuses on career and personal challenges as two couples (Maria and Brad; Sara and Alejandro) deal with anticipated and unexpected disruptions in their lives. These couples experience events and opportunities including returns-to-work after laborforce gaps, job changes, geographical relocations, infertility, unplanned business trips and workloads, and sleep deprivation during early child rearing years. As they devise strategies for managing these stressful situations both individually and collectively, they adapt to and transform their new normals by enacting communication resilience processes. Throughout the case, there are episodes in which they, and the children (Eden and Lucy), perform the five processes: crafting normalcy; using, maintaining, and creating new networks; backgrounding negative feelings while foregrounding productive action; utilizing alternative logics; and anchoring identities. They enact resilience for themselves and others, for the present and the future, and by reflecting upon their pasts.

INTRODUCTION

Rather than being traits, characteristics, or personality factors, a communication perspective on *resilience* sees this process as "constituted in and through communicative processes that enhance people's abilities to create new normalcies"

DOI: 10.4018/978-1-6684-3753-7.ch011

(Buzzanell, 2010, p. 9). In the *Communication Theory of Resilience (CTR)*, resilience is activated by *triggers*, or events and other disruptions, losses, deaths, transitions, and opportunities that might be mundane, such as going to a new restaurant in another part of town, or extraordinary and unusual, such as preparing for and coping with the aftermaths of hurricanes, wildland fires, tornadoes, extensive flooding, earthquakes, and mudslides (Buzzanell, 2018a, 2018b). To adapt to and/or transform the new normal that these disruptions seem to demand, people often engage in one or more resilience processes with other people. First, they may continue routines and rituals or create new ones along with language that indicates that that feel that they are experiencing some sense of normalcy (*crafting normalcy*). Second, they talk to and connect with others online and in face-to-face interactions (*using, maintaining, and creating new networks*). Third, they might feel upset, angry, betrayed, fearful, and/or devastated by something that happened yet they know that they need to pull themselves together and accomplish tasks that are necessary for them to survive and move beyond the disruption, such as locating water and food at a food pantry if family providers have lost their sources of income (*backgrounding negative feelings while foregrounding productive action*). Fourth, they may find silver linings, humor, and/or workaround or creative and improvisational procedures for handling the consequences of disruptions (*utilizing alternative logics*). Finally, they may make sense out of disruptions and their own parts in resilience processes by attending to salient identities, such as parent or friend, when everything else about life seems to be in disarray (*affirming identity anchors*).

Besides resilience, "It's Just a Part of Life" also is a case about *work-life*, specifically *work-family, communication* that can develop patterns for sustainable "balance" or perform satisfactory career and paid labor activities as well as personal life interests such as home, family, friendships, volunteering, and leisure. Work-life communication incorporates many tensions and contradictions that show up in conflicts, opportunities, and desires for flexibility in organizational policies (Putnam et al., 2014) and as problematics for research studies (Kirby et al., 2003). Communication and interdisciplinary studies have examined work-life balance through a variety of terms like boundaries, gendered household tasks, and caregiving. What is important to note is that work-life balance and forms of caregiving (e.g., fatherhood, motherhood, aunting, and creation of families where there are no legal or biological connections) are different based on race, ethnicity, nationality, class, gender, type of jobs and industries, and other differences (Bochantin, 2016; Buzzanell & D'Enbeau, 2009; D'Enbeau et al., 2010; Ellingson & Sotirin, 2010; Garwood, 2022)

CASE STUDY: IT'S JUST A PART OF LIFE

Maria heard the front doorbell and rushed to get her capris on. If she hadn't gained those 10 pounds, she might have an easier time with the zipper. As she was holding in her breath, she heard the doorbell ring again.

"Augh", Maria exhaled as she finally fully stuffed herself into her pants. She realized that she was still able to breathe and gave thanks for small blessings. She looked out the glass panel set in the front door to see the brown delivery truck. She opened the front door to the usual UPS delivery person in her neighborhood.

Maria smiled, "Hi Chris!! It's good to see you and to get the package I've been waiting for. These items have been out of stock for ages!!"

Chris replied with a laugh, "I'm grateful to you, Maria, for keeping UPS in business." Maria agreed as she signed the required form. As Chris walked down the sidewalk to the truck, Chris yelled, "Have a great weekend!" Maria watched as Chris hopped into the truck and took off.

Maria looked around before shutting the door. The skies were blue without a single cloud. The constant sunshine and palm trees took a little getting used to after living in the Midwest for just about all her adult life. But it was a good getting used to. And it had already been a few years since she and Brad moved to Florida. Brad had remarked that the sunshine helped with her seasonal affect disorder—who knew that the sadness and fatigue she experienced every winter up north actually had a name! As she was growing up, her mom just said that she and Maria liked to hibernate for the winter but Maria's withdrawal from everyone and inability to drag herself out of bed during the bleak seasons seemed more severe than her mother's.

So Maria and Brad moved to Florida through a confluence of happy happenstance.

Maria mused to herself, "it's just amazing how things work out". She surprised herself by talking out loud. She'd better stop doing that or people would wonder about her! However, she was well aware that these turns of good fortune didn't happen for everyone. She, Brad, and her children were grateful. She remembered how much her parents sacrificed for her to get a good education. They came to the United States from Venezuela before she was born. They settled in the Midwest because of job opportunities and good schools for Maria and her siblings. They struggled financially but made a good home. They wanted their children to live out their American dreams. Maria tried. Like her mother, Maria made sure that she prepared meals for the local food kitchen and donated to local community needs. For Maria, these donations went to hurricane relief and homeless shelters in her new city. Her dad had worked very hard and she didn't see him much when she grew up. He said, "you might not have everything you want, but you have everything you need." He was proud that he could put food on the table and a roof over their heads.

A smile crossed Maria's face along with a touch of sorrow when she thought how happy her parents would have been to see her now.

Maria's luck unfolded in unexpected ways. When Brad got his Florida job offer, she had been able to transfer to a brand new office of Global Laboratories. This position was not the pharmaceutical sales rep position she had when she returned to work after staying home with Eden and Luciana (nicknamed Lucy) for three years. She was pleasantly surprised when Global Laboratories wanted to hire her back. She had had a good record but didn't think workforce re-entry would be so smooth. It just took an updated resumé and LinkedIn profile, and some emails to former colleagues and bosses about being references for her job applications.

Then she received a message from a colleague of a former colleague thrice removed named Bev. It turned out that Bev was in HR recruiting for upper corporate levels.

Bev began the message by asking, "Would you be interested in returning to pharmaceutical sales? I've talked to some people you used to work with. They spoke very favorably about you." Maria enthusiastically responded, "yes!" She filled out the necessary paperwork, interviewed virtually, and began a week and a half later. She enjoyed her job and hadn't considered a change until Brad found out about a new opportunity that led to a job offer.

When Brad got his job offer, Maria zoomed with her bosses to let them know that she and her family were thinking about moving to Florida. Her bosses surprised her by immediately offering her a managerial position in a new office that they planned to open in the same city to which Maria and Brad were moving. They explained that they wanted someone who was very knowledgeable about the company and its products and services—however, an added bonus for this new office is that Maria spoke Spanish and would understand some aspects about the population demographics from South America as well as Mexico and Cuba. Maria was still amazed that re-entry and what turned out to be a transfer and promotion worked out so well.

She said a quick prayer of thanks that their move went so easily. Brad had really wanted the yellow mid-Century ranch-style house that needed a new roof. It also needed to have a couple of old trees taken down or, at least judiciously pruned, as Brad put it, in case of tropical storms and hurricanes. But there were house features like the huge main bedroom and built-in bookcases in the office that she loved immediately. Plus the yard had lots of palm trees and bromeliads in bloom, and big pool in the backyard. She suspected that the house was overpriced despite what their realtor said. But even if they had stayed in the Chicago area, they would have had to buy a different house and prices where escalating. The condo that Maria and Brad bought when first living together was near great restaurants, clubs, and art galleries. But their lifestyles were changing. They had gone around and around in conversation about what to do and where to move. The condo and location just weren't conducive to a family with small children. Their condo also wasn't near good public schools. The job offers and relocation packages put an end to their indecision.

So they sold their condo, packed up some personal items, and arranged for company-paid movers to take their belongings from Chicago to Florida. Maria and Brad made a vacation trip out of it. They stopped at Abraham Lincoln's birthplace and a bourbon distillery tour in Kentucky that was family friendly. They discovered a moonpie shop in downtown Chattanooga. They went to underground caverns and ate peaches at roadside markets. When they arrived in Florida, the girls swam in the pool with their floaties while Brad "lifeguarded" and Maria unpacked the sheets to make beds and dig out a few kitchen items for the first night in their new home. Eden jumped up and down, asking, "can we have a picnic outside by the pool?" and so they did. Maria thought that it was the best family vacation they had ever had. Their time together seemed to set the mood for their new life in Florida.

Their girls, Eden and Lucy, seemed to adjust very quickly to their new home. They enjoyed weekend outings to the many attractions and Gulf beaches less than an hour's drive from their home. They enjoyed authentic Latin, Spanish, Peruvian, and Mexican grocery stores and mom-and-pop restaurants. Maria had missed her friends in the Midwest. But she had to admit that she enjoyed the Florida winter weather, the near constant sunshine, and the heated pool. She did not miss icy sidewalks and streets. She also found that her friends were delighted to come and visit her. She had been warned by a new neighbor, "you'll have more visitors than you ever expected living here," and it was true.

In fact, she remembered, having visitors was why she had a package in her hand. Alejandro and Sara were coming and she bought some blow-up pink flamingo drink holders to float in the pool while they were visiting. Eden and Lucy were excited to see their Auntie Sara who always remembered the girls' favorite candies.

Just last night during their weekly Facetime "party", Eden quizzed Sara on where they would go while Alejandro and Sara were in town. From the other room, Maria overheard Eden, now 8 years old, remark, "Auntie Sara, I think that we should go to the aquarium in Clearwater again. There are new rescued animals. I also want to look at the dolphins with prosthetic tails. I am still sad that Winter died. But I am excited that I can swim virtually with her and do the musical tribute. Mom explained what a tribute is and that makes me happy."

Maria imagined what Sara said in reply. She heard Eden say, "you know, going to the aquarium would help me learn what I have to do to be a marine biologist. I can talk to the scientists at the aquarium." Sara chuckled to herself—Eden knew just what angle to use to get what she wanted. Lucy, aged 6, loudly seconded the ideas and added that she would like to get salt water taffy after they left the aquarium and went to Clearwater beach. So it was settled.

Now, Alejandro and Sara would arrive in an hour. Their flight from Chicago was on time. Brad was picking them up at the airport while Eden and Lucy were putting their school papers away. She glanced into their blue bedroom with the bunk beds. Eden and Sara were arguing over who would wrap up a small gift for Sara. Their curly brown hair moved from side to side as they shook their heads in disagreement. Maria figured that they could battle it out themselves. She had other things to do.

Maria thanked her lucky stars for Alejandro and Sara. She surprised herself by talking out loud again. A couple of weeks after Maria and Brad moved to Florida, Sara called and said, "we know you aren't set up but we want to come and help. Besides we are interested in exploring the beaches. AND I've been reading about the sunken gardens in St. Petersburg with all kinds of exotic plants and trees. It's one of the oldest roadside tourist attractions in the United States."

Maria ran her hand through her hair and murmured, "we have to unpack."

She was looking at herself in a mirror she was unpacking and added getting her hair colored to her "to do" list. The grey streaks were taking over and she hated how tired the grey made her look. Not that she wasn't tired. She was. She listened as Sara continued talking.

Sara was in the middle of countering Maria's arguments, "we can help you put up pictures. You know how good I am at finding the best local farmers markets and microbreweries! There's even a Saturday Market in Ybor City where chicken roam free. And the Spanish restaurant there is the oldest in the United States!"

Maria laughed, "I do *not* believe that the chickens roam free!"

But Sara had done her homework, "Believe!! These chickens are protected by a Tampa ordinance. It's illegal to harm them. Look, it'll be an adventure!!"

Maria agreed and so they had their first visitors to their new home.

During the visit, Eden and Lucy enjoyed the company and helped to rearrange furniture in the house. Alejandro and Brad brought tables and chairs with tropical flowered cushions for the lanai. Sara and Maria debated which of the nearby afterschool programs would be optimal for the girls.

That visit ended too soon as far as Maria was concerned.

To commemorate the visit, the two couples started a new tradition of picking up some junky Florida yard "art" whenever Alejandro and Sara came. They started with kitschy pink flamingos and now had brightly colored metal toucans, parrots, and other decorations. Alejandro and Sara flew in frequently given the low-cost no-frills direct flights into nearby airports. They kept bathing suits and some casual clothes and flip flops in the guest bedroom that now had a sign on the door with their names.

Maria was grateful, especially for that first visit. Brad had been putting in long hours at work meeting people and becoming certified for Florida safety inspections that differed from what he had been doing in Chicago.

It bothered her that both she and Brad often put in such long hours. Each of them was ambitious and liked being at the top of their occupations. Each of them hated negotiating who had extra hours to work—often sighing with the question, "how late do you have to work tonight?" Maria felt badly that she didn't have the energy her mother did to do all the child and home labor while also working full-time in the family restaurant. Her mother said that it was what women did. Besides her father was at the restaurant even longer hours than her mother.

The worst work-family "balance" questions—whoever named it "balance" must have been insane, Maria mused--were accompanied by glaring facial expressions when one of them had to take work calls during evening family time. Actually, Maria didn't mind taking the calls because she could solve problems quickly. She often thought of these times as just breaks from her usual work and household routines. She thought of them as "sneaking" work time and having a party when she had a glass of wine while chatting with colleagues in the evenings. She remembered some sort of corporate women's networking talk on "working lite" or something like that. She could identify with what the speaker described the women entrepreneurs doing to stay on top of their game.

Without their previous safety nets in Chicago, inevitably Maria and Brad had to negotiate how they'd handle sick childcare and school closings, especially during the COVID-19 pandemic. Neither felt good about the outcomes of these discussions. Maria wondered how they might "negotiate" differently. There had to be a better way. It hardly seemed like a negotiation—it seemed like one of those forced choice exams she took in college where she always felt that she had to select the lesser of two evils.

Even so, Maria thought that the new jobs were good for them, just as the frequent visits by Alejandro and Sara seemed good for the other couple.

Maria remembered the day when Alejandro and Sara surprised Maria and Brad by Facetiming them in the middle of a weekend afternoon. Maria saw their names pop up on her iPhone and answered with a "Hey, I hope you are calling to tell us that you are coming to visit!!"

But Sara tearfully told them that she and Alejandro set a deadline for the decision about having a child and now they were moving on. After years of medical tests and procedures, Alejandro and Sara had given up hope of getting pregnant. Even their parents had stopped asking about grandchildren and lighting candles at church.

Sara seemed so crushed, "We wanted to tell you both first. Nothing took and with no assurances of future success, we've decided to stop all the fertility treatments."

Alejandro simply remarked, "it is what it is", adding that he hated that phrase but that they were done trying. He looked tired. He added, "it's just a part of life. Not everything can be perfect."

Alejandro and Sara explained, "we both felt that the strain of always trying to have sex at the right moment for conception was wrecking our marriage and our professional lives. Who ever thought having sex was so much work! We know we have options—adopting, fostering, or something else. We are taking it one decision at a time."

Maria wondered what she would have done if she and Brad hadn't been able to have Eden and Lucy. Sure, they had enjoyed their pre-children time together. She reminisced about Sunday brunches and waking up mid-morning on weekends. It seemed like someone else's life. It sure wasn't their lives now. They always thought that they'd have children. What would they have done if they couldn't have Eden and Lucy? Maybe they would have buried themselves in their work. Maybe they would have adopted or gotten a dog. Maybe they would have gotten divorced.

Maria thought about the women at her corporation who decided to be voluntarily childless. They seemed to enjoy their lives and didn't act as though there was anything missing. The one complaint she heard these women voice was that their bosses and co-workers assumed that they could pick up the slack if anyone missed work or had to pick up their sick kids from daycare. They resented everyone's assumption that they had no responsibilities outside of work. On the other hand, Maria knew from looking at salary reports and reading the research that child-free professional women made just as much as, if not more than, men, who enjoyed the "fatherhood premium," whereas women with children faced the dreaded "motherhood penalty." These women made choices. In fact, one Black co-worker omitted any mention of her preschoolers. All of this was different from being involuntarily childless like Alejandro and Sara.

Maria admired the way Alejandro and Sara handled their disappointment. During their call that weekend afternoon, Alejandro and Sara proposed their solution to having a family.

Sara said, "we'd like to be the best uncle and aunt ever."

Alejandro added, "the two of us can get our kid fix and then hand Eden and Lucy back to you, all sugared up and spoiled. We watched how our parents did this grandparent thing with our siblings' children and we think we'd be excellent in these roles. We'd simply have to visit you more often. When the girls get older, they can fly to Chicago and spend the week with us. What do you think?"

Maria and Brad didn't even have to discuss the issue. They both grinned broadly at the iPhone screen and yelled "yes"!!

They knew how much Alejandro and Sara loved Eden and Lucy. They had even listed Alejandro and Sara as their children's guardians in their wills and other documents if anything should ever happen to them. Since Maria and Brad didn't come from large families and Brad didn't really keep in touch with his, making Alejandro and Sara "family" seemed like a natural and healthy thing for all of them to do.

When Brad got off the call, he leered at Maria and deepened his voice. "Well, little lady, how about travelling the skies with me to a remote but luscious tropical island with no cell service when Alejandro and Sara had Eden and Lucy for the week." His one eyebrow went up with his attempted leer.

Maria broke out laughing, "you are so out of your seduction game. You better hope nothing happens to me so that you don't have to go on the dating market!"

Maria quickly got serious, "Brad, if we have a week alone together, the one and only thing I can think about right now is that I want to sleep and sleep and sleep."

Brad tried to look like he was both leering and shocked at the same time, "you mean we won't have endless romps in the bed, on the beach, in the …"

Maria started laughing again so hard that she had tears rolling down her cheeks. She managed to quip, "dream on, Brad!"

They stopped bantering as Lucy came into the room. She had drawn an unflattering picture of Eden and scribbled "Eden is a butt holl" in red crayon at the bottom.

After correcting Lucy's spelling and telling her not to call her sister names, Brad agreed that sleep would be a treat. He commented further, "I hope our desire to sleep when we have a weekend or more alone doesn't mean that we are getting old."

Maria smiled at this memory from a conversation that seemed lifetimes ago. She could imagine them getting old together. She thought that she'd walk in the neighborhood holding Brad's hand, just as her paternal grandparents did when she was a child visiting them. She wondered what it would be like to be married to Brad for decades and to be empty nesters. She could barely imagine having a day to herself or to them as a couple.

She and Brad talked later that evening about what they would do during the summer week that Sara and Alejandro had the girls. Since having the girls, Maria felt perpetually sleep deprived—night feedings, poopie diapers, sick kids throwing up all over the bedclothes in the middle of the night, racing to school with forgotten paperwork, and more. But there also were early morning snuggles to make up for the other stuff. She and Brad agreed that even having a staycation would be worthwhile.

Maria was unwrapping the flamingo cup holders when Brad called.

Brad started by saying, "Maria, I'm on speaker phone."

Maria could hear Alejandro and Sara yelling out hellos in the background.

Brad continued, "I'll be home with Alejandro and Sara in about 15 minutes."

Maria could hear Brad sucking in a breath. She knew what he was going to say next was something she did not want to hear. She resented the fact that she wouldn't be able to growl at him while Alejandro and Sara were in the car.

Brad blurted out, "I wanted to give you a heads up about a call I just received. You know that news about the safety effects of climate change on beach communities?"

Maria said, "yes". She waited for the bad news.

"Well, we've expanded our scope to aging cities with old infrastructures that can't handle flash flooding, droughts, and fires. I'm going to have to fly out on Sunday afternoon for some briefings with officials in DC. I wanted to give you notice right away."

Maria sighed. She knew Brad would have to go. She also knew that he hated to be away from the girls so much and would do anything to avoid these conversations with Maria.

Maria asked anyway, "why can't Cerise handle this trip this time? You have been training her and she is great at these meetings."

Brad commented, "I thought of Cerise. The problem is that she is on a design team with an urgent deadline. There just isn't any other way."

Alejandro interrupted to say, "Hey, Maria, we were eavesdropping, of course! We'd love to have some alone time with the girls if you need to work late or whatever."

Sara interjected, "Lucy told me that she is into baking. I'd love to bake and cook with Lucy. It could be a surprise meal one night while Brad is gone."

Alejandro continued, "This would give Sara and me the chance to fix dinner with them and check out some bakeries. We can take the girls to that Greek fishing village in Tarpon Springs. We have wanted to go there and look at the sponges and fishing boats. We are dying for baklava."

Maria replied, "Let's talk some more when you get here." Maria thought she was well past her teenage FOMO days but still felt sad that she wouldn't be able to go on the excursion with them. Maria added before hanging up, "I'll regret not going. You know that."

Maria knew that this plan would help her keep on top of the recent influx of orders and new personnel in her office. She just wasn't ready to admit it yet.

Alejandro and Sara arrived shortly afterwards and there was mass chaos with everyone talking at once. After Sara opened her gift—a refrigerator magnet with a photo of Eden and Lucy—Maria commented, "Brad and I have to figure out a longer-term solution to times like these. We'll have pool-side suggestions tonight with red sangria and Cuban sandwiches!! Until then, help me inflate the rest of these flamingo cup holders!!"

CASE ANALYSIS AND DISCUSSION

As "It's Just a Part of Life" begins, Maria is preparing for out-of-town visitors who frequently visit her and her family in Florida. Maria reflects about how she and Brad ended up changing jobs and relocating to the Tampa Bay region as well as how their friends, Sara and Alejandro, have become not only frequent guests but also family members. Maria considers herself, her partner, Brad, and their children,

Eden and Lucy, to be very fortunate insofar as the many disruptions or stressors in their lives have worked out advantageously for them. They realize that they are very lucky. Not everyone has such a relatively easy time in these circumstances: trying to find employment after a labor force gap for child rearing, relocating to a new city in a different region of the United States, or finding short- and long-term solutions for work-family balance. But they and their friends have interacted with each other for the *social support*, or human and non-human resources and networks that can provide assistance (see Burleson et al., 2014) that they have needed during these and many other disruptions, opportunities, and changes. In doing so, they have (a) communicatively constituted resilience (Buzzanell, 2010, 2018a, 2018b) and have engaged in (b) work-life communication that displays patterns for sustainable "balance."

Specifically, Maria and Brad enact resilience processes that make up the Communication Theory of Resilience (CTR). For example, they enacted resilience by utilizing alternative logics when they looked upon their relocation trip from Chicago to southern Florida as their "best family vacation" whereas others might have focused on the lengthy drive and getting stuck in traffic around Atlanta or other cities. Similarly, Sara and Alejandro could have dwelled on their failed fertility treatments and childlessness but they reframed the situation as opportunities to be the best aunts and uncles for Eden and Lucy (and possibly legal guardians for these children if anything should happen to Maria and Brad; see Ellingson & Sotirin, 2010). Before they could reframe their feelings of loss and disappointment, Sara and Alejandro first needed to background their negative feelings. This doesn't mean that they denied or repressed their emotions. It means that they acknowledged that they could honor or legitimize their feelings as part of their ability to move on with their lives, in other words, they constructed productive action, like planning trips to visit Maria's family. In these examples and many others throughout the case, there are instances where a particular resilience process becomes prominent but, more often than not, resilience processes happen sequentially and/or simultaneously.

Moreover, the case indicates that children learn how to enact resilience. Parents, friends, teachers, and other people and non-human agents like films, books, and social media can assist children and adults in cultivating strategies that help people reintegrate after losses or disruptions so that they constitute or communicatively create new normal that can be advantageous for themselves and others. As one example, Eden discusses her sadness that Winter, the dolphin with a prosthetic fin who was featured in Disney films and who lived in the aquarium in Clearwater, Florida, died. For a child, the loss of animals and people in their everyday lives and in media can be heartbreaking. Yet, Eden was able to background these feelings as well as look forward to swimming virtually with Winter and enjoying a fun and, seemingly, career developmental trip to the Clearwater aquarium. She is able to do so because her immediate and extended family have resources and support her in her feelings and aspirational career identity (thus aligning with the affirming identity anchors process in CTR). These kinds of resources and support are known as protective factors for resilience in communication and interdisciplinary literatures. Many children and adults who have had traumatizing experiences and live in poverty or without food, safe homes, water, and other needs might have difficulty enacting resilience processes. This idea is alluded to when Maria often expresses thoughts and prayers of thanks for her life and for the sacrifices that her immigrant parents made so that she could have a good life.

Throughout, there are many examples of how the case characters performed resilience to cope with and transform their new normal but the important part is that they do not enact resilience alone. Constituting resilience communicatively means that others assist individuals and group members in grappling with changes and disruptions. For example, Sara and Alejandro envisioned themselves as parents for years (affirming identity anchors), yet all their attempts to conceive failed. Readers do not know what they might do in the future but, for the time being, they have decided to be an aunt and uncle to Eden and Lucy to the delight of Maria, Brad, Eden, and Lucy. They actively envision their new roles as commitments to themselves and to the other family. In this way, they create family and community not only in discourses or talk (e.g., "Auntie Sara") but also materially (e.g., legal documents, gifts, signs on the bedroom door indicating that the space within belongs to Sara and Alejandro).

In addition, another new normal in this case that requires others for enactment from across time, place, and generations is the *calling* for second and third generations of immigrants to live the better lives for which their family members had sacrificed, namely lives without political and religious oppressions and with the basic necessities for life (Sánchez Sánchez, 2021). Maria thinks back to how happy her parents who had immigrated from Venezuela would be to see her current life and family. She reflects on the struggles that they endured to make her good life possible. She also pays it forward by doing community service, such as donating money to local shelters and preparing meals for local food kitchens. These acts are necessary because resilience is a collective enterprise, especially as individuals and groups communicate to transform their current realities into new normals that are more diverse, more resourced discursively and materially, and more inclusionary of perspectives from the Global South and other lenses not as readily accessible in dominant Western societies like the United States.

The case also demonstrates work-life balance. This phrasing often is contested meaning that scholars and non-academicians recognize that work and personal life are not "balanced" insofar as they are rarely, if ever, equally valued and performed in life. Furthermore, work-life sets up only two domains when people have varied interests and role responsibilities. Finally, it's not work itself or family and other personal life activities that are "imbalanced" but how people prioritize their lives, schedule their time, and think about one part of life while supposedly being present or actively involved in another (e.g., when parents might be thinking about product launchs or their social media presence to boost their entrepreneurial business while taking their children on a neighborhood walk or on vacation).

With regard to the case, there are several incidents where work-life (im)balance comes into play. Maria tries to sneak time to engage in her paid labor while also doing home work which might include doing laundry, shopping, mowing the lawn, doing dishes, and other activities. At times she feels pleasure in her paid labor while also enjoying another activity such as conversations over a glass of wine with well-liked colleagues thus creating a kind of social event while they all are discussing business (Bourne & Forman, 2014). She does not seem to regard these times as *work-family spillover* where the activities of one domain spilling over or being transferred into the other domain such that there do not seem to be boundaries (Buzzanell, 2019) nor does she seem to feel exploited by the capitalistic business milieu in which she needs to labor outside of "work hours" just to keep up with correspondence and other tasks. However, there may be other interpretations of her behaviors and musings, especially during the episode when Brad calls her while driving Sara and Alejandro from the airport to Maria and Brad's house.

When Brad calls Maria, both of them experiences *work-family conflict* in which the role requirements and social norms for one domain, such as family, can produce strains, temporal disconnects, and behavioral incompatibilities with the other domain, such as paid employment (Greenhaus & Beutell, 1985). Brad anticipates conflict when he needs to tell Maria that he must travel unexpectedly ("I wanted to give you a heads up…") and it seems as though these kinds of incidents have been happening over weekends and evening family time for his job despite the best efforts of Brad and Maria. Both want to share earnings and caregiving obligations (Pedulla & Thébaud, 2015) and to use policies that provide flexibility without lowering their competence ratings and promotability because they cannot live up to the "*ideal worker*" who labors 24/7/365 seemingly without any non-work obligations or interests (Acker, 1990; see also Putnam et al., 2014).

Finally, Maria and Brad exhibit some communicative patterns that indicate that they may be able to negotiate more effectively to have more sustainable and fulfilling lifestyles. For instance, they have ongoing conversations about managing work-life priorities, demands, time, and opportunities. They seem to have developed communal support, or capital, through their frequent talk and interactions as well as affirmations of their relationship that would enable them to contend with disruptions (Afifi, 2018). They are well aware that there are systemic considerations that are unfair such as when white professional men are paid more than women with dependents and often more than men of color (i.e., "*fatherhood premium*" and "*motherhood penalty*", see Luhr, 2020). Maria also notes that single adults without dependents, particularly dependent children, have to navigate workplace expectations about their presumably unlimited time to engage in paid labor (Casper et al., 2016). Brad and Maria also have resources for childcare, health care, and other benefits from their employment. Furthermore, they have support systems like Sara and Alejandro.

DISCUSSION QUESTIONS

1. Maria and Brad seem to have ongoing "negotiations" whenever they have work-family conflicts. They both have high work involvement and desires for high family involvement. Maria engages in "working lite." They also seem to engage in negotiations that are more or less successful in the short- and long-term. Yet they can't seem to strike a reasonable solution or "balance" for this phase in their lives. Moreover, the COVID-19 pandemic added extra stress to their work-family balance. What might they do more effectively?
2. There are a number of everyday and major disruptions, stressors, and opportunities that can upend careers and personal life. These disruptions are called triggers in the Communication Theory of Resilience (CTR; Buzzanell, 2010, 2018a, 2018b). CTR theorizes five processes through which people interact online and offline and use language and routines to create new normals. These processes are: crafting normalcy, creating alternative logics, backgrounding negative feelings while foregrounding productive action, using and maintaining communication networks, and affirming identity anchors. What were the disruptions in Maria and Brad's lives? What about Alejandro and Sara's lives? In both cases, was there one disruption or were there "cascading triggers" or multiple disruptions happening over time and place? What did they do, as individuals and family members, to create new normals? In some disruptive cases, how might they engage differently in these five processes to co-construct more satisfying and sustainable new normals?
3. What are the motherhood and fatherhood penalties and premiums that Maria mentioned?
4. Despite their frustrations, Maria and Brad seem to have it pretty good. What might happen in this case if they didn't have the financial means and relational safety nets to manage their relocations, job changes, good quality schools, vacations and leisure times with friends and family?
5. Maria was born in the United States but her parents immigrated from Venezuela. How might she be living out Sánchez Sánchez's (2021) generational callings by working hard to be successful? How might these callings amplify stressors around employment and work-family balance?

REFERENCES

Acker, J. (1990). Hierarchies, jobs and bodies: A theory of gendered organizations. *Gender & Society*, *4*(2), 139–158. doi:10.1177/089124390004002002

Afifi, T. D. (2018). Individual/relational resilience. *Journal of Applied Communication Research*, *46*(1), 5–9. doi:10.1080/00909882.2018.1426707

Bochantin, J. E. (2016). "Morning fog, spider webs, and escaping from Alcatraz": Examining metaphors used by public safety employees and their families to help understand the relationship between work and family. *Communication Monographs*, *83*(2), 214–238. doi:10.1080/03637751.2015.1073853

Bourne, K., & Forman, P. (2014). Living in a culture of overwork: An ethnographic study of flexibility. *Journal of Management Inquiry*, *23*(1), 68–79. doi:10.1177/1056492613481245

Burleson, B., Albrecht, T., & Sarason, I. (1994). Communication of social support: Messages, interactions, relationships, and community. *Sage (Atlanta, Ga.)*.

Buzzanell, P. M. (2010). Resilience: Talking, resisting, and imagining new normalcies into being. *Journal of Communication*, *60*(1), 1–14. doi:10.1111/j.1460-2466.2009.01469.x

Buzzanell, P. M. (2018a). Communication Theory of Resilience: Enacting adaptive-transformative processes when families experience loss and disruption. In D. Braithwaite, E. Suter, & K. Floyd (Eds.), *Engaging theories in family communication* (2nd ed., pp. 98–109). Routledge.

Buzzanell, P.M. (2018b). Organizing resilience as adaptive-transformational tensions. *Journal of Applied Communication Research, 46*(1), 14–18. .1426711 doi:10.1080/00909882.2018

Buzzanell, P. M. (2019). Work/family spillover. In J. Ponzetti & S. M. Horan (Eds.), *Encyclopedia of interpersonal and family relationships* (pp. 915–918). Macmillan.

Buzzanell, P. M., & D'Enbeau, S. (2009). Stories of caregiving: Intersections of academic research and women's everyday experiences. *Qualitative Inquiry*, *15*(7), 1199–1224. doi:10.1177/1077800409338025

Casper, W., Marquardt, D., Roberto, K., & Buss, C. (2016). The hidden family lives of single adults without dependent children. In T. Allen & L. Eby (Eds.), *The Oxford handbook of work and family* (pp. 182–195). Oxford University Press.

D'Enbeau, S., Buzzanell, P. M., & Duckworth, J. (2010). Problematizing classed identities in fatherhood: Development of integrative case studies for analysis and praxis. *Qualitative Inquiry*, *16*(9), 709–720. doi:10.1177/1077800410374183

Ellingson, L. L., & Sotirin, P. J. (2010). *Aunting: Cultural practices that sustain family and community life*. Baylor University Press.

Garwood, E. (2022). Queering the kinship story: Constructing connection through LGBTQ family narratives. *Feminist Theory*. doi:10.1177/14647001211059521

Greenhaus, J. H., & Beutell, N. J. (1985). Sources of conflict between work and family roles. *Academy of Management Review*, *10*(1), 76–88. doi:10.2307/258214

Kirby, E., Golden, A., Medved, C., Jorgenson, J., & Buzzanell, P. M. (2003). An organizational communication challenge to the discourse of work and family research: From problematics to empowerment. *Annals of the International Communication Association*, *27*(1), 1–44. doi:10.1080/23808985.2003.11679020

Luhr, S. (2020). Signaling parenthood: Managing the motherhood penalty and fatherhood premium in the US service sector. *Gender & Society*, *34*(2), 259–283. doi:10.1177/0891243220905814

Medved, C. E. (2004). The everyday accomplishment of work and family: Exploring practical actions in daily routines. *Communication Studies*, *55*(1), 128–145. doi:10.1080/10510970409388609

Pedulla, D., & Thébaud, S. (2015). Can we finish the revolution? Gender, work family ideals, and institutional constraint. *American Sociological Review*, *80*(1), 116–139. doi:10.1177/0003122414564008 PMID:26365994

Putnam, L., Myers, K., & Gailliard, B. (2014). Examining the tensions in workplace flexibility and exploring options for new directions. *Human Relations*, *67*(4), 413–440. doi:10.1177/0018726713495704

Sánchez Sánchez, V. (2021). "Dando las Gracias a Mis Papás": Analyzing the enactment of callings across generations of Latinx Immigrants. *Journal of Communication*, *71*(6), 976–1000. doi:10.1093/joc/jqab037

ADDITIONAL READING

Hintz, E., & Brown, C. (2020). Childfree and "bingoed": A relational dialectics theory analysis of meaning creation in online narratives about voluntary childlessness. *Communication Monographs*, *87*(2), 244–266. doi:10.1080/03637751.2019.1697891

KEY TERMS AND DEFINITIONS

Communication Theory of Resilience (CTR): Process of reintegration after loss or disruptions (known as triggers) to communicatively construct new normalcies.

Work-Life Balance: Popular and academic term that implies that there are two domains in people's lives (paid labor and personal life activities) that are supposed to be equally present, valued, and performed.

Appendix: Supplemental Teaching Materials

CHAPTER 1

1. How does Valerie make communication decisions to manage privacy boundaries while assimilating into school and subsequently work? What are organizational factors that influence these decisions?

Valerie uses organizational socialization processes to observe how students and co-workers communicate positive emotions and competence. These observations cause Valerie to enact privacy boundaries around her true emotions and mental health concerns by masking negative emotions and faking positive emotions to blend in.

2. While Valerie sees her mental health and anxiety as private, how do her communication patterns make this information public in unexpected ways?

Valerie unknowingly exposes her mental health concerns through her nonverbal behavior and tone of voice. For example, Valerie erupts and is short with Alicia in the library and Valerie tears up when she is late on the project deadline.

3. When Valerie confided in Alicia about her mental health, what were the benefits and risks of this decision? How did Valerie communicate in ways to minimize the risks?

Valerie experiences relief after confiding to Alicia and realizes there are resources and support available. The disclosing risk is that Alicia becomes a "co-owner" and could share Valerie's mental health information. To mitigate this risk, Valerie explicitly asks Alicia to promise to keep the information secret.

4. Considering organizational socialization phases, which phase seems most important to learning communication norms about CPM and why?

Valerie draws most heavily on the anticipatory socialization and encounter stages as she observes others to learn expectations about expressing emotions and sharing information. This information allows her to blend in with others, but not address her mental health needs.

5. How are vocational and role anticipatory socialization both beneficial and problematic for mental health disclosures as individuals enter and metamorphosize into organizations?

Individuals can use vocational and role anticipatory socialization cues to obtain positions and blend in with existing organizational members. However, masking emotions and relying on passive socialization communication strategies (i.e., observations, receiving directions) may result in misunderstandings and missed opportunities to gain resources.

CHAPTER 2

1. What is the overall problem presented in this case?

The overall problem in the case is how leaders can better communicate with individuals who have received a mental health diagnosis(es). The focus is on microaggressions and how a leader can be well-intentioned but make statements that are considered disrespectful to their subordinates. Implicit bias can lead to microaggressions which, if communicated by a leader, can have significant negative implications for an organization.

2. What are the factors affecting the problem(s) related to this case?

Mental health, limited time to finish the marketing plan, a missing team member, and an untrained manager are major factors. The combination of these issues set up Chris to be less than understanding and unable to communicate well with Jo about being out sick and not helping with the campaign.

3. Discuss managerial and organizational issues and resources related to this case. In particular consider the following: 1) what costs/benefits would you see from adding integrity training to what Skymad International already does; and 2) if individuals like Jo leave a company what does a company have to do to recruit a new person? Does this add more cost to the company in the long run if individuals like Jo keep leaving?

The organization does not demonstrate an inclusive climate. To do this, everyone, including Chris, should receive both compliance and integrity training. Training can be expensive (students can look up consulting companies that conduct organizational training to get examples of cost) but without it, employees like Jo may leave. When an individual leaves an organization, that organization now incurs more cost in the form of: posting a job; reviewing applicants; interviewing applicants; training new employees; and waiting until the employee knows the job well enough to make meaningful contributions. Training is expensive, especially training that would be ongoing like Skymad would benefit from. But, a more inclusive climate can help improve the communication between managers, subordinates, and co-workers and potentially reduce costs due to the loss of employees.

4. What examples of Assumption of Inferiority, Patronization, and Fear of Mental Illness types of microaggressions are demonstrated in the case?

When Chris tells Jo they should take a few more days off, this could be perceived as an Assumption of Inferiority because Jo may now feel unneeded or believe that Chris thinks Jo is incapable of doing the job. A Patronization microaggression may be when Chris tells Jo they are a "good" employee. This could be a compliment or a judgment, Jo interprets it to be a judgment. Fear of a Mental Illness microaggression could be when Chris sees Jo's expression of emotion (tears) as part of their mental illness and not because Jo was experiencing a "normal" and acceptable emotion. The Case Analysis section includes some analysis of microaggressions in the case but it is important when discussing the microaggressions to have a fluid understanding of how the three types of microaggressions may be communicated. One student may see a statement as patronizing which another student does not view to be patronizing. This is crucial to the discussion of microaggressions because students will most likely think of microaggressions they have experienced, whether related to mental health or not, and they may have interpreted those microaggressions differently. The power to the conversation is not to label microaggressions but to encourage students to discuss their impact on an individual

5. Consider the gender of Chris and Jo. If Chris was male and Jo was female, how might that influence the perception Jo has of the microaggressions. After you consider this, flip the scenario and think about if Jo was male and Chris female. How do the dynamics of the situation, the microaggressions, and the gender of the leader and subordinate alter the perceptions of microaggressions and/or the potential outcome?

This question leaves room for students to explore the intersectionalities of gender, power, and mental illness. More women than men are diagnosed with mental illness and if a woman is the subordinate with less perceived power and say that woman already feels that they may not be valued because of their gender, the microaggressions may be perceived as even stronger aggressions than if the subordinate was male and the leader was female. In reverse, if a female leader is communicating microaggressions, may the male subordinate not take it as seriously as did the female subordinate who had a male boss? OR, could it be that a male with a mental illness perceives even more stigma because males have been diagnosed less frequently than females. This could lead a to a male responding even more strongly to the microaggressions. Finally, what gender do students assign the leader and subordinate? Do students assume the leader to be male more often than they assume the leader to be female? What about the subordinate? Implicit biases may be found among students when this is discussed. The gender of Chris and Jo was purposefully left open so that these areas could be explored as well as to avoid fostering implicit bias with regard to gender, power relationships, the communication of microaggressions, and mental illness.

6. How do you respond to the use of the word "subordinate" when referring to people in Jo's organizational role/position? How does the word "subordinate" communicate about the power differential in a leader-member exchange and how can the perception of being a subordinate to another individual lead to potential perceptions of inferiority even without microaggressions and/or amplify the impact of a microaggression?

This question is focused on encouraging students to discuss the importance of a leader's communication and awareness of how what they communicate can have an unanticipated impact. The understanding of one's power or even privilege can lead to better awareness in how one communicates. By students discussing the power of this word alone, coupled with potential microaggressions, students may be able to learn the perception of power can impact the perception of communication.

7. What is the final solution that can be recommended to the management of the organization described in the case? Provide your arguments in support of the recommended solution.

The organization needs to train employees on implicit bias, microaggressions, and train leaders on how to demonstrate more empathic-concern. One discussion or group assignment instructors could do here would be to have students research the websites and find others given in the Solutions and Recommendations sections and share the pros and cons for each of these suggestions.

CHAPTER 3

1. How does Todd protect his private information in the workplace? What private information does he choose to disclose? What private information does he choose to conceal?

Todd uses several tactics to protect his private information. First and foremost, he does not disclose his mental health condition to his colleagues and as such, has firm boundaries. Next, Todd is careful not to share too much regarding his personal beliefs related to mental illness with his colleagues. Todd chooses to share some personal information related to the loss of his daughter but conceals information about his mental illness.

2. Todd struggles with the stigma surrounding mental illness. What types of stigmatizing language does Noland use to reinforce Todd's beliefs regarding the stigma associated with mental illness?

Noland uses phrases like "attention-seeking" and "crazy" to refer to mental illness and therapy. These types of comments reinforce some of the self-stigma Todd feels regarding his own mental health journey.

3. What risks does Todd associate with disclosing his mental illness in the workplace? Do you believe his fears surrounding the stigma of mental illness are justifiable?

Todd believes that sharing his mental illness in the workplace will be met with discrimination and scrutiny. Todd sees his mental illness as a risk to his credibility that could impact his livelihood.

4. How does Todd's profession as a financial advisor add complexity to the case? Does one's profession significantly impact the risk associated with disclosing a mental illness in the workplace?

Todd's career as a financial advisor complicates the case since professionals who are in charge of managing finances are held to high standards in society. As such, Todd is particularly worried about clients or colleagues finding out about his mental illness since he does not want to be viewed as incompetent in his work.

5. If you had a friend managing a mental illness who was considering disclosing it within their workplace, what advice would you give that friend? What concerns would you have if your friend's mental illness was known to their colleagues/ clients? What benefits do you believe your friend might experience as a result of disclosing?

When it comes to providing friends with advice, it is always a challenge to ensure that the information provided is supportive and validating. Listen to a friend's concerns about sharing mental illness in the workplace and then respond with the potential risks and benefits that could result from the disclosure. Be sure to validate the feelings of the individual who is struggling with the issue and ensure to withhold judgment.

CHAPTER 4

1. How does Suzie conceptualize herself as being similar or different from her coworkers?

In Suzie's view, she sees herself as most similar to Veronica since they both are dealing with disabilities. In this vein, she almost positions Cindy as being better than her when Cindy is able to say the right thing even when Kathy can't.

2. Should Suzie tell her coworkers about her ADHD? Should she tell her supervisor, Kathy? What are the pros and cons associated with disclosing her difference?

This could go either way. If she does tell them, she risks being viewed as the stigma, and if she doesn't, she may have a harder time, and her coworkers may still just think she's "trying too hard."

3. What are some of the things that Suzie does to help manage her ADHD while also benefitting the office and others she works with?

One example is when she makes a calendar/schedule for the different roles. This wasn't previously written down and seemed like it was probably causing holes in the system since various tasks were left seemingly unfinished.

4. What organizational tensions exist that might keep Suzie from disclosing her ADHD?

Her coworkers go on about her notes several times and seem overly concerned about them. Given this, it's unlikely they'd react positively to other measures, such as recording meetings or writing down directions.

5. If Jared doesn't know that Suzie has ADHD, is he bullying her or discriminating against her? Would your answer change if Jared did know Suzie had ADHD? Why?

Maybe, but probably not since he treats Veronica similarly and she has a visible disability. Regardless of whether it's technically discrimination, Jared is an issue and negatively contributing to the work environment.

6. If Suzie were to disclose her difference, what kind of accommodations could she ask for?

She may request getting directions in written form, having someone share meeting minutes with her after meetings, recording meetings, additional time to complete tasks, and work from home options to minimize distractions.

CHAPTER 5

1. What is the overall problem presented in this case?

The organization fails to address implicit ableism in its workplace culture. This issue results in the isolation and mistreatment of an organization member with an invisible disability. Louisa then must face the complicated challenge of managing her organizational identity.

2. What are the factors affecting the problem(s) related to this case?

Institutional bias against people with disabilities is an ongoing problem in the larger society that contextualizes this organization. Additionally, workers bring their own internalized ableism to the organization if left unaddressed.

3. What are some of the emerging technologies that should be considered in solving the problem(s) related to the case?

Normalization of different assistive and accessible technologies within the organization could promote inclusion. For example, allowing a Zoom option for anyone to use in all meetings would prevent people with disabilities from feeling singled out if they are the only one requesting Zoom access for a meeting.

4. How do various factors of communication perpetuate ableism in organizations?

Organizational culture, internalized ableism, and interpersonal dynamics all influence ableism in an organization through communication. Multiple levels of communication should be considered when an organization seeks to promote diversity and inclusion in the workplace.

5. What is the final solution that can be recommended to the management of the organization described in the case?

The organization should promote an organizational culture of inclusivity by: requiring education about ableism in the workplace, addressing organizational entry and exit tactics that prevent diversity, and acting decisively when discrimination against a person with a disability takes place.

CHAPTER 6

1. What emotions are evident in this case study? How do the emotions vary among the characters?

Amy's emotions include apprehension, contentment, frustration, defensiveness, joy, happiness. Beau's emotions include concern, pride, fear, frustration. Craig's emotions include irritation, resignation, intrigue, wonder.

2. In terms of Miller et al.'s (2007) five types of organizational emotions (*emotional labor*, *emotional work*, *emotion with work*, *emotion at work*, and *emotion toward work*), which types are evident in this case study? Discuss examples.

Amy talks about how she and other guides "put on a happy face" with clients sometimes (emotional labor). Amy truly loves the work that she does and that shows in her interactions with clients (emotional work). Amy enjoys friendships with Dana and Everett while Beau enjoys his friendship with Craig (emotion with work). Amy's apprehension about seeing her brother shows up in her discussion with coworker Dana (emotion at work). Amy feels fulfilled by her job, Beau feels proud of his work accomplishments, and Craig feels frustrated by his work demands (emotion toward work).

3. How is work-life spillover illustrated through positive and negative emotions in this case study? Using specific examples from the case study, what are some benefits and drawbacks of work-life spillover?

In terms of positive emotions, Amy is happy to learn of a job opportunity from her client/friend Everett while Beau uses the pride he feels for her work accomplishments to convince Amy that she needs a new career path. In terms of negative emotions, Craig feels frustrated and overwhelmed by his boss's demand that he work during his vacation while Amy feels nervous about her brother's visit, sure he will judge her for her choice to be an adventure worker. Benefits of work-life spillover include the blurring of work and leisure. Drawbacks include constant availability and overwork.

4. What choices are the characters facing, and how do those choices relate to emotions and work-life spillover? What do you think they should choose?

Amy must choose what to do next. Will she stay with her adventurous lifestyle or opt for a more secure and predictable career? Meanwhile, Craig must decide whether to continue his work at A1 Strategies or quit so he can try out adventure work.

5. How do the concepts of organizational emotion and work-life spillover apply in your own life? Discuss examples.

Answers will vary but should include examples of how work permeates personal life and vice versa.

CHAPTER 7

1. In what ways did Kim experience convergence, divergence, or overaccommodation with other co-workers?

Kim experienced convergence with Chen (e.g., shared experiences, decreasing distance via verbal and non-verbal cues), divergence with Jennifer (e.g., lack of verbal responsiveness), and overaccommodation (e.g., overly slow and enunciated speech based on incorrect assumptions) with Sophia.

2. What do you think could be the motives for convergence, divergence, or overaccommodation demonstrated in the case?

Responses here could vary. Issues such as cultural backgrounds or power difference between Kim and Jennifer could be brought into discussion. In the case of overaccommodation, stereotyping about racial/ethnic minority could also enrich discussion.

3. How do you think convergence, divergence, and overaccommodation in the interactions between Kim and her colleagues/supervisor impacted her relationships with each?

Convergence with Chen made Kim feel closer to her. Divergence experienced with Jennifer made Kim feel even more distant from her. Overaccommodation from Sophia surprised Kim and caused her to question the support she would receive from this supervisor.

4. If you were in Kim's position, would you respond with exit, voice, loyalty or neglect? Why?

Responses here could vary. Students may be able to draw from their own work experiences to explain their selected action(s).

5. Do you think Kim will transfer to another organization? Why? Or why not?

Responses here will vary.

6. Would Kim's decision be different if she had a more positive or negative experience with this organization? What could the organization do to improve Kim's experience?

Yes, Kim seemed to want to stay at this organization and was committed to her job. There may be training programs or other initiatives the organization can devise to improve communication in this workplace, perhaps by fostering a more inclusive environment.

CHAPTER 8

1. If you were Shawna, how would you have responded to the microaggression?

Responses will vary.

2. Do you agree with Shawna's friend Tabitha that we have to pick our battles and not respond to every microaggression?

Responses will vary.

3. If you could speak with John about his comment, what would you tell him?

Responses will vary.

4. Have you ever been on the receiving end of a microaggression? If so, what type was it, and how did you respond?

Responses will vary.

5. What can organizers of professional academic conferences do to combat microaggressions?

Responses will vary.

CHAPTER 9

1. Have you ever experienced and/or witnessed the development of a close relationship in the workplace? If so, explain how social penetration theory and/or expectancy violations theory can be used to explain the process using key terms.

Responses will vary.

2. What stage of the social penetration process are Linda and Sam in at the beginning and end of the case?

At the beginning of the case, Linda and Sam are at the exploratory affective stage. As they progress throughout the case, they move into the next stage of the social penetration process. By the end of the case, the two are in the de-penetration stage, as evidenced by the actions of Linda. Linda is ignoring Sam, indicating a transgression has taken place.

3. What expectations were violated in the case?

Sam (inadvertently) violates Linda's expectations about their relationship. Linda expects something such as gender identity to be disclosed by this point in their relationship while Sam feels the need to hide their gender identity as explained by transgender standpoint epistemology.

4. What does the future look like for John and Linda?

John and Linda will have to talk about what happened. He will ask for transparency and give transparency in return. As John sticks to his values, he will most likely explain to Linda his view and how he would proceed. It is possible there will be disciplinary action and diversity training for Linda and the organization as a whole.

5. What "layers of the onion" are disclosed throughout the case?

The outer layer of the onion is demonstrated through the visible features of Sam and Linda. Sam presents themselves as a man and Linda as a woman. Linda appears older while Sam appears younger. As they move further into the layers of the onion more person things are revealed such as Linda's son with autism and Sam's true gender identity.

6. How might you handle identity negotiations in the workplace? For example, are there aspects of who you are that you may be (un)comfortable disclosing to everyone in your workplace? How do you think you would respond to certain types of identity disclosures from co-workers (e.g., Sam's identity as in the case)?

Responses will vary.

CHAPTER 10

1. What could managers and supervisors do to create a climate where employees are more comfortable to speak about difficulties and thus increase resilience as they go through hardships? Are the long-term benefits of resilient employees worth the short-term interruptions to work?

Managers and supervisors can create a supportive communication climate where employees can speak about hardships without expecting they will be penalized or suffer additional loss, such as being forced into fewer paid hours. Short-term interruptions dealing with one employee's hardships can lead to long-term benefits of a more cohesive and resilient team.

2. What is the difference between a trait theory of resilience and a communicative theory of resilience? Which theory do you subscribe to? Which do you think most managers subscribe to?

The trait theory argues that there is something inherent in the individual that allows them to be resilient through hardships, whereas the communicative theory argues that anyone can build resilience through the interactions they have with others.

3. In what ways did you see the communication processes of Buzzanell's communication theory of resilience play out in the cases of Fran and Tess? Which individual do you think showed the higher level of resilience and why?

Fran and Tess both demonstrated resilience and showed evidence of the five communication processes in the communication theory of resilience. Tess was able to build her resilience more quickly because she communicated right away about her needs, but both women took some time to come to a new understanding of normalcy after cancer.

4. How do you think managers should assign work to those employees they know are going through major hardships? What are the positive and negative effects of limiting work for cancer patients?

Talking to employees about their ability to work during hardships is key rather than just assuming. Fran demonstrated that losing the extra work was detrimental to her financially and emotionally rather than helpful. It is important to hold these conversations with employees so that the best decision can be made for them and the organization's needs.

5. How has your personal view of resilience changed after exploring these cases? How could you employ this new insight in your own work life?

The communication theory of resilience stresses that resilience is something we build with others rather than an individual trait. This can help those who are facing trauma, loss, and hardship build confidence in their ability to be resilient as they interact with others during this time.

CHAPTER 11

1. Maria and Brad seem to have ongoing "negotiations" whenever they have work-family conflicts. They both have high work involvement and desires for high family involvement. Maria engages in "working lite." They also seem to engage in negotiations that are more or less successful in the short- and long-term. Yet they can't seem to strike a reasonable solution or "balance" for this phase in their lives. Moreover, the COVID-19 pandemic added extra stress to their work-family balance. What might they do more effectively?

Maria and Brad might have conversations in which they routinize, improvise, and restructure their actions on daily and weekly bases (see Medved, 2004).

2. There are a number of everyday and major disruptions, stressors, and opportunities that can upend careers and personal life. These disruptions are called triggers in the Communication Theory of Resilience (CTR; Buzzanell, 2010, 2018a, 2018b). CTR theorizes five processes through which people interact online and offline and use language and routines to create new normals. These processes are: crafting normalcy, creating alternative logics, backgrounding negative feelings while foregrounding productive action, using and maintaining communication networks, and affirming identity anchors. What were the disruptions in Maria and Brad's lives? What about Alejandro and Sara's lives? In both cases, was there one disruption or were there "cascading triggers" or multiple disruptions happening over time and place? What did they do, as individuals and family members, to create new normals? In some disruptive cases, how might they engage differently in these five processes to co-construct more satisfying and sustainable new normals?

For Maria and Brad, some disruptions are births of children, relocations, job changes, and unexpected position demands that upend weekend plans with family and friends. For Alejandro and Sara, the major disruptions are their decisions not to pursue further infertility treatments. Both couples utilize the resilience processes in ways that seem satisfactory to them and also come together for a short-term solution to Brad's unexpected business trip that incorporates all five CTR processes. However long-term strategies to create new normals that anticipate, cope with, and transform work-family stressors still need to be accomplished.

3. What are the motherhood and fatherhood penalties and premiums that Maria mentioned?

Generally speaking, men are paid more when they become fathers, whereas women are paid less when they become mothers with the reasoning that women often engage in more childcare and house work which could prevent full commitment to career and paid labor.

4. Despite their frustrations, Maria and Brad seem to have it pretty good. What might happen in this case if they didn't have the financial means and relational safety nets to manage their relocations, job changes, good quality schools, vacations and leisure times with friends and family?

Maria and Brad have protective factors on which they can rely if something unexpected happens in their lives. Besides anticipating and planning for potential disruptions, they might also further develop their communication networks in online and offline spaces.

5. Maria was born in the United States but her parents immigrated from Venezuela. How might she be living out Sánchez Sánchez's (2021) generational callings by working hard to be successful? How might these callings amplify stressors around employment and work-family balance?

Maria realizes how much her parents sacrificed to enable her and her siblings to have better lives in a new country, namely, the United States. She may feel called or compelled to work hard to fulfill her parents' dreams for their family. She seems to have balanced career, work, and calling demands but aiming to do all well at all times could add an extra burden in Maria's work-life negotiations.

Glossary

Ableism: The belief that there is a perfect version of what a human should be; a person is considered "able" if they can meet these expectations (Chs. 2, 5).

Adventure Workers: Individuals who work short-term adventure jobs or perform work on a seasonal basis to support an adventurous lifestyle (Ch. 6).

Anticipatory Socialization: The first stage of the organizational socialization process that involves communication encounters prior to entering an organization and how those exchanges shape expectations of organizational member behaviors (Ch. 1).

Assistive Technology: Any computer software or hardware that is designed to assist people with a variety of disabilities or conditions; for example, magnifying software for someone who is visually impaired to make documents accessible or notetaking software for someone with ADHD who has trouble focusing (Ch. 5).

Attention-Deficit Disorder or Attention-Deficit/Hyperactivity Disorder (ADHD): A chronic, lifelong condition that affects attention, hyperactivity, and impulsiveness (Chs. 4, 5).

Boundary/Work-Family Border Theory: Theories that explain how boundaries and the characteristics of boundaries influence the degree of separation between an individual's work and the rest of life (Ch. 6).

Bystander Effect: Social phenomenon where a group of people who have witnessed an injustice fails to act because each one assumes that someone else will step in, resulting in no intervention from witnesses (Ch. 5).

Communal Coping: Viewing hardship suffered by one person as a stressor to be acted upon collectively (Ch. 10).

Communication Networks: People around an individual who are in regular communication with that individual and who may hold useful information or other means of support (Ch. 10).

Communication Privacy Management (CPM) Theory: Explains that individuals experience a dialectical tension between keeping information confidential and being open to predict communication disclosure decisions; factors such as privacy ownership and privacy control predict if individuals will experience privacy turbulence when dealing with personal information (Chs. 1, 3).

Communication Theory of Resilience (CTR): Process of reintegration after loss or disruptions (known as triggers) to communicatively construct new normalcies (Chs. 10, 11).

Convergence: Communicative adjustments to become similar or closer to an interlocutor (Ch. 7).

Dialectics: Tensions that arise in relationships or within individuals that require balancing two opposing forces (Ch. 10).

Disclosure: The act of revealing private information to another individual (Chs. 3, 4).

Discrimination: Unfair treatment of individuals based on an aspect of one's identity (e.g., race, gender, mental health diagnosis) (Ch. 3).

Divergence: Communicative adjustments to become dissimilar from an interlocutor (Ch. 7).

Emotion at Work: Emotion that spans the boundaries of the workplace and home; emotion employees take from work to home and vice versa (Ch. 6).

Emotion Toward Work: Emotion employees feel about their organization, job, or tasks they perform at work (Ch. 6).

Emotion With Work: Emotion generated from relationships and interpersonal interactions in the workplace (Ch. 6).

Emotional Labor: An employee's display of inauthentic emotion performed on behalf of an organization to increase profits (Ch. 6).

Emotional Work: An employee's display of authentic emotion that aligns with the organizational expectations (Ch. 6).

Emotions: One's temporary reaction to a person, event, or situation (Ch. 6).

Empathic-Concern Leadership: A leadership style in which the leader spends an appropriate amount of effort getting to know followers or subordinates and, through knowing them, demonstrates concern for them as individuals (Ch. 2).

Encounter Stage: The third stage of the organizational socialization process that occurs when individuals become new members of an organization and use direct and indirect communication strategies to learn what it means to be an organizational member and what behavior is appropriate (Ch. 1).

Expectancy Violations Theory: A communication theory focused on the behaviors of individuals and expectations of norms situated within interactions that violate communication norms and rules (Ch. 9).

Generalized Anxiety Disorder: A medical diagnosis characterized by excessive or unrealistic anxiety about two or more aspects of life (work deadlines, work pressures, social relationships, etc.) (Ch. 2).

Ideal Worker Norm: A societal belief that professionals should be fully committed to their work and rewarded for their commitment (Ch. 6).

Invisible Disability: Disability that is not immediately apparent to other people (for example, chronic pain is an invisible disability since an onlooker cannot see it); has different challenges than a visible disability (Chs. 4, 5).

Leader-Member Exchange Theory (LMX): LMX is focused on the quality of the interactions and, thus, relationships between leaders and their subordinates (Ch. 2).

Loyalty: A response to a deteriorating work environment by passively waiting for improvement (Ch. 7).

Managerialism: An ideology and social structure in organizations that privilege rationality over emotionality to achieve corporate and managerial values; characterized by control of employees' emotions (Ch. 6).

Managerialist Discourses: Language (spoken and written) that supports managerialism (Ch. 6).

Metacommunication: Hidden messages that imply the demographic group in question is not respected or valued, but the target of the message is viewed as an exception (Ch. 8).

Metamorphosis Stage: The third stage in the organizational socialization process when an individual feels like a full-fledged organizational member (Ch. 1).

Microaggressions: A statement that is considered disrespectful and possibly discriminatory by a person in the marginalized group with whom the microaggression is directed (Chs. 2, 8).

Minority Stress Theory (MST): Posits that as a result of marginalization, people experience unique stressors that affect their relational quality and well-being and will use specific maintenance strategies to manage the added stress (Ch. 4).

Negative Emotions: Temporary reaction that causes one to feel upset, sad, angry, fearful, or anxious (Ch. 6).

Neglect: Negligent work behaviors in response to a deteriorating work environment (Ch. 7).

Neurodivergent: Describes a person with a neurodevelopmental disorder or disability such as autism or ADHD; used as an inclusive term to celebrate neurological differences rather than pathologize them (Ch. 5).

Neurotypical: Describes a person without a neurodevelopmental disorder or disability (Ch. 5).

Nontraditional Worker: Individuals who work transient jobs, such as freelancing or contracting (Ch. 6).

Organizational Anticipatory Socialization: This occurs during the first stage of the organizational socialization process in the anticipatory socialization stage and involves refining general expectations by obtaining information specific to a particular organization (Ch. 1).

Organizational Culture: Social norms and values within an organization (Ch. 5).

Organizational Exit: The fourth and final stage of the organizational socialization process when an individual leaves an organization for a variety of reasons (Chs. 1, 7).

Organizational Socialization: This four-stage model explains how individuals learn about, enter, become members, and leave organizations, including specific communication behaviors that are prevalent during each of the stages (Ch. 1).

Overaccommodation: A failed attempt at accommodation that is perceived as demeaning by the listener (Ch. 7).

Positive Emotions: Temporary reaction that causes one to feel uplifted, happy, joyful, energized, or confident (Ch. 6).

Privacy Boundaries: Barriers created through communication rules that delineate what personal information belongs to individuals and others and how that information is allowed to be shared (Ch. 1).

Privacy Control: When an individual has the right to contain or disclose personal information (Ch. 1).

Privacy Ownership: When an individual believes that information belongs to themself or specified others (Ch. 1).

Privacy Turbulence: When boundaries around personal information are ruptured because individuals have different understandings of information ownership and control (Ch. 1).

Private Information: Any information that can make an individual feel vulnerable if it is revealed to another individual (Ch. 3).

Risk/Benefit Assessments: Individuals anticipate potential negative consequences and positive outcomes to determine if they will share private information (Ch. 1).

Sensory Needs: Commonly describes some people's sensitivity to noise or light due to a variety of factors; some neurodivergent people are easily overstimulated by excessive sound or brightness, so they utilize tools such as earplugs or sunglasses to keep from becoming overwhelmed (Ch. 5).

Social Penetration Theory: A communication theory positing the trajectory of interpersonal relationships evolving in a path like structure, progressing from superficial to intimate through the use of self-disclosure (Ch. 9).

Social Support: An interpersonal communication process that ameliorates the harmful effects of stress on an individual experiencing various hardships. Social support can include both verbal support and tangible, practical support (Ch. 10).

Stigma: Any attribute that leads others to regard one as being lesser or disgraced in society (Chs. 3, 4).

Traditional Worker: Individuals who work full-time hours and have predictable schedules over the long-term.

Vocational Organizational Anticipatory Socialization: This represents part of the first stage of the organizational socialization process in the anticipatory socialization stage and involves communication-related to how individuals learn what it means to be a member in a particular field, industry, or type of position (Ch. 1).

Voice: Constructive actions for improvement of the situation by making it known to management (Ch. 7).

Work-Life Balance: Popular and academic term that implies that there are two domains in people's lives (paid labor and personal life activities) that are supposed to be equally present, valued, and performed (Chs. 6, 11).

Work-Life Conflict: Occurs when an individual does not have adequate work-life balance; responsibilities in the workplace interfere with personal life and vice versa (Ch. 6).

Work-Life Crossover: Emotions experienced by an individual *and* their relational partners (e.g., family, friends, coworkers) when work and/or life interfere with the opposite domain (Ch. 6).

Workplace Accommodations: Tools that organizations are required to provide to people with disabilities use to help them do work-related tasks; for example, someone who uses a wheelchair might be provided with a ground floor office that is easily accessible to them (Chs. 4, 5).

About the Contributors

Jessica A. Kahlow (Ph.D., University of Wisconsin-Milwaukee) is a Teaching Faculty at the University of Wisconsin-Milwaukee. Her research concentrates on neurodiversity and new media in interpersonal and organizational contexts. Her work has been published in the Review of Communication Research, Computers in Human Behavior, Human Communication and Technology, and other journals and book chapters.

* * *

Greg G. Armfield received his Ph.D. in Communication from the University of Missouri-Columbia in 2004. From 2004 to 2008, he was an Assistant Professor at Angelo State University. In 2008 moved to New Mexico State University, where he currently holds the rank of Associate Professor and serves as Department Head for Communication Studies. Dr. Armfield has authored or co-authored over thirty refereed journal articles and book chapters, which can be found in the Journal of Communication, the Journal of Media and Religion, Speaker and Gavel, and the Journal of Communication and Religion. Dr. Armfield is the co-editor of two books exploring ESPN: The ESPN Effect and ESPN and the Changing Sports Media Landscape, published by Peter Lang. He also edits Communication in Action with Dr. Eric Morgan. Dr. Armfield is a member of the editorial board for the International Journal of Business Communication and continues to research organizational communication and sports.

Victoria L. Bray (B.A., University at Albany) is a graduate student pursuing a Master of Communication at the University at Albany. Her main areas of research interest include workplace communication, digital/new media communication, and marketing practices.

Patrice M. Buzzanell (PhD, Purdue University) is Professor of Communication, University of South Florida. She studies resilience, gendered careers, work-family, and design for ethics and inclusion. She published 4 books and over 300 articles, chapters, and engineering education proceedings. She is a National Communication Association Distinguished Scholar, Fellow (and Past President) of the International Communication Association, and Past President of the Organization for the Study of Communication, Language and Gender and the Council of Communication Associations.

Suzy D'Enbeau (Ph.D., Purdue University) is an associate professor in the School of Communication Studies at Kent State Universities. She publishes in three areas: how social change organizations navigate competing goals in varied contexts ranging from domestic violence prevention to transnational feminism; how gender is problematized in organizing and popular culture; and how qualitative inquiry challenges researcher identity and analyses. She is an associate editor of Management Communication Quarterly.

Donna M. Elkins (Ph.D., University of Kentucky) is a Professor of Communication and Director of the Center for Teaching and Learning at Spalding University in Louisville, KY. Her research interests include socialization of organizational newcomers, self-disclosure in the workplace, and balancing privacy when seeking social support online. Her most current research interest focuses on the communication processes used to build resilience when leaving an organization and starting a new business.

Courtney D. Fallon (MA, Missouri State University) is a graduate student in Communication at Missouri State University. Her research and writing interests lie at the intersection of organizational communication and rhetoric. In these disciplines, she studies how systems of power and oppression are maintained through communicative practices.

Patricia E. Gettings (PhD, Purdue University) is an assistant professor of communication at the University of Albany, SUNY. Her research explores the ways in which individuals communicatively manage their relationships with organizations, and how these practices influence outcomes like identity, relational quality, and organizational inclusiveness.

Eletra S. Gilchrist-Petty (Ph.D., The University of Memphis) is Professor and Chair of the Communication Arts Department at the University of Alabama in Huntsville (UAH). She is the author of three books and more than two dozen other publications. Gilchrist-Petty has held several offices with the National Communication Association (NCA), including chair of the African American Communication and Culture Division and committee memberships on the NCA Teaching and Learning Council, Affirmative Action and Intercaucus Committee, and Legislative Assembly. She is also chair of the Southern States Communication Association's Committee on Diversity, Equity and Inclusion. Gilchrist-Petty is, furthermore, a past NCA Division winner of the Top Research Journal article and recipient of the UAH Distinguished Teaching Award.

Emily Godager (M.A., University of Wisconsin-Milwaukee) is a PhD student in the Department of Communication at the University of Wisconsin-Milwaukee. Her research concentrates on topics in organizational communication, including organizational socialization and intersections of work and life.

Anne P. Hubbell received her Ph.D. in Communication from Michigan State University in 2000. She started at New Mexico State University in 2000 as an Assistant Professor. At NMSU, she served as a Department Head for two departments and as an Interim Associate Dean for the College of Arts and Sciences. She was promoted to Full Professor in 2016. She is currently serving as an Associate Dean in the William Conroy Honors College at New Mexico State University. Dr. Hubbell has authored or co-authored over 35 refereed journal articles and book chapters, which can be found in Health Communication, Case Book in Organizational Communication, Communication Quarterly, California Journal of Health Promotion, Communication Monographs, Communication Studies, Journal of Health Communication, and the Journal of Community Health. Dr. Hubbell regularly reviews articles for Health Communication and the Journal of Immigrant and Minority Health.

Alexis Madson (B.A., University of Wisconsin-Milwaukee) completed an honors research project which focused on communication privacy management theory to better understand how students navigate requesting help and securing resources for mental health concerns in an educational context.

Andrea L. Meluch (PhD, Kent State University, 2016) is an Assistant Professor of Business and Organizational Communication in the School of Communication and Department of Management at The University of Akron. Her research focuses on the intersections of health, organizational, and instructional communication. Specifically, she is interested in issues of organizational culture, mental health, and social support. She has published in Communication Studies, Communication Education, Southern Communication Journal, Qualitative Research in Medicine & Healthcare, Journal of Communication in Healthcare, and the Journal of Communication Pedagogy. She has also authored/co-authored more than a dozen book chapters and encyclopedia entries.

Seulgi Park is a doctoral student in the Department of Communication at the University at Albany, SUNY. Her research interests lie at the intersection of health, interpersonal, and intercultural communication. She is interested in health communication and health disparities, patient-doctor communication, and healthcare engagement among immigrant populations, especially focusing on Korean immigrants in the US.

Kari J. Pink (B.A., University of Wisconsin-Milwaukee) is a master's student in the Department of Communication at the University of Wisconsin-Milwaukee. Her research focuses on organizational communication. She works full time as director of marketing and communications, donor relations at the University of Wisconsin-Milwaukee.

Sarah E. Riforgiate (Ph.D., Arizona State University) is an Associate Professor of Communication at the University of Wisconsin-Milwaukee. Her research concentrates on communication pertaining to public/paid-work and private-life. Her work has been published in Communication Monographs, Journal of Family Communication, Management Communication Quarterly, Communication Teacher, Journal of Communication Pedagogy and other journals and book chapters.

Index

R

S

T

V

W

www.ingramcontent.com/pod-product-compliance
Lightning Source LLC
LaVergne TN
LVHW081324300926
849161LV00008B/1866
* 9 7 8 1 6 6 8 4 3 7 5 3 7 *